UNDERSTAN
MARTIN

CW00393187

LAP 18

Understanding Contemporary British Literature
Matthew J. Bruccoli, Series Editor

Volumes on

UNDERSTANDING
MARTIN
AMIS

SECOND EDITION

James Diedrick

University of South Carolina Press

© 2004 University of South Carolina

Cloth edition published by the University of South Carolina Press, 1995
Paperback edition published in Columbia, South Carolina, by the
University of South Carolina Press, 2004

Manufactured in the United States of America

08 07 06 05 04   5 4 3 2 1

Library of Congress Cataloging-in-Publication Data

Diedrick, James, 1951–
    Understanding Martin Amis / James Diedrick.— 2nd ed.
        p. cm. — (Understanding contemporary British literature)
    Includes bibliographical references (p.) and index.
    ISBN 1-57003-516-4 (pbk. : alk. paper)
    1. Amis, Martin—Criticism and interpretation. I. Title. II. Series.
PR6051.M5Z62 2004
823'.914—dc22   2003017456

For Jeffrey and Katherine

Contents

Editor's Preface

The volumes of *Understanding Contemporary British Literature* have been planned as guides or companions for students as well as good nonacademic readers. The editor and publisher perceive a need for these volumes because much of the influential contemporary literature makes special demands. Uninitiated readers encounter difficulty in approaching works that depart from the traditional forms and techniques of prose and poetry. Literature relies on conventions, but the conventions keep evolving; new writers form their own conventions—which in time may become familiar. Put simply, *UCBL* provides instruction in how to read certain contemporary writers—identifying and explicating their material, themes, use of language, point of view, structures, symbolism, and responses to experience.

The word *understanding* in the titles was deliberately chosen. Many willing readers lack an adequate understanding of how contemporary literature works; that is, what the author is attempting to express and the means by which it is conveyed. Although the criticism and analysis in the series have been aimed at a level of general accessibility, these introductory volumes are meant to be applied in conjunction with the works they cover. They do not provide a substitute for the works and authors they introduce, but rather prepare the reader for more profitable literary experiences.

M. J. B.

Acknowledgments

Since writing the first edition of this book in 1994, I have made many friends and accrued several debts. I wish to express special gratitude to my colleague Hunter M. Hayes of Mississippi State University for his unfailing generosity, his wide knowledge of contemporary literature, and his bibliographic acumen. The denizens of the Martin Amis Discussion Board (http://amisdicussion.albion.edu) have provided years of insight and incitement, and have significantly enriched this study. Among them Simon Brockwell, Bill Jarmell, Jim Murphy, Stephen Pepper, Geoff Northcott, Jeremy Sheldon (author of *The Comfort Zone*), Euan Stuart, and Julia Wells deserve special mention. Chris Sampson scoured British newspaper databases and provided much important information. Professor Geoff Cocks of Albion College, author of *Psychotherapy in the Third Reich,* helped improve my analysis of *Time's Arrow,* as did Professor Richard Menke of the University of Georgia. A British Academy Travel Grant administered by the Newberry Library in Chicago allowed me to conduct research in London during the fall of 2001. The Faculty Development Committee at Albion College gave me the gift of time by awarding me a sabbatical during the 2001–2002 academic year. This book was written with the support of the Howard L. McGregor Professorship administered by Albion College.

UNDERSTANDING
MARTIN AMIS

CHAPTER 1

Understanding Martin Amis

At the turn of the millennium, Martin Amis surprised nearly everyone. In *Experience: A Memoir* (2000), Amis descended from the lofty perch of the satirist—where he had reigned supreme for nearly thirty years—to take up residence in what W. B. Yeats called the "rag and bone shop of the heart." Eschewing the savage wit and cool ironic distance that characterize much of his fiction, he invited the reader into his domestic life in all its amplitude, contingency, and suffering. Verbal artistry is second nature to Amis—the preeminent prose stylist of his generation—and in *Experience* he does not, as he asserts in the memoir's introductory chapter, speak "without artifice"[1]; but he does grant access to some of the primal scenes of his emotional life. These include a series of shocks and losses he experienced in the 1990s, culminating in the 1995 death of his novelist father, Kingsley Amis. Before his father died, Amis's ten-year marriage to Antonia Phillips broke up, in part because of his relationship with Isabel Fonseca (whom he married in 1998); he

Throughout this study, quotations from Amis's books will cite page numbers parenthetically. These citations will usually refer to the most widely available paperback editions: Penguin in the case of *Money: A Suicide Note* and *The Moronic Inferno and Other Visits to America,* Harmony in the case of *Visiting Mrs. Nabokov,* and Vintage International for all others. The page numbers in the Vintage International editions correspond to those of the American hardback editions.

discovered that his beloved cousin, Lucy Partington (who had been missing since Christmas 1973), was a victim of the serial murderer Frederick West; he met for the first time with his first daughter, Delilah, born in 1976, who had been raised by her stepfather and only informed of her relation to Amis in 1995; and he severed ties with his longtime agent, Pat Kavanagh, over the much-publicized negotiations for a large advance on his novel *The Information,* in the process ending his close friendship with Kavanagh's husband, the novelist Julian Barnes. All of these events are treated with remarkable candor in *Experience.*[2]

In addition to its merits as autobiography, *Experience* sheds illuminating light on Amis's entire literary oeuvre. By writing about what he has called "my missing"—Lucy Partington and Delilah Seale (whose mother committed suicide shortly after her daughter's birth)—Amis reveals the subconscious sources of his preoccupation with women lost to murder or suicide, which begins as early as *Dead Babies* (1975).[3] His surprisingly forgiving portrayal of his father, which reclaims him from the mere caricature of reactionary opinions he became (or posed as) in his last decade, helps explain the paternal anxieties that recur in his writing—and why so many absent, errant, or abusive fathers haunt the pages of his novels. Finally, the narrative voice that echoes throughout *Experience*—characterized by empathy, self-criticism, and a discriminating intelligence—dissociates Martin Amis the man from the male protagonists that populate his best-known novels, driven and derided as they so often are by malice, envy, and spite. It serves as a reminder, in the words of the poet Craig Raine, that "you can't judge Amis by the cruel comic style of his books,"[4] and it offers a corrective to the reader who would confuse the narrators of his first-person novels with their creator.

Experience is destined to become a classic literary autobiography, and it earned Amis some of the best reviews of his career.[5] But it did not put to rest the critical reservations that have dogged his reputation from the start. For many, Amis's militant aestheticism—succinctly expressed in the title of his 2001 volume of literary reviews, *The War against Cliché: Essays and Reviews, 1971–2000*—limits his artistic reach. As early as 1977 Amis approvingly summarized Anthony Burgess's distinction between "A" and "B" novelists:

> The A novelist . . . is interested in character, motive and moral argument, and in how these reveal themselves through action. . . . The spunkier and more subversive B novelist, however, is quite interested in these things but is at least as interested in other things too: namely, the autonomous play of wit, ideas, and language.[6]

If any doubts remained that Amis is a "B" novelist, he dispelled them in a 1985 interview: "I would certainly sacrifice any psychological or realistic truth for a phrase, for a paragraph that has a spin on it: that sounds whorish, but I think it's the higher consideration."[7]

Adam Mars-Jones, long one of Amis's most perceptive critics, acknowledges Amis's stylistic virtuosity, but also tallies its costs:

> No one works harder on a sentence than Martin Amis, and no one stores up more pleasure for the reader with his phrasing. But sometimes it seems that the need to stamp each sentence with his literary personality defeats his ambition as a literary artist. This is perhaps a peculiarly modern artistic

dilemma. Fear of inauthenticity can lead to inauthenticity of a different sort, not an unsigned painting but a painting composed entirely of signatures.[8]

As literary editor David Sexton has said, Amis "believes only the author matters. But only books that live independently of their authors can live after them: if you don't give life to your characters, they can't give it back to you. Amis is trapped in his own book, its sole inhabitant."[9]

These criticisms also help explain what often happens when Amis turns to nonfiction and assumes the voice of cultural sage. Here his trademark voice and charged language are often inadequate or inappropriate to the subject, whether it be nuclear proliferation or the 2001 terrorist attacks on the United States. The portentous and overreaching "Fear and Loathing," published just one week after thousands died when passenger jets slammed into the World Trade Center and the Pentagon, is a particularly egregious example. Verging on self-parody, Amis describes the collapse of the towers as "the apotheosis of the postmodern era," declares in a bizarre neologism that the glint of the second plane was "the worldflash of a coming future," and sums up the damage with glib machismo: "Manhattan looked as though it had taken ten megatons." He also genuflects before two of his favorite American novelists (Saul Bellow and Don DeLillo) before placing a final seal of pseudo-significance on his ruminations, recording the date of the attack as "the eleventh day of the ninth month of 2001 (the duo-millennial anniversary of Christianity)."[10]

A similar striving for significance can be detected in Amis's fiction from the mid-1980s on. John Lanchester has written that "something . . . has gone astray in Amis's fiction since his masterpiece, *Money,*" adding that the novels since then "have tended to have a mix of superbly good writing with false notes and a straining for effect or largeness. They have combined brilliant comedy with serious preoccupations that often feel worked up."[11] Lanchester believes this is because Amis took to heart John Updike's damning assessment, originally published in 1978, that the elder Amis's "ambition and reputation alike remain in thrall to the weary concept of the 'comic novel.'"[12] Martin Amis has sought escape from this imprisonment through satire. But while this has purchased him greater range of subject matter, the cost has been emotional diminution. His work is fueled by disgust at the grotesque perversions and excesses wrought by postindustrial capitalism, but it often lacks a compensatory engagement with the intricacies of the human heart. To quote Mars-Jones again, satire is "the only genre which invites and requires negative emotion, the one in which empathy is dilution and blunder."[13] The remainder of this chapter, and much of this study, will explore the sources, expressions, achievements, and limitations of Amis's satirical impulse—as well as his fitful, artistically daring departures from the genre.

From the first, Martin Amis's literary sensibility was shaped by his father's career, his father's waywardness, and his father's neuroses. He was born on August 25, 1949, just five years before *Lucky Jim* brought transatlantic fame to Kingsley and transatlantic travel to his family. During the nine years he lived in South Wales, his father's friend, the poet Philip Larkin, made frequent visits to the Amis household (and served as godfather to Martin's older brother Philip). In 1960 he spent a formative year in America when his father was hired to teach creative writing at Princeton. Two years later Kingsley (whose "sexual recklessness," Martin would later write, "often approached the psychotic" [*Experience,* 81]) abandoned his wife Hilly and his family for the novelist Elizabeth Jane Howard.[14]

This was not the first time Kingsley's behavior made a formative impression on him. In *Experience* he recounts a remarkable parent-child role reversal:

> When I was a child I would sometimes hear my father in the night—his horrified gasps, steadily climbing in pitch and power. My mother would lead him to my room. The light came on. My parents approached and sat. I was asked to talk about my day, school, the games I had played. He listened feebly but lovingly, admiringly, his mouth open and tremulous, as if contemplating a smile. In the morning I talked to my mother and she was very straight. "It calms him down because he knows he can't be frightened in front of you."
>
> "Frightened of what?" "He dreams he is leaving his body."
> It made me feel important—up late, holding the floor, curing a grown man: my father. It bonded us. (180)[15]

Both the intimate knowledge of masculine compulsion that informs Amis's novels and the paternal anxieties that marked them from the late 1980s through the late 1990s can be traced to primal scenes such as this one.

During his young adult life, however, much of Martin Amis's imaginative energy was devoted to emerging from his father's shadow as a writer in his own right. Significantly, it was his stepmother Elizabeth Jane Howard, not Kingsley, who persuaded the teenage Martin to turn from comic books and video games to serious reading, introducing him to the novels of Jane Austen and helping him enroll in a series of "crammers" that prepared him for university entrance exams (*Experience*, 150).[16] From 1968 to 1971 he attended Exeter College at Oxford University, where his tutors included Jonathan Wordsworth, a direct descendant of the poet William Wordsworth, and Craig Raine, whose poetry gave rise to an influential literary movement known as the Martian School (see chapter 3 for the influence of this school on Amis's fiction). Like his father before him, he graduated with first-class honors in literature. Just three months out of Oxford, he was hired to write book reviews for the distinguished weekly the *Observer,* where his byline regularly appeared alongside those of Anthony Burgess, Stephen Spender, W. H. Auden—and Kingsley Amis. He was hired by the paper's literary editor, Terence Kilmartin, who did not let Amis's family connections sway him. "I gave him a book to review, a tryout, and I showed it around. People thought it was the work of someone who'd been reviewing for twenty years."[17]

In 1973 Amis joined two other prestigious British journals. He became an editorial assistant at the *Times Literary Supplement* (where he was named fiction and poetry editor in 1974),[18] and he began reviewing books for the *New Statesman,* where literary editor Claire Tomalin hired him as her assistant. She remembers his great agility with words. "It was great fun to work with that. Martin could so easily have stayed in Oxford and had an academic career. . . . He is very, very clever and had a terrific intellectual arrogance."[19] Beginning in 1974, Amis also wrote for Ian Hamilton's short-lived but legendary arts-council supported journal, the *New Review,* which also published the early work of Julian Barnes, Ian McEwan, Shiva Naipaul, and poet laureate Andrew Motion.[20]

Amis remained with the *New Statesman* for seven years. He was named assistant literary editor in 1975 and literary editor in 1977. In 1979 he resigned to write full time. His association with the *New Statesman* was the most significant of his journalistic career. It secured his reputation as a member of London's literary intelligentsia and solidified his left-liberal political credentials. Amis's friendships on the paper bear out this latter point— in 1976 he and two of the *New Statesman*'s most committed "Trotskyists," James Fenton and Christopher Hitchens, formed what they called the 26 Club (all three were twenty-six at the time). Amis now looks back on that time with a mixture of nostalgia and humility. "We did think we were a hot trio," he says. "The 26 Club! Now we almost weep with embarrassment."[21]

When he left Oxford, Jonathan Wordsworth had challenged him to either produce a novel within the year or return to Oxford for an advanced degree and a career as a university don. The result was *The Rachel Papers,* published in November 1973, which won the Somerset Maugham Prize for best first novel (as Kingsley's first novel, *Lucky Jim,* had done before it) and launched Amis's career as a fiction writer. Recalling this time, Amis marvels at his youthful stamina. "I had a huge amount of intellectual energy when I came down. . . . My head was full of literature, and longing to write. I wrote that novel in a year of evenings and mornings, while writing quite a number of reviews and keeping a full-time job."[22] In 1980, having published three novels and sold one screenplay, Amis resigned from his editorial position at the *New Statesman* to write full time, although he has continued to publish nonfiction in England and America, including essays and reviews in the *Observer,* the *Guardian,* the *Times* (London),[23] the *Independent,* the *London Review of Books,* the *New York Times Book Review,* the *Atlantic, Esquire, Vanity Fair, New York,* the *New Yorker,* and *Talk.*[24]

Amis himself later acknowledged that his family name guaranteed that he would get at least one novel in print: "Any London house would have published my first novel out of vulgar curiosity" (*Experience*, 25).[25] His rapid rise to prominence made him the target of attacks in the popular press (the satirical journal *Private Eye* took to calling him "Smarty Anus," and some attributed his early success to nepotism) even while many lesser writers strove to imitate his style. "His mixture of precocity, great intelligence, and wide sexual success is bound to provoke envy," Julian Barnes said in 1990. "People try to write like Martin. There's something very infectious and competitive about it."[26] Between 1981 and 1994, Amis published four more novels, four volumes of nonfiction, and a collection of short stories on the theme of nuclear terror. In 1984 he married the American philosophy professor Antonia Phillips. They had two sons: Louis, born the same year, and Jacob, born in 1986.

By the mid-1980s, bolstered by his critical successes as novelist and journalist, his aphoristic brilliance in interviews, and his influence on a rising generation of British writers, Amis had achieved the status of what David Flusfeder has called the "Author-as-Cultural-Event." Like Graham Greene, John Updike, Saul Bellow, Kurt Vonnegut, and Gore Vidal before him, Amis had come to represent "something that seems intrinsic to them and their writing, yet goes beyond both: an attitude, a moral system, a state of mind."[27] This celebrity status has not always had a salutary effect on his work, as the antinuclear polemics he wrote in the mid- to late 1980s attest, but it did guarantee his primacy in the London literary scene—and his increasing marketability.

This fact was not lost on his father. *The Letters of Kingsley Amis*, published in 2000, amply documents Kingsley's resentment and envy in the face of his son's literary ascent. In a 1979 letter to Philip Larkin, Kingsley asks, "Did I tell you Martin is spending a year abroad as a TAX EXILE? Last year he earned £38,000. Little shit. 29, he is. Little shit." Earlier letters refer to "lazy Martin" or "Savage little Mart"; one reports that "Scoundrelly Mart has sold his novel to the Yanks for $3,000 advance. Pretty good, eh?" In 1982 Kingsley indicts Martin and several of his peers, asking Larkin, "Have you actually tried to read Clive Sinclair and Ian McEwan and Angela Carter and M**t**m**? Roll on is all I can say boyo. Fucking roll on." And in 1984, the year *Money* was published, he told Larkin "of course Martin Amis is more famous than I am now."[28] Although Kingsley did go on to win the coveted Booker Prize for his 1986 novel *The Old Devils* (a prize that has thus far eluded Martin), his son's reputation eclipsed his own for the remainder of his life.[29]

By the mid-1990s, however—engendered in part by his continuing literary successes and his virtual omnipresence as a public figure—press opinion had begun to echo some of Kingsley's privately expressed resentment. His checkered personal life and his alleged greed in seeking an $800,000 advance for his 1995 novel *The Information* provided ammunition, and critics increasingly complained of his arrogance and "laddishness"— qualities that novelist A. S. Byatt memorably summarized as "male turkey-cocking."[30] Amis's longtime friend and fellow novelist Salman Rushdie has described the phenomenon in stark terms. "There is a thing that happened to Martin which periodically happens in England when the public print rounds upon the public figure and tries to tear him apart. It really has nothing to do with the money. It's just 'This guy has had it too good for too long—let's murder him.'"[31] Rushdie made this statement in 1995, three years before the *Times* (London) published an account of Amis's marriage to Isabel Fonseca. The article constitutes a reductio ad absurdum of the Amis animus, implicitly accusing Amis of greed, parsimony, vanity, and disloyalty. It is characterized by the kind of sneering tone usually reserved for the tabloids:

> Martin Amis, the millionaire novelist, has secretly married his American heiress girlfriend in a ceremony costing just £106.
>
> Amis and Isabel Fonseca, 36, got married at a register office in Westminster London, last week without telling most of their friends.
>
> The author is renowned not only for his literary talent in works such as *The Rachel Papers* and *London Fields,* but also for a headline-grabbing £500,000 book advance and a £20,000 new set of teeth. His wedding, nevertheless, cost considerably less.[32]

In the context of ad hominem attacks like this one, it is not surprising that Amis has downplayed his skirmishes with his father over aesthetics and politics.

Kingsley, Martin, and Literary Paternity

It is no exaggeration to claim that every aspect of Amis's career—his hard-edged persona, his stylistic virtuosity, his patriarchal assumptions, his compulsively expressed devotion to the work of Vladimir Nabokov and Saul Bellow—is grounded in his uniquely charged relationship to his father. Indeed, not even Kingsley's death in 1995 has lessened its intensity, as the afterword to *Koba the Dread: Laughter and the Twenty Million* demonstrates (its title: "Letter to My Father's Ghost"). The complex question of Martin Amis's "anxiety of influence" in relation to his father, and his father's generation, is central to an understanding of his fiction. The phrase "anxiety of influence" derives from the writing of literary theorist Harold Bloom, who places the Oedipal struggle between literary "fathers" and "sons" at the symbolic center of all relations between writers, texts, and their predecessors. In Bloom's view (which, like Freud's theorizing, is unrepentantly and reductively phallocentric), a writer unconsciously perceives his most significant precursors as potentially castrating father figures, and thus employs strategies intended to disarm them. These typically involve taking up the literary forms of the precursors, revising, recasting, and displacing them.[33]

In Martin Amis's case, of course, this symbolic conflict assumes a literal dimension. It even comes complete with primal scenes of rivalry in which texts substitute for other extensions of the male self—their concealment and display all part of the filial competition. Kingsley reported that when his son was still living at home, "whenever I walked into a room where he was writing, he immediately put his hand over the paper in the typewriter."[34] This account implies a father's interest turned back by a son's suspicion, but the son's way of representing the situation shifts the emphasis radically: "My father, I think, aided by a natural indolence, didn't really take much notice of my early efforts to write until I plonked the proof of my first novel on his desk."[35]

In the wake of his father's death, Martin has increasingly described their relationship as a close one, "based on humor and good nature and generosity and support."[36] In his afterword to

Koba the Dread, he goes so far as to assert that "if our birth-dates had been transposed, then I might have written your novels and you might have written mine" (270). During his lifetime, however, Kingsley vehemently and publically criticized Martin's work and his aesthetic allegiances. Complaining to one interviewer of a "terrible compulsive vividness in his style," Kingsley claimed that he could not finish his son's novels. "It goes back to one of Martin's heroes—Nabokov. I lay it all at his door—that constant demonstrating of his command of English."[37] Julian Barnes has called Kingsley's public attacks scandalous, adding "it's a hurt that will never go away," although Christopher Hitchens maintains the rancor was largely theatrical.[38] Martin himself, who never rose to the bait of his father's barbs in public, noted that his father read only three of his novels, and sent the others "windmilling through the air after twenty or thirty pages," adding philosophically that "older writers should find younger writers inimical, because younger writers are sending them an unwelcome message. They are saying, 'It's not like that anymore. It's like this.'" But he also admitted to David Flusfeder in 1997 that he was stung by his father's unwillingness to read his novels: "How could he be so incurious about me?"[39]

One result of this rupture has been a search for substitute literary "fathers."[40] Beyond their intrinsic merit, the essays Martin Amis has written on such writers as J. G. Ballard, Saul Bellow, Norman Mailer, Vladimir Nabokov, V. S. Pritchett, Philip Roth, John Updike, and Angus Wilson reveal a writer obsessed with (male) precursors. With a few exceptions (Jane Austen, Iris Murdoch, Fay Weldon, Joan Didion) Amis's impressive collection of literary essays and reviews concerns male writers.[41] According to Bloom's theory, the proximity and intensity of his father's influence have led him to seek a series of father substitutes whose influence he can acknowledge without filial conflict.

The aesthetic allegiances of the writers Martin Amis most admires are clearly opposed to those of Kingsley, whose fiction conforms to the mode of "classic" (as opposed to modernist) realism as David Lodge defines it. In this sense, the rivalry of the two novelists has implications that reach far beyond individual psychology. "Classic realism," Lodge writes, "with its concern for coherence and causality in narrative structure, for the autonomy of the individual self in the presentation of character, for a readable homogeneity and urbanity of style, is equated with liberal humanism, common sense, and the presentation of bourgeois culture as a kind of norm."[42] Among other things, classic realism strives for verisimilitude, the artfully constructed illusion of reality, achieved in part by a balanced, unified combination of authorial speech and represented speech. The author seeks to fade into the background as the reader is immersed in narrative detail. The opening of chapter 13 of Kingsley's *Lucky Jim* (1954) is representative:

> Dixon paused in the portico to light the cigarette which, according to his schedule, he ought to be lighting after breakfast on the next day but one. The taxi he'd ordered was due any minute. If by the time he'd finished his cigarette Christine had still not appeared, he'd just ask the taximan to take him to his digs, so whatever happened he'd be in a car soon.[43]

By contrast, postmodern texts typically call attention to their status as fictions, as verbal constructs. The language of such texts calls attention to itself, and the author—or an author surrogate—is often present as a character in the narrative. Consider the opening of Martin Amis's first-person novel *Money* (1984):

As my cab pulled off FDR Drive, somewhere in the early Hundreds, a low-slung Tomahawk full of black guys came sharking out of lane and sloped in fast right across our bows. We banked, and hit a deep welt or grapple-ridge in the road: to the sound of a rifle shot the cab roof ducked down and smacked me on the core of my head. I really didn't need that, I tell you, with my head and face and back and heart hurting a lot all the time anyway, and still drunk and crazed and ghosted from the plane. (7)

Amis's language becomes a kind of character here (and in his other novels)—self-conscious, virtuosic, vying for attention with the plot and the other characters. Amis transforms nouns into verbs ("sharking," "ghosted"), invents a new model of car ("Tomahawk"), and describes its encounter with a cab in a way that evokes America's violent past and present ("across our bows," "Tomahawk," "rifle shot"). The inanimate world itself comes vividly to life in Amis's reifying prose: the very roof of the cab is called into action during America's assault on the narrator (who has just arrived in New York from London).

These formal and stylistic differences between father and son reflect significant ideological oppositions as well. In 1990, explaining why Kingsley, once a member of the Communist party, became so outspokenly conservative in the 1970s and 1980s, Martin positioned himself far to his father's left:

The thing about him and his contemporaries—these former Angry Young Men, all of whom tend to be right-wing now— is that while they weren't born into poverty, they didn't have much money. Then they made some money, and they wanted to hang on to it. And they lived through a time when the left was very aggressive and when union power made life unpleasant. There are many aspects of the left that I find unappealing, but what I am never going to be is right-wing in my heart. Before I was even the slightest bit politicized, it was always the poor I looked at. That seemed to be the basic fact about society—that there are poor people, the plagued, the unadvantaged. And that is somewhere near the root of what I write about.[44]

Amis reminds the reader here that historical developments have played a part along with Oedipus in determining the differences between his outlook and his father's, as he does at the beginning of *Einstein's Monsters* (1987): "I was born on August 25, 1949: four days later, the Russians successfully tested their first atom bomb, and deterrence was in place. So I had those four carefree days, which is more than my juniors ever had" (1). As he said elsewhere, "post-1945 life is completely different from everything that came before it. We are like no other people in history."[45] More recently, Amis has disavowed the leftist politics that characterized his fiction and journalism in the 1970s and 1980s. His postmillennial journalism, from his essays on the implications of the September 11, 2001, terrorist attacks to his ruminations on the British monarchy, evince a shift to the right, and in *Koba the Dread* he goes so far as to make the preposterous claim that he is not "ideological." (271). Since no human being is free from ideology, this last claim deserves to be treated with skepticism.

Martin Amis and Postmodernism

The first of many orphans to wander through Amis's fiction appears in his second novel, *Dead Babies* (1975). His first name is Andy, and he gives himself his last name, Adorno, "after the German Marxist philosopher whose death had brought so much despondence to the commune in the summer of 1972, when Andy was just a boy" (179). Amis is doing more here than merely commemorating the death of a great thinker. *Dead Babies* is about the violence and brutality that is unleashed, even partly produced, by an age of ostensible social liberation. In this sense, it is a fictional counterpart to Theodor Adorno and Max Horkheimer's great work *Dialectic of Enlightenment* (1947), the first two sentences of which could serve as an epigraph for much of Amis's fiction: "in the most general sense of progressive thought, the Enlightenment has always aimed at liberating men from fear and establishing their sovereignty. Yet the fully enlightened earth radiates disaster triumphant."[46]

Adorno is central to any discussion of postmodernity, because he has had a formative influence on the philosophical assumptions of postmodern thought. *Dialectic of Enlightenment* argues that the "reason" enshrined during the Enlightenment as a force of liberation from superstition, as an agent of human mastery over the world of contingency, is a reductive form of reason, a discourse that is itself enslaving. Since Enlightenment "reason" takes a specific, Eurocentric incarnation of consciousness, of thinking, as the norm, it is also racist and imperialist, seeking to impose its standards and practices onto all regions of the world. Well before Michel Foucault, Adorno, and Horkheimer insisted that "power and knowledge are synonymous." Their subsequent claim that "Enlightenment is totalitarian" is the seed from which much postmodern theory grew, informed as it is by a rejection of totalizing claims and a suspicion of the uses to which they are put.[47] Martin Amis's discussion of the Nazi's "Final Solution" in his afterword to *Time's*

Arrow reflects this thinking: "The offense was unique, not in its cruelty, nor in its cowardice, but in its style—in its combination of the atavistic and the modern. It was, at once, reptilian and 'logistical'" (168). Rather than an antithesis of Enlightenment ideas, the Holocaust represents one of its faces. Calling Amis's fiction "postmodern," then, involves far more than stylistic analysis, since his style is inseparable from, and embodies, his larger social outlook.

It is important to remember that aesthetic postmodernism can never be separated from, is always already implicated in, political postmodernity. While the roots of the postmodern may be found in Enlightenment thinking, recent historical developments have definitively shaped the postmodern concerns of writers like Amis. Indeed, some theorists of postmodernity define the term this way exclusively. For Sven Birkerts, three historical conditions have been definitive: the existence of the "actual and psychological" fact of the nuclear age and the possibility of human annihilation that has dominated power relations and political agendas since the Second World War; the cumulative effects of the Western world's shift from "industrial mechanization to information processing"; and the saturation of western societies by electronic media, "particularly television."[48]

All three of these developments have dealt blows to the Enlightenment-inspired fiction of individual autonomy, stability, and agency, and this is another aspect of the postmodern condition. Writing about Philip Larkin's reputation, Amis notes that "Larkin the man is separated from us, historically, by changes in the self. For his generation, you were what you were, and that was that. It made you unswervable and adamantine. My father has this quality. I don't. None of us do. There are too many forces at work on us."[49] The increasingly fluid, unstable nature of selfhood is one of Amis's central subjects. Although the concept of the self, or personal identity, as something fluid, changeable, and shaped by external conditions goes back, at least, to David Hume, and has been a staple of modern literature and psychology for nearly a century, Amis writes here as if it is a recent phenomenon. What has, in fact, changed is the forms of mediation that shape identity, as he has acknowledged elsewhere. "Modern life . . . is so mediated that authentic experience is much harder to find. Authentic everything is much harder to find. . . . We've all got this idea of what [life] should be like—from movies, from pornography."[50]

This observation helps explain Amis's much-quoted assertion that "motivation," an essential element in the traditional novel, is "a shagged-out force in modern life. . . . A. C. Bradley and that whole school of humanistic criticism tell us that people behave for reasons, whereas—if you read the *Sun* every day, and keep your wits about you in the street—you see that motivation has actually been exaggerated in, and by, the novel: you have something much woollier than motivation."[51] It is not so much that motivation does not exist; rather, traditional humanist conceptions of conscious motivation have been questioned by much postmodern thought, replaced in part by psychoanalytic notions of unconscious drives and structuralist theories of the socially conditioned nature and shape of subjectivity itself.

In this sense the work of Jacques Lacan, Juliet Mitchell, and Michel Foucault is more important than that of Sigmund Freud in understanding Amis's fiction, especially Lacan's insistence that language structures the human subject, mediating all relations to the other and the real as well as defining it.[52] Not only is language central to Amis's aesthetic—"style is morality," he has insisted[53]—but his first-person narratives virtually dramatize the ways in which language systems and the cultural ideologies that shape them in turn shape consciousness. All of Amis's novels emphasize the degree to which cultural conditions condition character—especially the characters of Anglo-American males living within what Frederic Jameson has called "the cultural logic of late capitalism."[54]

Approaching Amis's novels as texts that dramatize the interrelationship of language and ideology offers a way of directly addressing the two most persistent charges leveled against his work: that he has never discovered a subject equal to his stylistic virtuosity, and that he harbors a deep (if unconscious) animus toward women.[55] Admittedly, his mode of caricature is discriminatory; his men are typically colossal in their absurdity, while his women are absurdly diminished. But his novels have always come to query masculinity, not to praise it. It is no accident that the first essay in *The War against Cliché*—in a section titled "On Masculinity and Related Questions"—includes a hilariously scathing review of the poet Robert Bly's book *Iron John: A Book about Men*, which accuses Bly of wanting "to establish, or re-establish, a world where men are so great that women like being lorded over" (7). Amis concludes this review with a reminder, if any were needed, that his own evolving views of gender both derive and depart from those of his father: "Feminists have often claimed a moral equivalence for sexual and racial prejudice. There are certain affinities; and one or two of these affinities are mildly, and paradoxically, encouraging. Sexism is like racism: we all feel such impulses. Our parents feel them more strongly than we feel them. Our children, we hope, will feel them less strongly than we feel them. People don't change or improve much, but they do evolve" (9).

Denaturalizing gender and gender relations is consistent with the effect of postmodern discourses generally, since, as Linda

Hutcheon has noted, they "manage to point to conventions as conventions and thus to de-naturalize the things we take as natural or given."[56] "What you're always looking for," Amis has said of his novelistic quest, "is a way to see the world differently."[57] If life has changed profoundly in the late twentieth century, it follows that the forms that represent life must change as well. Every novel Amis has written is, at one level, a critique and modification of the subgenre(s) in which it participates. Of his first novel, Amis has said that "the only twist I was conscious of giving to the adolescent novel—the genre to which *The Rachel Papers* belongs—is that Charles Highway is a budding literary critic, whereas the narrators of such novels are usually budding writers."[58]

Actually, this "twist" serves to embody the novel's central concern with self-consciousness, mediation, and inauthenticity. His second novel, *Dead Babies,* is a grotesque variation on the country house novel, set, like most of Jane Austen's novels (or those of P. G. Wodehouse), on a country estate, and concerned with the (ill) manners of a group of the young and the privileged. The head of this estate is a man who seems to represent the quintessence of Enlightenment reason, culture, and civility, but who is revealed as a moral monster by the end of the narrative. In *Time's Arrow,* technically his most audacious novel, Amis subverts the science fiction genre, creating a reverse-chronology narrative whose structure itself, by undoing historical progression, mimics the progress-denying catastrophe that was the Nazi Holocaust.

Narrative Strategies

Because of the didactic connotations of the word, Amis is wary of calling himself a satirist: "the shape of my novels are all comic, or anti-comic, but certainly not anything else, not tragic or even satirical."[59] Yet the evidence of his major novels reminds the reader of D. H. Lawrence's admonition: "trust the tale, not the teller." Amis is in many ways a postmodern Jonathan Swift, wielding the weapon of what Northrop Frye has called "militant irony" with the same controlled, merciless precision as Swift himself. Consistent with his skepticism toward totalizing explanations and moral positions, however, Amis's irony is far less stable than Swift's. A voice of moral and religious certainty can be heard behind the masks of Swift's personae; beneath the raucous bluster of Amis's narrators, expressions of fear and nihilism bid for the reader's attention. Precious little is ever affirmed in his novels. As Mars-Jones has written, Amis's "mighty triptych" of novels about urban life (*Money, London Fields, The Information*) constitute "a love poem to West London from which love is excluded. . . . Only in satire . . . could [Amis] write so many pages . . . full of commandingly vivid detail, none of it sensuous. Not a sensation enjoyed, hardly even a tune heard with pleasure, no food taken into the body without latent or patent disgust."[60]

This is half of the truth of Amis's satirical energies. It does not account for the aesthetic pleasure his writing offers, the lyrical beauty that paradoxically emerges from his confrontation with urban squalor. His achievement, as Mars-Jones notes, has been "to separate verbal beauty from the cause it has traditionally served, to detach lyrical language from the lyrical impulse."[61] Amis is one of the greatest urban portraitists in English prose, and his lyrical voice soars highest when he is imagining cities as malevolent or sordid places. During his whirlwind book tour of the United States in *The Information*, for instance, Richard Tull rides a cab from the airport into

Chicago, "the only city that really frightened him," and Amis is expansive:

> Chilling Chicago awaited them in its vapors and gray medium, deeply massed and square-shouldered on the vague horizon. They heaved on, five yards per heave, along Kennedy Expressway. The five lanes coming into the city were all blocked and the five lanes going out of the city were all blocked; between these two great metal Mississippies of steam and suffering, of spiritual durance, there lay a railtrack on which brightly lit and entirely empty trains sped past in both directions. No one ever used the trains. They had to be in the cars. Americans were martyrs to the motors; autos were their autos-da-fé. Never mind what cars have in store for us globally, biospherically; cars—our cars—hate us and humiliate us, at every turn, they humiliate us. Types of car drivers (timid, pushy) are also types of sufferers: the silent, the permanently enraged, the apparently equable, those who persuade themselves that they are running the show (known as "motorists"), the snarl-prone, the oath-casting, the sullen, the erased. . . . They drove on. (247)

By the time Richard arrives in New York, he is feeling diminished and humiliated, and the narrator's description of the city is meant to mimic his condition. It does so, but the style of the description achieves a perverse sublimity: "Manhattan, as they neared it from the north, looked like a coda to the urban-erotic, the garter and stocking-top patterning of its loops and bridges now doing service as spinal supports and braces, hernia frames. Above it all, the poised hypodermic of the Empire State" (288).

As this second example indicates, Amis's novels are often "double-voiced," a term coined by Mikhail Bakhtin to describe the interrelationship between two sets of voices and attitudes: those of the characters, and those of the author. Bakhtin identifies several subcategories of double-voiced speech in fiction, three of which are central to Amis's novels: stylization, parody, and *skaz* (Russian for oral, vernacular narration).[62] When employing stylization, the author adopts (and typically heightens) an existing style of speech while narrating a character's actions, to suggest how the sensibility of that character is shaped by that mode of language and thought. In the following description from *Dead Babies,* Keith Whitehead has just set fire to the stack of pornographic magazines that have fueled his onanistic desires, and Amis renders the scene in the debased language of sentimental romance:

> He watched the last of his lucent girlfriends curl in on herself, rise yearningly on the stirred embers, erase in black smoke, and shrink to a charred and wizened ball. He poked the scattering fire with a stick. They were all dead now, his girlfriends . . . the one with the tenderly veined breasts, the one that looked like a woman he had sometimes seen in the village, the one with the impossibly concave pants, the one with the deep and pleading eyes, the one whose lips had seemed to say . . . No, they were all dead, dead, and their ashes strewn upon the wind. What will my nights be now? he thought. (138–39)

Parody adopts a style in order to reverse its affective intent. Here, by contrast, the language is an accurate index of Keith's pathetically thwarted longings, thoroughly mediated by soft-core pornography.

Although Amis came under the sway of D. H. Lawrence early in his career, he has more recently assailed him for his anti-Semitism, racism, and misogyny (*Experience,* 117). In *London Fields,* Amis parodies a lyrical passage from Lawrence's *The Rainbow* in order to satirize Keith Talent's squalid pursuits. Rendering the harmony between the Brangwens and their Nottinghamshire land, Lawrence writes that they

> came and went without fear or necessity, working hard because of the life that was in them, not for want of the money. . . . They were aware of the last halfpenny, and instinct made them not waste the peeling of their apple, for it would help feed the cattle. But heaven and earth was teeming around them, and how should this cease? They felt the rush of the sap in spring, they knew the wave which cannot halt, but every year throws forward the seed to begetting, and, falling back, leaves the young-born on the earth. They knew the intercourse between heaven and earth, sunshine drawn into the breast and bowels, the rain sucked up in the daytime, nakedness that comes under the wind in autumn, showing the birds' nests no longer worth hiding. . . . They took the udder of the cows, the cows yielded milk and pulse against the hands of the men. They mounted their horses, and held life between the grip of their knees, they harnessed their horses at the wagon, and, with hand on the bridle-rings, drew the heaving of the horses after their will.[63]

In his parody, Amis imbues Keith's consciousness with a similar sense of harmony and "natural" rhythms:

> The days passed. Though making himself no stranger to pub or club Keith drank nothing and worked hard because of the

life that was in him. He sensed the pulse and body of the street-trade and heard the cars lowing in the furrows. Like new corn the young Swedes and Danes formed lines at his stall, and were reaped. He walked dog and burped baby and drew the keening of wife after his will. The hot macadam pulled on his shoes, like desire, and he had the surety a man knows when there is a sickly Saudi granny in the back of the Cavalier. He harkened to the chirrup of fruit-machine and the tolling of pinball table, humped the dodgy goods and defrayed life's pleasures with sweat of brow and groin and armpit, knew also the firm clasp of Analiese's ankles around his neck, the coarse reassurance of Trish Shirt's hair in his fist. And ever dazed from staring at the sun, the source of all generation. Heaven and earth was teeming around him. And how should this cease? (114)

The reader need not know the source of the style Amis is parodying to understand that the lyrical language is seriocomically at odds with Keith's pursuits.

First-person vernacular narration, or *skaz,* is a common mode of narration in Amis's novels. *The Rachel Papers, Success, Money, Time's Arrow,* and *Night Train* are pure examples of *skaz:* dramatic monologues in which first-person speakers are given full voice and free range, while the author's perspective is implied through irony. The speakers in these quasi-confessional narratives are granted imaginative license to express their most private thoughts, no matter how asocial. In *Success* and *Money,* Amis has created characters in the tradition of Dostoevsky's Underground Man: manic, profane, perversely perceptive. Their very estrangement from conventional society sheds a harsh but illuminating light on the unexamined assumptions of their worlds.

Terry Service, the lower-middle-class orphan who narrates half of *Success,* embraces this tradition in the following yowl of pain: "I want to scream, much of the time, or quiver like a damaged animal. I sit about the place here fizzing with rabies" (52). He calls himself a "quivering condom of neurosis and ineptitude" (142), but he possesses an acute sense of the price to be paid for social success. Raging against his upper-class foster brother, he speculates about what robbed him of "all soulfulness and feeling and heart," turning him into "the little bundle of contempt, vanity and stock-response you pass yourself off as, all the stuff that simply got to you before anything else could" (88). The nakedness of these characters' desires, resentments, and fears throws into ironic relief the assumptions and values of respectable society. Their speech is also an implied dialogue with an implied reader, one of the ways Amis directly engages the reader in their stories, implicates the reader in them, and elicits a mixed response that often combines identification, revulsion, and judgment. In these ways, Amis speaks obliquely "through" his first-person narrators, without offering a definitive judgment of them or the social forces that have shaped them. He leaves both these tasks to the reader.

CHAPTER 2

Nasty Things Are Funny
The Rachel Papers; Dead Babies; Success

Amis's first three novels constitute an informal trilogy. It is possible to identify all three as apprentice works—although this label does an injustice to the stylistic assuredness of *The Rachel Papers* and the rigorously controlled formal structure of *Success*. All three vividly capture masculine appetites, anxieties, and dreads, rendering the rage for "socio-sexual self-betterment" among urban youth with an unerring eye for the shaming detail. They also demonstrate remarkable verbal inventiveness (including a marriage of the demotic and the literary that had a major influence on late twentieth-century British fiction), although in the first two an uncertain control of tone often results in pastiche.[1] They often brilliantly render male misogyny, although it is not always clear where satirized sexism ends and authorial antifeminism begins.[2] Finally, all three constitute a set of opening variations on Amis's great fictional theme—what Adam Phillips has called "self-consciousness, as a threat and a promise (the furtive logic, the demonic secrecy people live by)."[3]

The Rachel Papers

The Rachel Papers (1973) is an audacious first novel. Written by a practicing literary journalist about a would-be literary critic, it makes high comedy out of its own self-reflexiveness. The novel's protagonist and narrator is a hyper-self-conscious nineteen-year-old poised, like his author was when he gave him life, on the brink of worldly success. Charles Highway travels the same educational road that brought Martin Amis to his vocation, and his interior monologues are peppered with the names of writers Amis studied, reviewed, or shared space with on the pages of *Observer,* the *New Statesman,* and the *Times Literary Supplement.* Charles's literary values, moreover, if not his moral ones, echo the early Amis, from his affinity for the grotesque to his unrepentant blurring of the boundaries between high art and popular culture, between measured poetic eloquence and the free verse of the street. The very first sentences of Charles's narration announce the presence of a distinctive voice—sly, inventive, brash, and self-deprecating by turns, in love with words and their power to shape experience: "my name is Charles Highway, though you wouldn't think it to look at me. It's such a rangy, well-travelled, big-cocked name and, to look at it, I am none of these" (3). Amis himself is being characteristically sly here, obliquely indicating that Charles's words are not an entirely reliable index of his character. Since no one's are, this does not prevent Amis from repeatedly speaking through Charles, whose admission that he dresses "not so much with taste as with insight" describes Amis's own fictional voice in this and subsequent novels, often raised in rude protest against the genteel tradition.

In the hands of a less gifted writer, this self-reflexiveness might have become tiresome self-indulgence. But *The Rachel Papers* possesses a ferocious verbal energy that animates every page, and its author has managed to transform his own artistic self-consciousness into a dramatic monologue on the subject spoken by a fully realized character whose obsessiveness becomes the stuff of serious comedy. The following account of

Charles's initial intimacy with Rachel is characteristic: "Only her little brown head was visible. I kissed that for a while, knowing from a variety of sources that this will do more for you than any occult caress. The result was satisfactory. My hands, however, were still behaving like prototype hands, marketed before certain snags had been dealt with. So when I introduced one beneath the blankets, I gave it time to warm and settle before sending it down her stomach. Panties? Panties. I threw back the top sheet, my head a whirlpool of notes, directives, memos, hints, pointers, random scribblings" (158).

In addition to the performance anxiety inscribed here, Charles's manner of speech and thought radiate beyond his single consciousness. Consider the "prototype hands" reference. Like his subsequent use of "memos" and "directives," "prototype" and "marketed" derive from the larger discourse of commodity capitalism. Henri Bergson's theory of comedy posits that human beings laugh at the spectacle of other humans reduced to automatons, which is one obvious source of the humor here.[4] There is something chilling about this comedy, however, since the dehumanization it captures has its source in a social and economic system. Charles's most intimate thoughts and actions are never wholly his own; they are conditioned by a cultural logic that penetrates even the unconscious. In the description above, Charles and Rachel are reduced to body parts, Charles's hands to defective products, his consciousness to an implementation plan.

The title of the novel is similarly double-voiced. It comes from Charles himself, yet it evokes more famous literary predecessors: *The Bickerstaff Papers* (Jonathan Swift) and *The Aspern Papers* (Henry James). The "Rachel Papers" are the mass of notes, diaries, and memoranda that Charles spends the last five hours of his nineteenth year shuffling and reshuffling. "If I run through, let's say, the last three months, and if I try to sort out all my precocity and childishness, my sixth-form cleverness and fifth-form nastiness, all the self-consciousness and self-disgust and self-infatuation and self- . . . you name it, perhaps I'll be able to locate my *hamartia* and see what kind of grown-up I'll make" (4). The novel's twelve chapters are structured by the clock, beginning with "7 o'clock: Oxford" and ending with "Midnight: coming of age." While each chapter is rooted in a precisely realized present, much of the novel's action takes place in a complex series of flashbacks ranging back in time from a few days to several years. By revisiting the past (or rather his literary rendering of it) Charles attempts to construct his currently older, supposedly wiser self. This narrative structure creates much of the comedy of self-consciousness that is *The Rachel Papers*. In the second chapter, for instance, Charles is already quoting his (two-month) younger self, who in his notebook titled *Highway's London* had found his room "oppressive, sulky with the past, crouching in wan defiance as I turned to look at it" (11). Re-reading this patch of purple prose, he responds with a verbal sigh: "My word." Charles's endless literary self-fashioning is more than a symptom of his self-consciousness; it is part of what Amis has called his own "genuine idea about modern life—that it's so mediated that authentic experience is much harder to find."[5]

As befits a novel about self-consciousness, the plot of *The Rachel Papers* concerns Charles's own obsessive plotting: to achieve his twin, intertwined desires of entrance to Oxford and Rachel Noyes. He achieves both, the first on the first attempt and the second (as Rachel's last name implies) after an initial rejection. But his efforts in both cases are so compulsively, self-consciously calculating that they nearly extinguish the genuine passion that may have originally motivated them. From the first, Rachel functions, at least in part, as a fantasy-projection of Charles's own upwardly mobile aspirations (her first name is a virtual anagram of his own). Unlike his current girlfriend, who works contentedly at a pet food store, Rachel is studying for university, and has a tony Hampstead address. Her apparent refinement holds the same allure for Charles as an Oxford degree, and her involvement with another man, an American, increases her desirability. By the time he wins her affections, however, he has already judged her wanting: "Rachel's character was about as high-powered as her syntax" (70). Reductively imagined by Charles, she *is* her prose. Midway through his account of their initial lovemaking, Charles's present-tense voice breaks in to record that his experience was nothing like that which D. H. Lawrence's novels celebrate; it was "an aggregate of pleasureless detail, nothing more; an insane, gruelling, blow-by-blow obstacle course" (152). Similarly, when Charles writes his Oxford entrance essays, Chaucer, Shakespeare, Blake, and Hardy become occasions for rhetorical performances designed to demonstrate his precocity and "characteristic knowingness" (185). Late in the novel he is finally brought up short by the Oxford don who evaluates these essays. His rebuke speaks to Charles's treatment of people as well as literature: "literature has a kind of life of its own, you know. You can't just use it . . . ruthlessly, for your own ends" (215).

This comeuppance is one of the ways Amis places distance between himself and Charles. The others are more subtle, and presume wide acquaintance with many of the writers alluded to in the novel. Of the more than one hundred authors and literary texts alluded to in *The Rachel Papers,* two are of crucial importance to the novel's themes: John Keats's "The Eve of St. Agnes" and Swift's "Cassinus and Peter." Keats's poem is a lushly sensuous rumination on the relationship between romantic desire and self-deception. As soon as Madeleine and Porphyro consummate their passion, wind and sleet assail the window panes of Madeleine's chamber, portending future troubles. Immediately after Rachel admits to Charles that she has lied to him about her father, and Charles has curtailed an admission of his own waning feelings toward her, Charles reports that "the wind outside, which had been strong all evening, started to make cornily portentous noises, cooed from behind the cellar door, fidgeted with the window-frames" (208).

In the previous chapter Charles was confronted by two graphic reminders of Rachel's bodily nature, and this fundamentally alters a relationship which he reports "had been . . . straightforward and idealized . . . utterly without candor" (181). This chapter is subtitled "The Dean of St. Patrick's," a reference to Jonathan Swift, and the unnamed poem that shapes this chapter is the once-infamous "Cassinus and Peter," a satirical portrait of a Cambridge undergraduate driven to hysteria by his discovery that his beloved "Celia, Celia, Celia shits!"[6] Unlike Cassinus, Charles is aware of the role self-deception plays in his desire, but the sexual double-standard still holds sway over him. Despite his longing for authenticity, his Keatsian desire to embrace pure sensation, few of Charles's experiences are direct ones. In one of his many moments of self-criticism, he indicts himself for this: "I will not be placed at the mercy of my spontaneous self" (180).

Charles's preternatural self-consciousness as he composes his one and only narrative is analogous to Martin Amis's own as he wrote his first novel in the shadow of his famous novelist father.[7] How to put oneself on the map, place enough distance between oneself and one's most significant precursor? Charles's conflicts with his father, his provisional reconciliation with him, and his success in fashioning his own narrative voice suggest some answers. Significantly, and despite the novel's focus on his pursuit of Rachel, Charles's relationship with his father forms the emotional center of the novel. This is made clear in the first chapter, when Charles notes that it is "strange" that "although my father is probably the most fully documented character in my files, he doesn't merit a note-pad to himself, let alone a folder" (8). He is present even (especially) in his formal absence, in other words. Like Kingsley Amis, Gordon Highway has spent some time lecturing at Cambridge, and he is also in the writing profession (he is the editor of a prestigious business journal). Charles subsequently informs the reader that he was thirteen when he discovered that his father had a mistress; that he has begun a "Letter to My Father" (Kafka wrote a famous letter of the same title) documenting his grievances against him; that his father is becoming a political reactionary. These are, of course, sources of familial tension familiar to Martin Amis. Charles's "rebellion" takes complex forms, including equal measures of moral disapproval, presumed superiority, and exaggerated difference on the one hand, and parody which sometimes turns into outright imitation on the other.

This is not unlike the relationship between *The Rachel Papers* and *Lucky Jim*. Both are first novels by gifted comic writers, and both bear many family resemblances, from mastery of dialect and dialogue to delight in comic incongruities. But *The Rachel Papers* is clearly, defiantly different than *Lucky Jim*. At first glance, the earlier novel might seem the more subversive: Jim Dixon is lower middle-class, anti-establishment, and anti-pretension, a would-be radical lecturer in history who calls into question certain class-bound pieties of British intellectual culture. It was written when its author was a member of the Communist Party, and it won him the label "Angry Young Man," applied to a handful of British writers who railed against the status quo in the fifties. Charles, by contrast, seldom meets a pretense he doesn't want to adopt, and he is all too eager to join the (intellectual) establishment. The genuinely radical student movements of the sixties have merely provided him with another pose to assume (that of the drug-savvy hippie) when the right social opportunity arises.

Yet for all his supposed subversiveness, Jim Dixon never questions the patriarchal, materialistic, even homophobic assumptions that inform his sensibility. Nor does his author. *Lucky Jim* conforms to the traditional comic paradigm (definitively outlined by Northrop Frye in his *Anatomy of Criticism*) in which a well-suited couple, attracted to one another but separated by various social barriers, overcome all obstacles to their union and end up in each other's arms. *Lucky Jim* is more comic romance than comic satire: Jim Dixon is treated with authorial sympathy throughout. His favorite maxim is "nice things are nicer than nasty ones,"[8] and the nicest thing in his world is the conventionally attractive Christine Callaghan. He is rewarded with her at novel's end, along with a job working in her uncle's office.

Charles Highway has clearly read *Lucky Jim,* because midway through the novel he explicitly rejects Jim Dixon's maxim and replaces it with his own down-and-dirty comic aesthetic: "surely, nice things are dull, and nasty things are funny. The nastier a thing is, the funnier it gets" (87). Expressed so crudely, this may sound like little more than an adolescent male's malicious sense of humor—and Martin Amis's way of tweaking his father. But it is, in fact, consistent with Charles's earlier aesthetic announcement: "I had begun to explore the literary grotesque, in particular the writings of Charles Dickens and Franz Kafka, to find a world full of bizarre surfaces and sneaky tensions with which I was always trying to invest my life" (62). The fictions of Dickens and Kafka often combine cruelty and laughter, of course. So do the satires of Jonathan Swift. What is emerging here is Martin Amis's own literary manifesto—one part exorcism of his father's precedent, one part declaration that his own comedy veers toward the grotesque.

Charles's assertion that "nasty things are funny" comes at the beginning of a chapter titled "Nine: the bathroom," in which he speculates about his "anal sense of humor" ("very common among my age group"). As he speculates further about its source, he suggests that it stems from a "sound distrust of personal vanity plus literary relish of physical grotesqueries" (87). This brings Swift to mind, whose own representations of bodily excesses are inseparable from his Christian humanism. Vanity was one of Swift's favorite satiric targets, and he deflates it by rubbing his readers' noses in the corruptibility of their fleshly selves. Amis's own aesthetic of the carnal in *The Rachel Papers,* however, is less moralistic, and more transgressive, than Swift's.

The Rachel Papers, in fact, consistently subverts aesthetic and moral norms, claiming they are the enemy of fictional realism. Charles's self-assessment late in the novel is typical of this posture:

So I am nineteen years old and don't usually know what I'm doing, snap my thoughts out of the printed page, get my

looks from other eyes, do not overtake dotards and cripples
in the street for fear I will depress them with my agility, love
watching children and animals at play but wouldn't mind
seeing a beggar kicked or a little girl run over because it's all
experience, dislike myself and sneer at a world less nice and
less intelligent than me. I take it this is fairly routine? (207)

This open-endedness characterizes the entire narrative
structure of *The Rachel Papers*. In chapter nine of the novel,
when his rival for Rachel's affections is out of the picture,
Charles interrupts his narration, warning the reader not to
expect conventional comic satisfactions: "in the following
phase, with the obstructive elements out of the way . . . the
comic action would have been due to end, happily. But who is
going to believe that any more?" In the world Charles and his
author inhabit, "we have got into the habit of going further and
further beyond the happy-ever-more promise: relationships in
decay, aftermaths, but with everyone being told a thing or two
about themselves, busy learning from their mistakes" (150). In
fact, *The Rachel Papers* frustrates even these last two expectations. Characteristically, Charles writes to Rachel to break off
their affair, and though she comes to confront him with his cal-
lousness, she stalks out of the room instead. Charles ends his
autobiographical narrative by refilling his pen, not taking moral
stock.

All of the potentially serious emotional scenes in *The
Rachel Papers* are similarly curtailed, or inadequately realized.
When Rachel initially declines Charles's advances, for instance,
his reaction is surprising ("I felt completely hollow, as if I were
a child" [84]), because glibness and calculation have so dominated his account of his relationship to her. Charles wants to

represent his affair (to the reader and Rachel) as his first emotionally serious relationship, but it is never convincingly rendered as such. Similarly, near the end of the novel Charles has a final confrontation with his father, which becomes a reconciliation. But Charles's emotional freight is so quickly unloaded, and his expression of solidarity with his father so pat, that it seems like another verbal pose.

Given the parodic nature of *The Rachel Papers,* this is not surprising. While the novel can be read as a (male) adolescent coming of age story, it can just as easily be taken as a parody of the genre, not to mention a parody of the kind of comic romance Kingsley produced in *Lucky Jim.* Parody is subversive, representing a rejection of social or aesthetic authority, but it doesn't elaborate alternatives. Unlike Jim Dixon, who clearly becomes the moral center of *Lucky Jim,* Charles Highway remains something of an enigma at the end of *The Rachel Papers.* He is not simply a satiric target; *The Rachel Papers* may be a satiric comedy, but it is not a full-fledged satire. Author and reader may laugh at Charles's excesses, but they are also implicated in them. *The Rachel Papers* is Amis's first achievement in that most demanding of narrative modes, the dramatic monologue—requiring that the novelist make his own voice heard through, and sometimes in spite of, the first-person narrator. It is a form Amis raises to the level of high postmodern art in several of his later novels, when his narrators bear fewer resemblances to him than Charles does. In *The Rachel Papers,* it is not always clear where Amis stands in relation to his narrator.

What is clear, however, is that at the level of verbal inventiveness and style, *The Rachel Papers* is the work of a major talent. This was publicly recognized in 1974, when the novel won England's Somerset Maugham Prize, and unexpectedly reaffirmed in 1980, when it was discovered that the American writer Jacob Epstein had plagiarized substantial portions of *The Rachel Papers* in composing *Wild Oats,* his own first novel. Amis wrote about his discovery of this theft in a 1980 issue of the *Observer.* In a thoughtful, nuanced rumination on the sometimes fuzzy line between allusiveness and plagiarism, Amis regretfully notes that Epstein stole much more than many of his words: he stole his style, which "is not something grafted on to ordinary language: it is inherent in the way a writer sees the world." After establishing the extent of Epstein's pilfering, Amis goes out of his way to praise Epstein as a "genuinely talented writer."[9] Actually, Amis is being generous. As Thomas Mallon notes in his lively, illuminating account of the case in his book *Stolen Words,* a comparison of these two novels demonstrates that it is Amis who possesses that rare gift—a genuinely distinctive literary voice, one that speaks incisively *of* as well as *to* its generation.

Dead Babies

In *Dead Babies* (1975), Amis moves from first to third person; from a precisely rendered present to an indeterminate near-future; from semi-autobiographical satiric comedy to full-blown Menippean satire. An epigraph from the third-century satirist Menippus alerts the reader to this last fact: "and so even when [the satirist] presents a vision of the future, his business is not prophecy; just as his subject is not tomorrow . . . it is today" (xii). The portentousness of this statement is an accurate index of the overly programmatic nature of *Dead Babies,* which constitutes a virtual encyclopedia of Menippean effects without ever fully succeeding as either satire or novel.[10]

Dead Babies is Amis's first and last experiment in formal satire, and it is easy to see why. It exhibits the same verbal inventiveness that characterizes *The Rachel Papers,* but little of its comic high spirits. In place of the fully realized Charles Highway, Amis presents ten minimally rendered characters, most of them suffering from "street sadness" and "cancelled sex," their outward liberation masking inward blight. And they are all forced to serve a satire that is less successful than the satirical comedy of *The Rachel Papers.* Nastiness proliferates—*Dead Babies* is not for the squeamish—but the novel is only fitfully funny. Despite these limitations, *Dead Babies* is full of interest— for readers of Amis as well as students of satire and the novel. It manifests Amis's ambitious experiments with genre, point of view, and voice as he moves beyond the autobiographical locus of his first novel and toward the wider social engagements of his later work.

Among other things, *Dead Babies* is a perverse variant on the British genre of the country house weekend novel made popular by P. G. Wodehouse.[11] The narrative spans three days, Friday through Sunday. Six English residents of Appleseed Rectory play host to a weekend revel featuring increasing amounts of alcohol, drugs, and thwarted sex. They are joined by a trio of Americans, a young woman from London, and the mysterious "Johnny," who turns out to be a double of one of the other characters. The authorial persona, who appears occasionally to remind the reader of his control over the other eleven, constitutes a shadowy twelfth character. The "dead babies" of the title refers to a variety of humanist beliefs that most members of the group have declared defunct. This phrase is evoked whenever any of these beliefs threaten the narcissistic ethos articulated most aggressively by Marvell Buzhardt. Buzhardt is American, a "postgraduate in psychology, anthropology, and environment at Columbia University," and the author of *The Mind Lab,* which promotes the hedonistic use of psychoactive chemicals. As the weekend proceeds he distributes a variety of these drugs to the Appleseeders, fostering in each an illusory sense of power and control. The increasingly outrageous, ultimately deadly effects of his prescriptions constitute Amis's judgment on the ethos that produced them.

As *Dead Babies* opens, the reader learns that Quentin Villiers, the lord of Appleseed estate, has been reading *Rameau's Nephew* by Denis Diderot. *Rameau's Nephew* is one of the great Menippean satires of the eighteenth century. Amis is here providing one of many intertextual clues to his own narrative program. Mikhail Bakhtin provides an extended definition of this form of satire in his book *Problems of Dostoevsky's Poetics,* which was reviewed in the *Times Literary Supplement* in 1974, during Amis's tenure as fiction and poetry editor.[12] The most important characteristic of the form, Bakhtin writes, "lies in the fact that the most daring and unfettered fantasies . . . and adventures are internally motivated, justified and illuminated here by a purely ideological and philosophical end—to create *extraordinary situations* in which to provoke and test a philosophical idea . . ." The testing of this idea or truth is given priority over "the testing of a specific individual or social-typical human character."[13] It is clear from the beginning of *Dead Babies* that the characters will be subordinated to the ends of satire. After briefly introducing the main English characters, the narrator announces "these are the six that answer to our purposes"(19). Later, answering the anguished soliloquy of the endlessly victimized Keith Whitehead ("who's doing it all to me, eh?"), the narrator is even more explicit: "you simply *had* to be that way . . . merely in order to serve the designs of this particular fiction" (146–47).

Menippean satire is a hybrid form. "The organic combination of philosophical dialog, lofty symbolism, fantastic adventure and underworld naturalism is a remarkable characteristic of the Menippea," Bakhtin writes.[14] Each of these elements is given play in *Dead Babies*. Amis stages several dialogues— "those conversations," he calls them, between Marvell and various Appleseed residents—which echo those of the two speakers in *Rameau's Nephew*. In Diderot's dialogue, one of the speakers is an unrepentant hedonist and hypocrite who insists his position is the necessary outcome of the materialist philosophy on which Enlightenment reason is founded. He is opposed by a speaker who clings to the belief that civic virtue is compatible with materialistic determinism. In *Dead Babies,* Marvell is the voice of hedonism, and he articulates certain au courant ideas of his generation. It is left to Quentin to oppose Marvell's post-humanist values, at least rhetorically. He defends love, monogamy, even feudalism, often sounding like an eighteenth-century English squire. He is an anachronism, in other words. Marvell, on the other hand, echoes another representative of the eighteenth century, one who has gained a certain currency in the twentieth: the Marquis de Sade. Sade's celebration of perversity was not a rejection of Enlightenment values so much as a dark variant of Enlightenment mastery over nature. In a similar sense, Marvell exemplifies one logical outcome of contemporary enlightenment thinking. He uses Andy Adorno's embrace of a guerilla theater group called the Conceptualists, who believe that "Other sex is to do with choice rather than urge," to argue that "perversion is justified—no, demanded—by an environment that is now totally man-made, totally without a biology"

(154). Marvell is a late-twentieth-century embodiment of the same presumptuous and reductive rationalism that satire has traditionally opposed.

Although his assumptions tend to dominate these philosophical dialogues, Marvell's "values" are implicitly critiqued by a pattern of "lofty" symbolism. *Dead Babies* is divided into three sections; the list of "main characters" is arranged so as to emphasize two groups of six and three; the action takes place over a three-day weekend; the sexual preference of the Americans is the ménage à trois; the neurosis (or psychosis) of each character is traced to the Oedipal triangle. The weekend orgy of sex, drugs, and depravity that constitutes the action of *Dead Babies* is a kind of infernal parody of the Last Supper, with presiding host Quentin Villiers ultimately revealed as the Antichrist (his last name evokes the word "villain" and anagrammatically contains the word "evil"). There is even a parody of the crucifixion when the long-suffering dwarf Keith Whitehead is roped to the blossoming apple tree in the rectory garden, where "two grimed hypodermics hung from his bloated arms" (187). "We're ecstatic materialists," crows Andy in a moment of drunken epiphany (140), but ecstasy is conspicuous only by its absence. In this extreme satire on countercultural liberation theology the sacraments of drugs and sex substitute for emotional or spiritual ones, but they never bestow even fleeting grace. For all the compulsive talk of, and graphically rendered attempts at, sexual congress in the novel, only one couple consummates their desire, and this event leaves the woman in tears.

Body fluids of all kinds flow copiously in *Dead Babies*, but they are not purgative. They express the varieties of personal and social disease produced by everything from parental neglect to the aestheticization of violence. In Menippean satire, as

Bakhtin writes, "the idea . . . has no fear of the underworld or of the filth of life,"[15] and Amis, providing proof, rubs the reader's face in it. The worst tendencies of the present are exaggerated and projected into a post-seventies future that has become a theater of cruelty, with the body as its stage. The simulated beating of an aged comedian that the Appleseeders witness at a venue called "the Psychologic Revue" is brutal and shocking, but it is mirrored to varying degrees in the pain and humiliation the characters visit on each other. Keith, described in the character list as "court dwarf," is fed experimental drugs by Quentin and Andy, who simultaneously delight in and learn from the spectacle of his reactions. Later, in back-to-back scenes of shocking detail, he is sexually assaulted by the three Americans. Physical anxieties and humiliations are commonplace in *Dead Babies,* from Giles Coldstream's dental nightmares to Andy's bouts of impotence, which strike hardest when he meets a woman he can't dominate. The narrator offers brief but graphic sexual histories for each character, and these, along with their physical eccentricities, define them. In a novel, this formula would seem hopelessly reductive. In a satire on narcissism, it serves to suggest what life has been reduced to.

The satire in *Dead Babies* is not quite so fixed as this reading has so far suggested. It is more than a conservative howl of obscene rage at moral decline (although, like all satire, it is motivated in part by conservative impulses). It is closer in spirit to the philosophical open-endedness of *Rameau's Nephew* than the stable moral ironies of Swift's *A Modest Proposal* (by titling his satire *Dead Babies,* Amis is aligning it with Swift's shocking *Proposal,* in which the speaker calls for the killing and eating of Irish babies). Swift always maintains a clinical distance from the characters and narrators who are the targets of his satire; Amis is, to varying degrees, complicit with his. This is registered in *Dead Babies* in varying ways, most noticeably in Amis's uncertain control of tone at crucial moments. While he strives for and usually maintains a coolly detached point of view, at times his judgment fails him, and his writing goes soft. Near the end of the novel, for instance, just before doom descends, the narrator abandons satire for bathos: "But pity the dead babies. Now, before it starts. They couldn't know what was behind them nor what was to come. The past? They had none. Like children after a long day's journey, their lives arranged themselves in a patchwork of vanished mornings, lost afternoons, and probable yesterdays" (164). Verbal triplets are characteristic of Amis's style; here they strive for a portentous tone that clashes with the novel's black comedy.

A more complex manifestation of this open-endedness can be found in the character of Quentin Villiers. Although he mouths the traditional pieties of love, commitment, and paternal responsibility, he actually represents a trap laid for the reader, a false alternative to the excesses of the others. His heart is the darkest of all. He is finally more like de Sade than Marvell himself: a monster of perversion and rapacity. Readers seeking safe harbor with Quentin find themselves alone and unprotected in the final storm. In an important sense Quentin, who combines civility and sadism, deference and control, who has one foot firmly planted in the eighteenth century, symbolizes the historical conditions that gave rise to the Marvells of the contemporary scene. In *Dialectic of Enlightenment,* Max Horkheimer and Theodor Adorno (Andy's namesake) argue that "Enlightenment is totalitarian," since the "reason" it enshrined provided the means for dominating nature and other men, masking that domination under the rubric of scientific rationalism. In this reading of the Enlightenment, de Sade can be seen as a radical truth teller. "Whereas the optimistic writers [of the Enlightenment] merely disavowed and denied in order to protect the indissoluble union of reason and crime, civil society and domination, the dark chroniclers mercilessly declared the shocking truth." Then Horkheimer and Adorno quote from de Sade's novel *Justine:* "Heaven vouchsafes these riches to those whose hands are soiled by the murder of wives and children, by sodomy, assassination, prostitution, and atrocities; to reward me for these shameful deeds, it offers me wealth."[16] At the end of *Dead Babies,* having killed his wife, Diana, and Marvell, Quentin sits in the Appleseed Rectory kitchen, waiting for Keith to arrive. He has arranged evidence that will implicate the Conceptualists in all the killings and free him from suspicion. "His green eyes flashed into the dawn like wild, dying suns" (206).

Quentin's case becomes even more interesting in light of the ways he is like his author. Most obviously, he is a man of letters. He edits a "satirico-politico-literary magazine" at London University. He is urbane, witty, and presides over the goings on at Appleseed Rectory like a combination reveler, entertainer, and sadistic ringmaster. Moreover, he bears the same family resemblance to his creator that Charles Highway does: "Quentin was an adept at character stylization, a master of pastiche, a connoisseur of verbal self-dramatization" (38). He is, in other words, a partial portrait of the artist as a young Martin Amis. Since Quentin is shown to be a subtle plagiarist in the reviews he writes for his magazine, there are also ways in which his depiction involves a degree of authorial self-interrogation. Amis has acknowledged that *Dead Babies* is derivative, noting in particular his debt to Anthony Burgess, Vladimir Nabokov, and William S. Burroughs.[17] In 1971, Stanley Kubrick's film version of Anthony Burgess's *A Clockwork Orange* was playing in London, and *Dead Babies* certainly partakes of that novel's dystopian vision of the future. That same year, in an *Observer* review titled "A Book of the Dead," Amis described the characters in Burroughs's *The Wild Boys* in terms that could apply to many of the blasted denizens of *Dead Babies:* "the ironist's version of nature without nurture, like Swift's Yahoos—filthy, treacherous, dreamy, vicious and lustful."[18]

Finally, Quentin's calculated ruthlessness in dispatching the other characters has an eerie parallel in Amis's own attitude toward them. *Dead Babies* is full of animus and condescension toward Amis's generation, and Quentin's final burst of murderous violence is its ultimate symbolic expression. In *The Rachel Papers,* Amis seeks to exorcise his father's generation; in *Dead Babies,* he enacts a similar ritual on his own.

Success

The narrative "doubling" characteristic of both *The Rachel Papers* and *Dead Babies* becomes an organizing principle in *Success* (1978), a novel which could be said to initiate a second informal trilogy in Amis's career even as it concludes a first. As a culmination of one series, *Success* represents a major formal advance. Gone is the stylistic patchwork, the occasional wavering of tone, the sometimes intrusive self-reflexivity that mark his first two novels. In their place is a rigorously controlled narrative consisting of parallel dramatic monologues spoken by feuding foster brothers: Gregory Riding and Terrence Service. Taken together, these monologues form an "X" whose intersection marks the death of Greg's sister Ursula, which both men have contributed to. It also represents the crossing point in the fortunes of each: while one brother falls in the world, the other ascends. As this geometry suggests, and even granting the precisely rendered differences between the two, they emerge as doubles of one another, much as Quentin and Andy do in *Dead Babies.* Only now such doubling is an explicit theme. Karl Miller describes the novel this way: "*Success* is an orphan delirium, and the first of three fictions, a series of turmoils, in which orphan and double meet."[19] The other two are *Other People: A Mystery,* and *Money: A Suicide Note,* which will be considered in separate chapters.

Success also manifests some significant intertextual "doublings." The first of these is hinted at in the book's dedication: "To Philip." Philip is the name of Amis's older brother, who was named after the poet Philip Larkin—a regular visitor to the Amis household during Martin Amis's childhood.[20] Martin Amis has written of Larkin's work with great admiration,[21] and Larkin's 1946 novel *Jill* anticipates *Success* in its focus on a young working-class man in awe and envy of his decadent, aristocratic Oxford roommate. In addition, Amis's treatment of the damage Terry suffers at the hands of his father, and Terry's own oft-repeated lament that he is "fucked up," constitute a narrative excursion into the nihilistic territory Larkin explored in his 1971 poem "This Be the Verse," with its bleak opening stanza: "They fuck you up, your mum and dad / They may not want to, but they do / They fill you with the faults they had / And add some extra, just for you."[22] In his own narration, Terry implicitly doubles himself with Oliver Twist, emphasizing the Dickensian qualities of his orphaned childhood, from the grim and violent squalor of his early years to his fairytale ascension into privilege when he is adopted by Gregory's wealthy family. Ultimately, however, Terry comes to resemble the Artful Dodger more than Oliver.

Vladimir Nabokov also inhabits the margins of *Success*. Its title is also the title of a novel by the fictional author featured in the first book Nabokov wrote in English: *The Real Life of Sebastian Knight*. Nabokov's novel is narrated by Sebastian Knight's half-brother, who searches in vain for the definitive truth about a person he feels he is virtually *becoming* by the end of his quest—a doubling echoed in a different register at the end of *Success*. In his first essay on Nabokov, published two years after *Success*, Amis claims that Nabokov's characteristic literary mode is the "sublime," focused not on some ideal world, but "directed at our fallen world of squalor, absurdity and talentlessness. Sublimity replaces the ideas of motivation and plot with those of obsession and destiny. It suspends moral judgements in favour of remorselessness, a helter-skelter intensity."[23] This description certainly applies to Amis's own procedures in *Success* (and most of his other novels), as does his comment about *Lolita* in a later essay: "it constructs a mind in the way that a prose Browning might have gone about it, through rigorous dramatic monologue."[24] As with all dramatic monologues, *Success* expects a great deal of the reader, who is left to construct the truth from the unspoken gaps in and between each narrative.

Success chronicles a year in the lives of Greg and Terry, who share a flat in Bayswater, a fashionable west London neighborhood. A chapter is assigned to each month. The novel begins in January and ends in December, emphasizing a cyclical pattern consistent with the place-trading fortunes of the two: in the end, as in the beginning, one is abject, the other ascendant. Each chapter is subdivided into alternating monologues; Terry speaks first, then Greg. (In a deftly self-reflexive touch, the first words of each brother, spoken as they pick up the phone in the first chapter at the beginning of their monologues, are "Terry speaking" and "Gregory speaking."[7, 15]).

Terry—a short, balding, unsuccessful but ambitious salesman —is a distant literary cousin of Little Keith in *Dead Babies*. Greg constantly refers to him as a "yob," a British slang term (an inversion of the word "boy") for a loutish male.[25] Greg—a tall, attractive, decadent, seemingly successful art gallery manager—bears a similar familial resemblance to Quentin Villiers. Terry was adopted at age nine by the philanthropic Mr. Riding after Terry's seven-year-old sister was murdered by his father: "I don't know whether my father killed my mother; but I bloody know he killed my sister, because I was there at the time and watched him as he did so. (Suck on that. It's easy enough to see what it was that fucked me up. I go on about all this a lot. I make no apologies. It's just too bad. I'm allowed to go on about it, on account of it fucking me up)" (25). His horrific past has bestowed him with a protective resilience, however, which Greg is forced to acknowledge as his own deceptions and self-deceptions begin to unravel and their fortunes are reversed. "And Terry. What is this with him now? No, *don't* tell me. Don't tell me he's becoming a success. NO, don't tell me that. . . . But the yobs are winning. And Terry, of course, is 'doing well.' He has shown that he will perform what is necessary to succeed" (184).

Despite their mutual malice, Greg and Terry's voices initially engage the reader with their immediacy, their dialectical authenticity, and their confessional intimacy. The foster brothers' narratives are dialogic: each speaker is intensely aware of the other speaker and of the reader. Their remarks are sprinkled with direct addresses to an assumed listener. "I'm drinking a lot these days," Terry says in the first chapter, adding "wouldn't you be?" (12). When his turn comes, Terry says of his decadent friends, "they're marvellous fun—you'll like them" (41). Each also intermittently quizzes or counsels the reader about his counterpart. "Has he said anything to you about it?" (45), Terry asks after reporting what Gregory has told him about his liaison with Terry's ex-girlfriend Miranda, and Greg wonders if Terry "has said anything about my sexual dispositions" (18).

Greg and Terry's repeated interrogatives function like hooks, pulling the reader into their perceptual worlds, their quandaries and queries. Terry's early questions are particularly endearing in this regard; he is a bit like Lemuel Gulliver, plopped down on this island earth as if from some other planet, puzzling through the streets of a strange land. "Sometimes I will turn, halfway along the stone corridor, to see that I am being followed by curious and unfriendly eyes. And once I'm down there, down in the streets of the earth, and the train bursts angrily out of its hole, and I try to join the people stacked inside—I keep expecting them to make some spontaneous gesture of protest, hardening their van to keep me out. (This can't be alienation, can it? I want to belong. I'm dying to belong)" (32).[26]

For a time then, and to differing degrees, the reader feels close to the two narrators, and implicated in their stories, almost as a relative would. Indeed, each speaks to the reader with the intimacy and special pleading that a sibling might, seeking an ally. Amis wants the reader to experience the way these two men think, and what they represent, from the inside, and the hothouse atmosphere induced by their narratives achieves this. So do the suggestions that they are symbolic doubles. Early in the novel, for instance, Terry notes the parallels in their family histories. "Mr. Riding and my father were the same age, and Greg's and my birthdays were only twenty-four hours apart; Ursula, Greg's sister, and mine were both seven at the time, and were alike the survivors of abbreviated twins—and so on" (27).

Other similarities emerge as the narrative proceeds. The benign neglect of Terry's aristocratic parents bequeathed him an emotional sterility to match Greg's barely controlled neurotic anxiety. Indeed, Terry's overt narcissism is ultimately matched by Greg's stealthier variety, which emerges fully only when he achieves the necessary social and economic status.

In chapter four, Terry had warned the reader that "Gregory is a liar. Don't believe a word he says. He is the author of lies" (88). It is the first of many explicit warnings in the novel, voiced by Amis through his characters, that his two narrators are unreliable, that the reader needs to be on guard. It is an especially apt warning in regard to Greg: the most shocking scene in the novel, his brutal seduction of Terry's would-be girlfriend Jan, turns out to be a product of Greg's delusional imagination. It is also one of the ways Amis engineers a progressive withdrawal of sympathy and identification from Terry and Greg, encouraging the reader to evaluate the underlying social and familial causes of their respective pathologies.

There is, in fact, something uncomfortably close about the intimate relationship initially established among foster brothers and reader in *Success,* and the reader's recognition of this coincides with consecutive revelations of the literal incest that exists at the corrosive center of the novel. Terry was nine when his sister was killed by his father. Greg was nine when he initiated an incestuous relationship with his sister Ursula. Abused and victimized women thus define the family histories of both characters. Through special pleading, Greg tries to convince the reader that his intimacy with Ursula is exempt from moral censure. With sneering superiority, he calls the prohibition against incest "a strip of warped lead from the gutter presses, a twitch in the responses of philistines and suburbanites, a 'sin' only in the eyes of the hated and the mean" (66). He claims that he and Ursula came together innocently in childhood, clinging to one another in the absence of parental warmth.

From Greg's earliest confessions, however, it is clear that incest is both the product and the embodiment of the pathological narcissism that forms the ground of his being. Greg's description of Ursula's response when he first caressed her alludes to Narcissus's own immobilizing stare into self-reflecting waters. It reveals more about his own desires than his sister's: "Ursula looked up at me encouragingly, her face lit by a lake of dreams" (68). In one sense all of the doubling in the novel, and all of the abuse and betrayal, double back to this primal moment. It initiates a kind of narcissistic withdrawal from the larger world and from other people that blights Greg's later life. As an adult, he is unwilling to face the fact that his continuing intimacies with his sister have emotionally maimed her and driven her to suicide. When he does turn his mind to her, his thoughts are self-damning, and reveal his essential infantilism. "Why does she cry so much *now*? What else can she be crying for but the lost world of our childhood, when it didn't seem to matter what we did?" (117).

Terry harbors a different kind of pathology. Significantly, it is well adapted to the world of late-1970s London, a world where "socio-sexual self-betterment" (as both Greg and Terry term it) is the ruling ethos. Thus it is not surprising that once Terry gains the social upper hand, he should take up where Greg has left off. He coaxes Ursula into his bed, pressures her to repeat sexual acts she performed on Greg, and hastens her self-destruction. Out of gratitude, he offers a kind of mechanical reciprocation, unaware that Ursula takes no pleasure in his advances. When she does finally come to him for sexual comfort, after Greg has permanently rejected her in a fit of jealous pique over Terry, their union is brief, fitful, and desperate. Terry's self-absolving description of their last conversation before Ursula's suicide precisely captures his own emergent sociopathology: "I merely pointed out, gently but firmly, that there was no sense in which I could assume responsibility for her, that you cannot 'take people on' any longer while still trying to function success-fully in your own life, that she was on her own now, the same as me, the same as Greg, the same as everybody else" (207).

The moral monstrosity spawned by this obsession with suc-cess is the central vehicle of Amis's social satire in *Success*. The novel was published the year before Margaret Thatcher rose to power as head of the England's Conservative Party; Terry and Gregory's acrimonious coexistence prophetically captures the increasingly intertwined, antagonistic relationship between the monied classes and their envious, entrepreneurial rivals. Gra-ham Fuller has said *Success* is "a parody of England's class war, with Gregory and Terry symbolizing the spiritual decay of the landed gentry and the greedy self-betterment of the 'yobs,'"[27] although it may be more accurate to see their animosity as rep-resenting the political struggle within the Conservative party itself. Certainly both Terry and Greg personify versions of the philistinism and greed that many of Thatcher's critics predicted would be her ideological legacy.

Success is acutely attuned to London in the late 1970s, whose streets Greg walks while observing, in his inimitably reactionary fashion, "the great bus-borne ecologies of fat-faced identical Germans, check-trousered colonials and arachnoid Arabs" (42) who wield increasing commercial power. Terry, on the other hand, is haunted by a fear of falling to the level of the "tramps" and "hippies" he passes on the streets, in whose stoned-out faces he glimpses his own potential fate. Sitting at his office desk, he gives in to paranoia about losing his job. "I see myself from behind, my craven tread, my hair, and beyond me, through the blue window, I glimpse that second figure up in the streets of the sky, that familiar, shuffling, grubby, mackintoshed caricature, Terry the Tramp" (39). Before long he begins encountering an actual tramp whose "orange-peel face is scored with trickly yellow lines from crying in the cold sun," and resolves to "speak to him soon and ask him what it's like" (65). When he does, his attempted charity is recognized for the self-serving condescension that it is, and answered with something more honest: naked, crude hostility. Near the end of the novel, Terry has one last meeting with this shadowy alter ego, and it measures the absolute depth of his moral fall. "I kicked him clumsily on the side of the head. I'd tried to keep my left foot on his hand—for extra tension—and half lost my balance in the process" (209). After brutalizing him, Terry takes a ten-pound note from his pocket and stuffs it in his hand. "A fair deal, probably. Fair for him and fair for me" (209–10). By the end of the novel, Terry's language, like everything else in his life, has been reduced to the level of commerce.

Terry's obsessive class envy is inscribed in his definition of "chippy," offered early in the novel: "it means minding being poor, ugly, and common" (57). Tom Paulin has argued that this definition remains unchallenged by the novel. "It is a term that recognizes and colludes with the authority of class, and it passively submits to the condition of being an anxiety-ridden *petit bourgeois*."[28] Yet it is important to remember that it is Terry and Greg who collude with the authority of class, not necessarily their author. Petit bourgeois anxiety is one of Amis's subjects. So is the misogyny that Graham Fuller attributes to Amis. Fuller rightly complains that the women characters in *Success* are little more than caricatures: "Ursula and Jan are pawns, a thin, mindless, upper-class waif and a voluptuous, sardonic, working-class strumpet." Then he commits a critical error that is common among readers of Amis: "In keeping with their creator's misogyny, they're discarded once they've served their purpose."[29] Terry and Greg's attitudes toward women are appalling; their behavior toward women is often shocking. Shock is one of Amis's favorite fictional strategies.[30] But this need not be confused with authorial misogyny. Certainly Amis can be faulted for a thinness of characterization when it comes to women, and a reductively binary view of gender that constitutes a form of sexism, but in *Success* Ursula and Jan are pawns in Amis's anatomy of male misogyny, not in his own sustained attack on women. This confusion of the author with his characters—in this case two first-person narrators whose voices necessarily dominate the novel—is an inherent danger of the dramatic monologue. In his subsequent first-person narratives, Amis will take additional steps to discourage such confusion.

CHAPTER 3

Entering the "Martian School"
Other People: A Mystery Story

Judged by its ambition and risk taking, *Other People: A Mystery Story* (1981) must be considered one of Amis's most important novels. Pursuing his quest to "see the world differently,"[1] Amis looks through the eyes (and ears, nose, taste, touch, mind) of a woman suffering from what seems to be amnesia. The novel consists of her experiences in contemporary London, and her encounters with a series of "other people," including her pre-amnesiac self, Amy Hide. This former self was morally corrupt and corrupting, whereas her "re-born" self, who takes the name Mary Lamb, is a moral innocent, discovering the world anew. Choosing a woman as his main character represents one kind of risk for Amis, and a major departure from his first three novels. Rendering the world primarily from her amnesiac perspective constitutes another. "When the past is forgotten," says the third-person narrator, a shadowy presence whose commentary punctuates the action of the novel, "the present is unforgettable" (56).

One of Amis's achievements here consists in making the familiar hauntingly strange. The subtitle of *Other People* suggests a kinship with one of the most enduring popular genres, but fans of Agatha Christie and other conventional mystery writers are in for some surprises. The reader is the only detective at work in *Other People,* and the literal mystery of Mary

Lamb's identity and fate is finally less important than the philosophical puzzles the novel pursues. *Other People* is a novel of existential mystery (the first half of its title alludes to Jean-Paul Sartre's play *No Exit,* with its famous line "hell is—other people!"), and it explores the enigmas of time, memory, sexual identity, evil, death—and other people.[2] To do so, the novel adopts the techniques of what came to be known as the "Martian School of Poetry." Its members include Craig Raine and Christopher Reid, whose poetry Amis promoted in both the *Times Literary Supplement* and the *New Statesman.* Amis's excursion into this representational territory is significant not only for what it helps him achieve in *Other People,* but because it looks ahead to similar experiments with language, imagery, and point of view in *Money, Time's Arrow,* and several of the stories in *Einstein's Monsters* and *Heavy Water.*

Poetic precedents are crucial to a full understanding of *Other People.* On December 14, 1979, a little more than a year before the appearance of his fourth novel, Amis published the poem "Point of View" in the *New Statesman.* Amis makes no claims for himself as a poet,[3] but this poem underscores the importance of the "Martian School" to the themes and techniques of his fourth novel. Its first stanza shockingly inverts perceptual and moral norms by imagining how deviants see other people:

> Policemen look suspicious to normal
> Murderers. To the mature paedophile
> A child's incurious glance is a leer
> Of intimate salacity; in more
> Or less the same way, live people remain
> As good as dead to active necrophiles.

The last stanza threatens to erode the boundaries separating "normal" from "deviant":

> If you don't feel a little mad sometimes
> Then I think you must be out of your mind.
> No one knows what to do. Clichés are true.
> Everything depends on your point of view.[4]

This poem, which reappears in prose form in *Other People* (186–87), enacts in miniature the "de-naturalizing" of conventional understanding that characterizes the novel as a whole.

Point of view is something that Craig Raine was also preoccupied with while Amis was conceiving *Other People*. In its 1977 Christmas issue, the *New Statesman* published Raine's poem "A Martian Sends a Postcard Home," reprinted in the October 20, 1978, issue when it shared the Prudence Farmer Award with Christopher Reid's "Baldanders" for best poem published in the *New Statesman* the previous year. *New Statesman* critic James Fenton invented the label "Martian School" to account for similarities between the two poets, writing that "the Martian's point of view is a useful fiction, but it is not unlike the poet's own, which insists on presenting the familiar at its most strange." He added that Raine "has developed . . . the phenomenological style. . . . The only activity is that of a free contemplation, without ulterior motive, eager if anything for the most improbable discoveries."[5] "A Martian Sends a Postcard Home" (which became the title of Raine's 1979 volume of poetry) begins by rendering the Martian's first encounter with the world of books ("Caxtons" alludes to William Caxton, the first printer of books in English):

> Caxtons are mechanical birds with many wings
> and some are treasured for their markings—
>
> they cause the eyes to melt
> or the body to shriek without pain.
>
> I have never seen one fly, but
> sometimes they perch on the hand.

Next the alien describes earthly weather patterns:

> Mist is when the sky is tired of flight
> and rests its soft machine on ground:
>
> then the world is dim and bookish
> like engravings under tissue paper.
>
> Rain is when the earth is television.
> It has the property of making colors darker.

The most celebrated description in the poem emerges from the Martian's encounter with a telephone:

> In homes, a haunted apparatus sleeps,
> that snores when you pick it up.
>
> If the ghost cries, they carry it
> to their lips and soothe it to sleep
>
> with sounds. And yet, they wake it up
> deliberately, by tickling with a finger.[6]

Like Raine's Martian, Mary Lamb/Amy Hide sees the world from an alien perspective. As the novel's center of perceiving consciousness, "she enjoys certain advantages over

other people." As the narrator says of her in a slightly different context: "Not yet stretched by time, her perceptions are
without seriality: they are multiform, instantaneous and random, like the present itself. She can do some things that you
can't do. Glance sideways down an unknown street and what
do you see: an aggregate of shapes, figures and light, and the
presence or absence of movement? Mary sees a window and a
face behind it, the grid of the paving-stones and the rake of the
drainpipes, the way the distribution of the shadows answers to
the skyscape above" (56). The perceptions of Mary/Amy and
her Martian predecessor hearken back to a much earlier poetic
tradition, one to which Amis has acknowledged his indebted-
ness: that of the Romantic poets.[7] In his *Biographia Literaria*,
Samuel Taylor Coleridge describes William Wordsworth's contribution to their collaborative volume of poetry, *Lyrical Bal-
lads,* in terms that apply to many descriptive passages in *Other
People*. As Coleridge describes it, Wordsworth sought to "give
the charm of novelty to things of every day, and to excite a
feeling analogous to the supernatural, by awakening the
mind's attention from the lethargy of custom, and directing
it to the loveliness and the wonders of the world before us; an
inexhaustible treasure, but for which in consequence of the
film of familiarity and selfish solicitude we have eyes, yet see
not, ears that hear not, and hearts that neither feel nor understand."[8]

When Mary leaves the hospital at the beginning of the
novel and encounters the urban mystery that London represents
to her, it has the effect of removing this film of the familiar:

Not too far above the steep canyons there had hung an imperial backdrop of calm blue distance, in which extravagantly

lovely white creatures—fat, sleepy things—hovered, cruised and basked. Carelessly and painlessly lanced by the slow-moving crucifixes of the sky, they moreover owed allegiance to a stormy yellow core of energy, so irresistible that it had the power to hurt your eyes if you dared to look its way (18–19).

In this passage the things people typically take most for granted in the urban and natural realms—skyscrapers, clouds, jet airplanes, the sun—are seen again as if for the first time. The human body is also made strange by Mary's loss of memory. She is struck by the wonderful strangeness of her mouth, that boundary-defying door of perception: "a thing that seemed to have no business there, too vital and creaturely against the numb contours of her face . . . from the inside she could trace the scalloped bone curved on to the hard inner lips. Was there anywhere else like that in your body, a place you could feel from the inside and outside at the same time?" (32). Moving inexorably from innocence to experience, "she got to know her body and its hilly topography—the seven rivers, the four forests, the atonal music of her insides . . . even the first glimpse of lunar blood left her unharrowed" (56).

The "free contemplation" of these early perceptions does not last long in *Other People*. For the most part they are confined to part One, which takes up fewer than forty pages. By part Two, which opens with a chapter titled "Gaining Ground," Mary begins adapting to the urban inferno that London resembles, for most of the other characters in the novel, a secular version of a place of the damned, filled with "violence, vagrants, vandals, and vampires" (124). Here Amis begins adapting his technique of "making strange" to satirical ends, revisiting the territory canvassed in *Success*. In her journey through London, Mary begins in the company of a group of winos and squatters (one of whom sings snatches of a nursery rhyme that provides her with her name) proceeding from the lower depths to a lower-middle-class family and finally to independence and an upperclass lover. The socioeconomic distinctions separating the characters she encounters are bridged by their essential moral similarities: no matter what their status, they are driven and derided by petty dreams and anxieties.

The satire that results from these encounters does more than echo that of *Success,* however. Amis's "Martian" style often produces a kind of anthropological irony that makes the familiar world seem like a foreign country. After Mary is taken in by the Bothams, for instance, she begins "reading in earnest." She reads everything, including the tabloid newspaper delivered to Mr. Botham,

> a dirty sheath of smudged grey paper that came and went every day. It was never called the same thing twice. There were pictures of naked women in it; and on the back pages men but not women could be bought and sold: they cost lots of money. In the centre pages someone called Stan spoke of the battle between cancer and his wife Mildred. Cancer won in the end, but heroism such as Stan and Mildred's knows no defeat. It was all about other places, some of them (perhaps) not too far away. It told of atrocious disparities of fortune, of deaths, cataclysms, jackpots. And it was very hard to read, because the words could never come to an agreement about the size or shape they wanted to be (57).

The novel is rich with ironic descriptions like this one, many of them small gems of concentrated implication. Pubs: "There was a stale, malty, sawdust heat, and an elusive device to hurt the ears; the wall of sound came and went at you very cleverly with deceptively brief intervals, never giving you time to rearrange your thoughts" (39). Romance novels: "The girls in the books in the cupboard were taunting parodies of the girls condemned to read them" (73). Television: "Mary was used to television by now, its contests, its suspended worlds, its limitless present of vociferous catastrophes" (137). Clothes: "Clothes were interested in . . . abundance and expertise . . . they told people about the soul they encased by dramatizing your attempted lies about money and sex" (155).

Other People departs from *Success* in generic ways as well. In contrast to the black-comic realism of its predecessor, *Other People* experiments with a form of gothic supernaturalism. During her wanderings through London, Mary has a series of encounters with a character named John Prince, who sometimes resembles a Dickensian spirit of Mary's past ("poor ghost," he tells her at one point, "come on. I'm afraid there's one more thing you must see tonight" [122]). Prince remains a mysterious presence throughout the novel; he is figured forth at various times as a policeman, Amy's former lover, the Prince of Darkness, and Amy's murderer. In this last role he serves as the narrator's dark double, carrying out the narrative design that casts Mary/Amy as sacrificial victim. Like a traditional gothic villain, Prince is part lover, part destroyer. He stalks Mary/Amy from the beginning of the narrative, and leads her into the dark labyrinth of the past that increasingly haunts her. His presence contributes an uncanny feel of *Other People* while pointing toward the novel's symbolic dimensions. So does Mary/Amy's dual identity. Like another of her literary predecessors, Robert

Louis Stevenson's Dr. Jekyll, Mary harbors within her "good" self a destructive alter ego—a female Mr. Hyde, as Amy's last name indicates. As these supernatural elements suggest, the meaning of *Other People,* as Amis has said, is "consistent but not . . . realistic."[9]

The fact that Mary is not suffering from simple amnesia, for instance, is intimated at the end of the first chapter. When she reaches the outskirts of London, she gives in to pain and fatigue: "this is it, she thought, this is my death" (19). As the careful reader will discover, this precisely describes the symbolic content of her narrative. Symbolically, Mary is linked to the protagonist of Coleridge's great supernatural poem, "The Rime of the Ancient Mariner." After the Mariner sins by killing the albatross, he enters the realm of "Life-in-Death," where he suffers the consequences of his past transgressions. He seems to be delivered from this state of purgatory near the end of the poem, only to be consigned to an eternal repetition of his experiences by telling his story to any listeners he can bring under his spell.

This pattern is echoed in *Other People.* Amis's own convoluted explanation of the novel alludes to the influence of both "The Rime of the Ancient Mariner" and another of Coleridge's poems, "Kubla Khan" (which describes a woman's "demon lover"):

The novel is the girl's death, and her death is a sort of witty parody of her life. In life she was Amy Hide, a character who was privileged in all kinds of ways and made a journey downward through society—as some very strange people do: downward mobility is largely a new phenomenon, and it's a metaphor for self-destruction which some people seriously do enact—and therefore her life-in-death is one in which she is terrifically well-meaning and causes disaster. In her real life as Amy Hide she was not well-meaning, and brought disaster on herself. The Prince character, the narrator, has total power over her, as a narrator would, and also as a demon-lover would. At the very end of the novel she starts her life again, the idea being that life and death will alternate until she gets it right: she will go through life again, she will meet the man at the edge of the road, she will fall into the same mistakes . . . but actually I wanted to suggest on top of everything else that she would in fact get it right this time.[10]

This last implication is expressed by Prince in his final words to Mary/Amy: "Try again, take care, be good. Your life was too poor not to last for ever. Get it right this time. Come, I'll be very quick" (222).

As Amis's remarks suggest, Mary/Amy is asked to carry a great deal of symbolic weight in *Other People*. Amis is on record as saying that the reader shouldn't identify primarily with the characters of a novel. "What the reader should do is identify with the writer. You try to see what the writer is up to, what the writer is arranging."[11] In *Other People*, Amis uses Mary/Amy to explore varieties of "otherness." On one level, Mary/Amy's literal estrangement is a metaphor for that of Amis's generation. A kind of emotional and moral "downward mobility" affects even the most privileged members of the twenty-something generation here. Like Mary/Amy, they seem to have lost touch with the past; their responses are likewise stunted. The narrator even compiles a new, secularized list of the seven deadly sins to apply to this generation: "venality, paranoia, insecurity, excess, carnality, contempt, boredom" (195).

During Mary/Amy's affair with the urban professional Jamie, which devolves into a gothic parody of romantic intimacy, her amnesia-induced dissociation is mirrored in his emotional numbness. Their lovemaking generates nothing beyond animal warmth. "He could remember what you did, but he couldn't remember what you did it for. And Mary couldn't remember either" (194).

Mary/Amy also allows Amis to explore gender more fully than in his previous novels (*Other People* is dedicated to his mother). "*Women* are the other people" (188), the narrator says at one point, and in *Other People* Amis attempts to imaginatively inhabit this otherness. At first, of course, the male/female dichotomy is a distinction without a difference, since Mary/Amy has forgotten her gendered identity along with everything else. It doesn't take her long, though, to observe that sexual aggression and violence are the special province of males. Soon after her release from the hospital, her friend Sharon pairs her with the petty criminal Trev, and after some serious drinking "Trev slammed Mary up against a wall and tried to cover her mouth with his" (45). As if to suggest such behavior is culturally relative, Amis has Mary/Amy answer Trev's subsequent aggression with her own self-preserving violence. In a particularly effective passage of "Martian" description, Mary/Amy offers this comically abstract description of male heterosexual desire: "She started to understand. His two wet red points wanted to get as close as they could to her, to get inside" (46). During her residence at the Church-Army Hostel for Young Women, and later in a house she shares with two other women, Mary/Amy wonders why the women she has observed do not cultivate their own forms of power. "How shameful, really, that when women tried to be free of men and strong in themselves, they just watched the way men were strong and copied that. Was there no second way to be strong, no female way? Mary was sure there must be. But perhaps not, or not any more, or not yet" (178). Although in much of his other writing Amis seems to maintain an essential-ist view of male-female differences, in *Other People* he imagines them to be culturally relative.

Amis pays a price for all this thematic ambition. The sym-bolic weight Mary/Amy carries in the novel is not unlike the albatross that hangs from the Mariner's neck: it restricts her autonomy and freedom of movement. Amis has partially com-pensated for this problem by making her an amnesiac, so that her largely affectless responses are consistent with her condition. But this does not eliminate the impression that she is primarily a narrative device rather than a character. As Alan Hollinghurst has written, "like Virginia Woolf, Amis elides authorial free-ranging intelligence with the restricted reactions of the protago-nist, and it is often hard to see where one becomes the other."[12] For instance, when the narrator, ostensibly rendering Mary/Amy's perceptions, writes that "ordinary people are really terri-bly strange, deep with dreams and infamies, or so Mary thought" (109), the concluding attribution seems disingenuous. This is clearly Amis's belief (one he has expressed in interviews), and Mary is its mouthpiece.[13]

Amis's wordplay in the novel hints at this. The first letters of Mary/Amy's two first names form the initials of Martin Amis, and as Evan Hunter has noted, "Amy Hide" is a near homonym for "Amis Hiding."[14] The doubling does not stop here. Just as Amy represents Mary's dark double, John Prince is the narra-tor's cruel counterpart. As Amis acknowledged in an interview, "the narrator is the murderer, and the writer and the murderer are equivalent in that each has the power to knock Amy off."[15]

The brief prologue that begins the novel, written in the form of a confession, foreshadows Prince's role in *Other People*. It also suggests a parallel between authorship and murder. "I didn't want to have to do it to her. I would have infinitely preferred some other solution. Still, there we are. It makes sense, really, given the rules of life on earth; and she *asked* for it. I just wish there was another way, something more self-contained, economical, and shapely. But there isn't. That's life, as I say, and my most sacred duty is to make it lifelike. Oh, hell. Let's get it over with." (9) "I feel a sort of guilt about creating characters, guilt about making them suffer," Amis has said,[16] and the epilogue filters Prince's mercenary determination through this regret.

As if in compensation, the narrator himself, never explicitly linked with Prince in the novel, expresses nothing but sympathy for Mary/Amy. In many ways, he and Mary/Amy are alter egos. Her estrangement from the world, for instance, is a less reflective version of his own. His alienation results from an unspecified emotional wound (he has "taken a smash" he tells us), and his responses fill the gaps created by Mary's affectlessness. Consider their separate ruminations on death. Mary's is strangely impersonal, unaffected by memories of loss:

> She wondered where the end of the world was and what the world ended with—with mists, high barriers, or just the absence of everything. Would you die if you went there? . . . She knew a little about death now. She knew that it happened to other people, to every last one of them. It was a bad thing, obviously, and no one liked it; but no one knew how much it hurt, how long it lasted, whether it was the end of everything or the start of something else. (59)

The narrator's parallel musings on mortality are poignant and historically conditioned; he voices a postmodern, existential angst: "*Is* there life after death? . . . If there is, it will probably be very like life, because only in life is there variety. . . . There will have to be many versions of death, to answer all the versions of life. There will have to be a hell for each of us, a hell for you and a hell for me. Don't you think? And we will all have to suffer it alone" (127).

In passages like this one Amis is clearly moving beyond the social satire of his first three novels (and the first part of *Other People*) and giving voice to a more generalized late-century malaise. In this sense, too, Mary/Amy's experiences serve as a vehicle—for a bleak existential vision. Her progressively disillusioning encounters with the world and with other people seem designed to justify the narrator's nihilistic commentary, which itself seems to derive from some unspecified sense of diminishment and loss. The emotional territory occupied by the last several chapters of the novel calls to mind the lines from yet another Coleridge poem, "Dejection: An Ode": "A grief without a pang, void, dark, and drear, / A stifled, drowsy, unimpassioned grief, / Which finds no natural outlet, no relief, / In word, or sigh, or tear."[17]

The depths of this disillusionment can be measured by Mary/Amy's changing relationship to books. Initially, they help her construct her understanding of the world, and lift her out of her "unforgettable" present. Later she decides that books are part and parcel of the corrupt world of "power, boredom and desire; . . . they all fawned and fed on the buyable present. What had she felt before? She felt that books were about the ideal world, where nothing was ideas but everything had ideality and the chance of moral spaciousness. But it wasn't so" (182).

As Victoria Glendinning commented in her 1981 review of
Other People, this view represents "a major loss of faith, for her,
for an author, for anyone."[18] Earlier in the novel, as Mary/Amy
is discovering anew the power of words, she imagined that they
constitute everything—the world, the self, the order of things:

> Each word she recognized gave her the sense of being re-
> stored, minutely solidified, as if damaged tissue were being
> welded back on to her like honey cells. Even now she knew
> that language would stand for or even contain some order, an
> order that could not possibly subsist in anything she had
> come across so far—that shadow driving across a colourless
> wall, cars queuing in their tracks, the haphazard murmur of
> the air which gave pain when you tried to follow it with your
> mind . . . *Reading* might well hold the key to any order the
> world disclosed, Mary felt. (40)

Amis certainly embraced these articles of artistic faith in writing
Other People, a novel that constantly reminds the reader of its
author's love of words as well as other books. Along with
Mary/Amy, Amis seems to be questioning this sustaining belief
at the end of *Other People.*

Or perhaps he is posing one last challenge to the reader,
this one calling for a rejection of the dualism that initially
seems to organize the novel. Throughout *Other People,* Amis
has challenged the epistemological dichotomies that structure
conventional wisdom, including such distinctions as male/
female, good/evil, even life/death. Mary/Amy's conclusion that
literature is about nothing but corruption assumes an absolute
boundary between literature and "moral spaciousness" that
Amis certainly does not recognize. He ends *Other People* with

a ray of hope, intimating Mary/Amy's rebirth. Prince's words light the way: "try again, take care, . . . get it right this time" (222).

CHAPTER 4

I Am All You Never Had of Goods and Sex

Money: A Suicide Note

Quarterly, is it, money reproaches me:
"Why do you let me lie here wastefully?
I am all you never had of goods and sex.
You could get them still by writing a few cheques."
—Philip Larkin, "Money"

In *Money: A Suicide Note* (1984) the materialist excesses of the late twentieth century are viewed through, and magnified by, the salacious leer of its narrator. "I'm addicted to the twentieth century," says the eponymous John Self, and during his narrative the reader vicariously experiences the damage this addiction inflicts on Self's physical body—and the larger social body he also inhabits. *Money* represents a highwater mark in Amis's career, building on the strengths of his earlier novels but far exceeding them in scope, depth of characterization, and organic unity. It also stands as one of the indispensable novels of and about its decade. In terms of narrative technique, *Money* is a vernacular dramatic monologue in the Russian *skaz* tradition. Dostoevsky's novella *Notes from Underground* is the master text of this tradition, containing a narrator whose bitter alienation from his society and its most cherished beliefs makes him a perversely perceptive critic of that society. Self is a literary descendant of Dostoevsky's protagonist, sharing the Underground Man's brutal, seamy honesty. This chapter will analyze the comic artistry of *Money,* including its figurative strategies, narrative voice, satirical motifs, and use of doubles and doubling.

Plot and Figurative Design

The plot of *Money* is deceptively simple. As the novel opens, in early summer, 1981, John Self arrives in New York to direct what he imagines will be his first major film. He is one of the new media hucksters who came of age in the freewheeling 1960s, and he struck it rich in the mid-1970s making a series of controversial TV commercials pedaling "smoking, drinking, junk food and nude magazines" (78). More recently, he has made a deal with the American producer Fielding Goodney to film a story based on his own life. During the six frenetic months his narrative recounts, Self turns thirty-five, shuttles between London and New York, meets with Goodney, auditions actors and screenwriters, and wallows in the fleshly vices his commercials celebrate.

Self is seriously involved with two women in the course of the novel: Selina Street (the most inspired of many inspired names in *Money*) and Martina Twain. Selina betrays Self with at least two men, and she ultimately stages Self's betrayal of Martina, who represented his only (faint) hope for renewal and reform. The other major character in the novel is one Martin Amis; Self hires him to rewrite the film's script, and they have many subsequent encounters. Self's high-speed, high-rolling life comes to an end when he discovers that Fielding has set him up: the money financing the film and his appetites is nonexistent, and all the contracts he signed with Fielding hold Self financially liable. He ends up back in London, broke, having survived a failed suicide bid.

Absent from this brief summary is the highly charged language, the arresting comedy, the figurative and thematic ingenuity that breathe life into every page of the novel. Consider the metaphorical implications of Self's hearing problem, for instance. At first, it seems to be a purely physical condition.

"Owing to this fresh disease I have called tinnitus, my ears have started hearing things recently, things that aren't strictly auditory. Jet take-offs, breaking glass, ice scratched from the tray" (7). Then these sounds begin to shape themselves toward meaning—odd music, strange languages—that Self cannot decipher. One morning he wakes up in a New York hotel room hearing "computer fugues, Japanese jam sessions, didgeridoos" (11). Later, sitting in a London pub called The Blind Pig, he hears strange sounds coming from the mouths of his fellow "Earthlings" (his name for human beings): "the foreigners around here. . . . They speak stereo, radio crackle, interference. They speak sonar, bat-chirrup, pterodactylese, fish-purr" (86). Is this tinnitus again? The curious reader, consulting a medical encyclopedia, discovers that tinnitus is a condition, not a disease. A "common complaint," it is "the annoying sensation of noise in the ear when no sound is present."[1]

Like so many of the details in *Money,* John Self's tinnitus constitutes part of larger pattern of implication that awaits the reader's discovery. Early in his narration Self describes "four distinct voices" competing for his attention. They represent a figurative extension of his tinnitus, filling his head with distracting noises. The first two render him *morally* hard of hearing: "First, of course, is the jabber of money, which might be represented as the blur on the top rung of a typewriter—£%¨@=&$—sums,

subtractions, compound terrors and greeds. Second is the voice of pornography. This often sounds like the rap of a demented DJ: *the way she moves has to be good news, can't get loose till I feel the juice—* . . ." (104). These two refrains nearly drown out all the other voices Self hears, leading to everything from hilarious comic confusions to searing betrayals to life-threatening catastrophes. They speak of an invaded Self, a programmed Self, a diminished Self—a "gimmicked" Self, to use one of his favorite terms.

The other two voices—one speaking in conscience-stung tones, the other in unquiet desperation—imply regret and possible reform. "Third, the voice of ageing and weather, of time travel through days and days, the ever-weakening voice of stung shame, sad boredom and futile protest. . . . Number four is the real intruder. I don't want any of these voices but I especially don't want this one. It is the most recent. It has to do with quitting work and needing to think about things I never used to think about. It has the unwelcome lilt of paranoia, of rage and weepiness made articulate in spasms of vividness: drunk talk played back sober" (104). Though Self is not aware of this, these two voices are in conflict with the first two. Taken together, all four voices constitute a fragmented, decentered Self.

Self thinks of these voices as an unwanted affliction, like his tinnitus, though he owns up to a small measure of responsibility for their presence. "All the voices come from somewhere else. I wish I could flush them out of my head. As with vampires, you have to ask them in. But once they're there, once you've given them headroom, they seem pretty determined to stick around" (104). This is because they come to *constitute* Self— who he is, how he sees and hears the world, how he relates to others. They represent his subjective experience of the world, what he calls his "private culture." And while the specifics of these voices (especially their ranking) precisely measure Self's character, they have a wider application. Their resonance suggests something about the dialogic design of *Money* itself.

Money can be read exclusively as a satirical novel, attacking the influence of capitalism on consciousness in the postwar west.[2] "I think money is the central deformity in life," Amis has said. "It's one of the evils that has cheerfully survived identification as an evil. . . . It's a fiction, an addiction, and a tacit conspiracy that we have all agreed to go along with."[3] In this reading John Self is both target and victim, a one-man carnival of junk taste and junk morality who has relinquished most of his free will by embracing commodity culture in all its pornographic excess. The fact that most of Self's pleasures are solitary and onanistic reinforces the sense that he is a prisoner of his own addictions. Amis's public statements about Self sanction this reading: "he has no resistance, because he has no sustenance, no structure."[4] The spectacle of Self's "private culture" —by turns appalling, savagely hilarious, touching, and contemptible—represents a tour-de-force of satiric representation. Self's narrative, written in 1981, is like an extended hangover following the orgy of the "Me" decade. At the same time, his unabashed entrepreneurial greed embodies the emergent ethos of the 1980s.

Few, however, will experience Self merely as a monster of wretched excess. He is so fully, triumphantly realized that most readers will warm to him in spite of themselves. Once Self enters the reader's consciousness, he takes up permanent residence there, like the best characters in Dickens. One method of this magic is what Amis has called the novel's "mad exuberance."[5] Self's conversations with other characters may be halting and fractured, but Amis has infused his soliloquies with a dazzling punk-poetic eloquence, a blend of what Ian Hamilton has called "low slang and high figurative artifice."[6] Moreover, *Money* frequently traverses the traditional boundary placed between a satiric persona and the reader. As his surname suggests, Self is meant to be broadly representative. Like his tinnitus, Self's experiences of temporal confusion, psychic fragmentation, and anxiety are common symptoms—of the postmodern condition that has shaped his voice as well as the voices of his fellow "Earthlings." In this sense the novel's 1984 publication date is significant: Orwell's great dystopic novel *1984* is a recurrent motif in *Money*. *1984* is a seminal postmodern novel, and *Money* extends Orwell's analysis of totalitarian ideology into the realm of postindustrial capitalist democracies. Unlike Orwell's protagonist, Winston Smith, Self lives in a "free" society (two of them, in fact). Like Winston, his responses have been conditioned— not by a state apparatus, but by an equally powerful economic system that shapes individual subjectivities, fetishizes objects, and commodifies relationships. His role in this system—as a maker of television commercials—puts him at the center of its mediating machinery. Jean Baudrillard's famous diagnosis of the "loss of the real" is apposite here, especially considering that Self's reality is both an illusion and an elaborate joke. In *Simulacra and Simulation,* originally published in 1981, Baudrillard claims that the "real" is now defined in terms of the media which constitutes it.[7] Laughing at Self, the reader is laughing at an exaggerated version of other selves as well.

Self's Voice

Doing justice to the novel's verbal artistry alone would require a separate essay, but some avenues worth further exploration can be suggested here. Amis has set severe limits on himself in *Money*, since his narrator is verbally challenged and resistant to literature, not to mention narrative structure ("in my state, you don't want things assuming any shape on you" [131]). He is also drunk a great deal of the time, which poses a serious threat to sustained narrative coherence. *Money*'s 363 pages contain no chapter titles or numbers; there are nine unnumbered sections, but the logic of these divisions is not immediately apparent. As a result, the novel's narrative seems messy, sprawling, unfocused—though never less than compelling. Self's exposition is roughly chronological, but it is punctuated by flashbacks, digressions, and frequent omissions. The latter occur when Self defers disclosing shaming events that have just happened to him. Repression decisively shapes his story, disrupting chronology, increasing narrative suspense, and leading to dramatic revelations throughout the novel.

There is method in this narrative sprawl, since among other things it convincingly captures Self's "private culture" in all its human density. Early in the novel, discussing his film outline with scriptwriter Doris Arthur, he breaks away from his transcription of their conversation, noting that he has given this speech so many times that he can speak while letting his mind "wander unpleasantly, as it always wanders now when unengaged by stress or pleasure." What follows perfectly conveys the associational twitchiness of Self's thought: "My thoughts dance. What is it? A dance of anxiety and supplication, of futile vigil. I think I must have some new cow disease that makes you wonder whether you're real all the time, that makes your life feel like a trick, an act, a joke. I feel, I feel dead. There's a guy who lives round my way who really gives me the fucking creeps. He's a *writer*, too . . . I can't go on sleeping alone—that's certain. I need a human touch. Soon I'll just have to go out and buy one. I wake up at dawn and there's nothing" (61). Like his autoeroticism, Self's self-examination is a constant in the novel. His self-awareness constitutes a kind of psychological doubling, captured in a sentence near the beginning of the novel: "Jesus, I never meant me any harm" (16).[8]

In terms of its verbal surface, *Money* mirrors Self's limitations while finding ways around them. Self favors simple words, short sentences, and clipped syntax (the only semicolon in his entire narrative occurs in its last sentence). Yet Amis achieves maximal effects from these minimal means. He employs allusion, parody, sudden shifts of tone, and comic irony so that Self's statements echo with additional, authorial implications. Amis satirizes Self by "doubling" Self's voice with his own throughout the novel, composing an artful counterpoint that resonates with implications beyond the range of his narrator's hearing. Self's explanation of the change he is experiencing under Martina's influence is representative of his staccato style —and Amis's "double-voicing": "I'm getting chicked. It would explain a great deal. I have tried in the past to feminize myself. I womanized for years. It didn't work, though on the other hand I did fuck lots of girls. Who knows? It if happens, it happens" (306). Unlike Self, Amis (and the ideal reader) recognizes that "womanizing" will not bring Self (or any male self) any closer to feminine, or feminist, understanding.

Repetition is Self's favorite rhetorical strategy, not surprising given his self-description ("that's my life: repetition, repetition" [29]). Fortunately for the reader and the novel's art, this repetition is never redundant. The word "money" and its variants, for instance, appear on virtually every page of the novel, since the cash nexus determines and shapes all of Self's experiences and relationships, but its uses are almost infinitely variable.

At one point, for instance, Self lists the titles of the few books he owns. It is one of many great comic lists in the novel, and it reveals how Self's money mania reduces all of culture to the same qualitative level. "*Home Tax Guide, Treasure Island, The Usurers, Timon of Athens, Consortium, Our Mutual Friend, Buy Buy Buy, Silas Marner, Success!, The Pardoner's Tale, Confessions of a Bailiffu, The Diamond as Big as the Ritz, The Amethyst Inheritance*" (67). Self notes that "most of the serious books are the accumulations of Selina's predecessors" (67), and that he has not read them. Those who have will recognize that they are concerned with the deforming influence of money—as is the novel Self is narrating. To Self, however, money is *formative*—especially of his language. After receiving his first letter from Selina in their two-year relationship, containing the postscript he finds so seductive ("P.S.—I'm pennyless"), Self realizes this is the first time he has seen her handwriting. He then wonders if she has seen his. "Had I ever shown her *my* hand? Yes, she'd seen it, on bills, on credit slips, on cheques" (69).

Self's phrase "my hand" is an example of the pervasive verbal doubling in the novel, a form of repetition manifested in punning, double entendres, double takes, double-talk, and inversion. "My hand" is a double entendre referring to Self's secrets as well as his penmanship. Amis constantly makes an artistic virtue out of Self's repetition compulsion, wresting poetic effects from his narrator's verbal habits. Self's use of the word "true" and its variants in the following passage is a telling example. It conveys the perverse depth of his emotional investment in money: "Selina says I'm not capable of true love. It isn't true. I truly love money. Truly I do. Oh, money, I love you. You're so democratic: you've got no favourites" (221). Later in the novel, when Self's money malignancy is in temporary remission, he uses repetition to express a different kind of long-ing. "Me, I don't like what I want. What I want has long moved free of what I like, and I watch it slip away with grief, with help-lessness. I'm ashamed and proud of it. I'm ashamed of what I am. And is that anything to be ashamed of?" (299). "I" is used eight times in four sentences here, effectively capturing its speaker's self-absorption. Moreover, Amis teases the reader into thought by reversing the order of the verbal pairs ("like/want" becomes "want/like") and by using "ashamed" three times in close succession but with entirely different connotations. The last sentence here carries an arresting comic charge (via verbal doubling) that effectively conveys Self's confused struggle to change.

Like his syntax, Self's vocabulary is rough and ready. It also reflects a dialectical doubling appropriate to his transatlantic background (his mother was American, and he spent several childhood years in New Jersey). Few of his words are more than two syllables in length, and many are of the four-letter variety. His word choices give his voice a unique accent nonetheless. Some of them are simply working-class Britishisms ("brill" for brilliant, "knackered" for exhausted, "sock" for apartment); some are favored Americanisms that take on an added charge coming out of a British mouth ("gimmick," "upshot"). Others are slang terms whose meaning Self expands ("rug" becomes his word for any hair, not just a toupee) or uses in an altered context ("redo" is generally used as a verb, and applied to renovation, but Self turns it into an all-purpose noun, as in "rug redo"—which translates as "haircut"). "Redo" and "rethink" are two of his favorite terms, reflecting his mechanistic self-conception (he refers to himself repeatedly as a robot, a train, and a cyborg). Most of these terms are conventionally masculine, if not macho, and so are his favored phrases, especially "butch it out" and "shagged out."

As Ian Hamilton has noted, Self's voice often "comes out sounding like Holden Caulfield done over by Mickey Spillane."[9] Or like Martin Amis. Readers familiar with Amis's other novels and nonfiction will notice that Self's voice often partakes of Amis's distinctive accents, from Martian-style descriptions to sharp social satire. Hamilton describes its tone as "an urban-apocalyptic high fever," adding that it is "somehow kept steady, helped across the road, by those old redoubtables—wit, worldly wisdom, and an eye for social detail."[10] These are qualities that inform Amis's writing generally. Yet for all of the vocal "doubling" whereby Amis's voice inhabits Self's, Self never seems a mere mouthpiece for his creator. He retains his uniqueness, as his description of Manhattan street life demonstrates: "I strode through meat-eating genies of subway breath. I heard the ragged hoot of sirens, the whistles of two-wheelers and skateboarders, pogoists, gocarters, windsurfers. I saw the barreling cars and cabs, shoved on by the power of their horns. I felt all the contention, the democracy, all the italics, in the air" (12). Self's language is visceral, elemental; even his more abstruse musings are experienced as sensations.

Satirical Motifs

As the preceding passage suggests, Self is especially expressive about machines. His fetishistic relationship to his sports car is the ultimate expression of this impulse. One of Amis's major satirical strategies in *Money* is his use of proper names; they evoke actual models or people while partaking of a wholly imaginary realm. Fielding uses a limousine called an *Autocrat;*

Martin Amis drives an *Iago 666*. These vehicles share the road with *Acapulcos, Alibis, Boomerangs, Farragos, Hyenas, Mistrals, Tomahawks,* and *Torpedoes. Fiasco,* the name of Self's purple sports car, sounds like a combination of an Italian *Fiat* and an American *Fiero,* while forming a word that describes the tenor of its owner's life.[11] In keeping with the novel's satire on commodity fetishism, Self invests his car with powers well beyond its mechanical function. "It's temperamental, my *Fiasco,* like all the best racehorses, poets and chefs" (64). It also inspires some of his best punk-poetry, as in this passage, which makes explicit the theme of doubling that echoes throughout the novel: "The car and I crawled cursing to my flat. You just cannot park round here any more. . . . You *can* doublepark on people: people can doublepark on you. Cars are doubling while houses are halving. . . . Rooms divide, rooms multiply. Houses split— houses are tripleparked. People are doubling also, dividing, splitting. In double trouble we split our losses. No wonder we're bouncing off the walls" (64).

Self's ignorance of the implications of many words, his own as well as those of other people, generates some of the novel's most wicked comedy. When Fielding tells him that they cannot sign the actress Day Lightbrowne to their film because she was recently date raped by her therapist, Self is stymied. "Date-raped, huh. What kind of deal is that? What, sort of with bananas and stuff?" (26) Later, after his first encounter with Martin Amis, Self visits a New York brothel called the Happy Isles. One of the prostitutes asks him his name, and he answers "I'm Martin" (97), confiding that he hates his own name ("I'm called John Self. But who isn't?" [97]). One lie leads to another, and to a comic misunderstanding. It turns out that the prostitute ("they call me Moby," she tells Self, parodying the opening sentence of *Moby Dick*) is a graduate student in English literature at a New York university. When Self tells her he is a fiction writer, she asks him what kind of fiction he writes. He hears her question as "John roar mainstream." He has never heard the word "genre," so he cannot hear her actual question as "genre or mainstream?" She has to spell out her meaning: "are they mainstream novels and stories or thrillers or sci-fi or something like that?" (98). It is the first of many instances where Self's ignorance of literature will get him in trouble. In fact, his subsequent rejection of this intimidating woman in favor of a less educated, more voluptuous prostitute named "She-She" anticipates his later, more fateful turn from the literary Martina to the pornographic Selina.

Throughout *Money,* Amis uses comic means to deepen the novel's themes. Nowhere is this more apparent than in his treatment of Self's relationship to high culture. Although Self has always turned a deaf ear to literature itself, he appreciates its commercial currency. One of his best-known television commercials was an ad

> for a new kind of flash-friable pork-and-egg bap or roll or hero called a Hamlette. We used some theatre and shot the whole thing on stage. There was the actor, dressed in black, with his skull and globe, being henpecked by that mad chick he's got in trouble. When suddenly a big bimbo wearing cool pants and bra strolls on, carrying a tray with two steaming Hamlettes on it. She gives him the wink—and Bob's your uncle. All my commercials featured a big bim in cool pants and bra. It was sort of my trademark. (70)

This is the first of many Shakespearean allusions in *Money,* all of which echo with seriocomic relevance to Self's situation. Like Hamlet's relationship to his stepfather, Self's relationship with his father is troubled and violent. In fact, Barry Self has recently taken out a contract on him—Laertes' employment of Rosencrantz and Guildenstern echoed in a pulp fiction mode. In addition, the revised script for the autobiographical film Self is attempting to make echoes the Oedipal dynamics of *Hamlet:* the son kills his father hoping to protect his mother. Beyond these plot parallels, Self's existential soliloquies—which often seem slightly crazed—crackle with a skewed insight that recalls Hamlet's own high-pitched dramatic monologues.

Othello is an even more pervasive motif in the novel. Self reports that just before he left for New York, he was told that Selina was cuckolding him. Later, when he reluctantly attends the opera *Othello* with Martina Twain, he assumes that Desdemona is cuckolding Othello, missing the point entirely. Self's subsequent summary of *Othello*'s plot is one of the novel's many brilliant parodies. It is also a signal example of how Amis "doubles" Self's voice, speaking through it of Self's character and limitations:

Luckily I must have seen the film or the TV spin-off of *Othello,* for despite its dropped aitch the musical version stuck pretty faithfully to a plot I knew well. The language problem remained a problem but the action I could follow without that much effort. The flash spade general arrives to take up a position on some island, in the olden days there, bringing with him the Lady-Di figure as his bride. Then she starts diddling one of his lieutenants, a funloving kind of guy whom I took to immediately. Same old story. Now she tries one of these double-subtle numbers on her husband—you know, always rooting for the boyfriend and singing his praises. But Otello's sidekick is on to them, and, hoping to do himself

some good, tells all to the guvnor. This big spade, though, he
can't or won't believe it. A classic situation. Well, love is
blind, I thought (277).

"He can't or won't believe it." Although Self finally resembles
Othello less than he does Roderigo, the lecherous spendthrift
and victim in Shakespeare's play, he is like Othello in his double
gullibility. He is (often willfully) ignorant of the complex web of
deception and double-dealing in which he is enmeshed. First he
discovers that Martina's husband has been sleeping with Selina
(later he will find that his best friend did too); then he learns that
"Frank the phone," the caller who has goaded and bedeviled
him during his time in New York, is none other than Fielding
Goodney, who ruins him financially. Goodney has no clear
motive for any of this, but then neither did Iago: he acted from
what Coleridge termed "motiveless malignity."[12]

The language of *Othello* actually extends to Self's final, violent confrontation with Goodney, though Self is deaf to the allusion. Self has brutally beaten the disguised Goodney, mistaking
him first for Frank the phone, then the redheaded woman who
has been following him. After the beating, he asks the crumpled
figure to identify itself. "'Oh damn dear go,' it seemed to say.
'Oh and you man dog'" (322). It is not until late in the novel,
when Self recounts this scene for the Martin Amis character during their chess game, that he is given a translation of these lines
from the play, spoken by Roderigo as Iago stabs him: "Oh
damned Iago. Oh inhuman dog." Amis remarks, "fascinating,"
adding: "pure transference" (347). Fluent in the language of
Freudian psychology, the Amis character recognizes that Goodney thought of himself as the wronged Roderigo and Self as
Iago. Even though Martina has given Self a book on Freud to

read, part of his "how-to kit for the twentieth century" (308), he does not yet understand Freudian terminology or Amis's comment. He even mistakes the *Othello* quotation for a reference to the Amis character's car (an *Iago* 666). "The cunning bastard, I thought. Oh, I caught that reference to his own little rattletrap. He's definitely after my *Fiasco*" (347). Not so: Amis, like every character in the novel save Martina, is just manipulating Self.

This reference to Self as an "inhuman dog" is no accident. It takes up and further extends a web of animal imagery that clings to Self throughout his narrative. A double-edged motif, this imagery functions to extend the satirical portrait of Self (so debased that he often seems subhuman) while simultaneously engaging the reader's imaginative sympathy for him. Self reads George Orwell's allegorical novel *Animal Farm* during his relationship with the bookish Martina Twain, and while its allegory is lost on him, the novel still strikes responsive chords. Well before he reads the book, he describes himself in animal terms. He stares at a barmaid with "the face of a fat snake, bearing all the signs of its sins" (14). Waking with a tremendous hangover (one of many), he enters the bathroom, emerging "on all fours, a pale and very penitent crocodile" (16). The pigs in *Animal Farm* clearly disturb him, however—doubtless because they remind him of his earlier self-characterization: "200 pounds of yob genes, booze, snout, and fast food" (35). He thinks of them with high distaste: "You should see these hairy-jawed throwbacks, these turd lookalikes, honking and chomping at the trough" (191).

Self *can* imagine aspiring to the status of a dog, on the other hand:

Where would I be in *Animal Farm*? One of the rats, I thought at first. But—oh, go easy on yourself, try and go a little bit easy. Now, after mature consideration, I think I might have what it takes to be a dog. I *am* a dog. I am a dog at the seaside tethered to a fence while my master and mistress romp on the sands. I am bouncing, twisting, weeping, consuming myself. A dog can take the odd slap or kick. A slap you can live with, as a dog. What's a kick? Look at the dogs in the street, how everything implicates them, how everything is their concern, how they race towards great discoveries. And imagine the grief, tethered to a fence when there is activity— and play, and thought and fascination—just beyond the holding rope. (193)

This entire passage precisely (and touchingly) describes Self, who earlier confided to the reader that he "longed to burst out of the world of money and into—into what? Into the world of thought and fascination. How do I get there? Tell me, please. I'll never make it by myself. I don't know the way" (118). The spectacle of Self relating to *Animal Farm* strictly as an animal story, and relating to it profoundly on that level, is one of the great comic conceits in the novel. It is comic, yet not simply condescending: the Self-referential image of the dog staked to its animal nature but yearning for the world beyond the restraining rope is a humanly compelling one and nudges the reader toward genuine sympathy.

Self's case is a hard one, however. He seems allergic to the sustained effort that thought requires. Like reading, for instance. "I can't read because it hurts my eyes. I can't wear glasses because it hurts my nose. I can't wear contacts because it hurts my nerves. So you see, it all came down to a choice between pain and not reading. I chose not reading. Not reading —that's where I put my money" (44). As a result, the world of complex thought remains out of Self's reach. Martina talks one evening about aesthetics, about the "reluctant narrator" in a novel, "the sad, the unwitting narrator"—Self, in other words. But he cannot understand what she is saying. "I could follow her drift for seconds at a time, until the half-gratified sense of effort—or my awareness of watching myself—intervened, and scattered my thoughts" (126).

When he does begin to make the effort, under Martina's tutelage, he begins to glimpse the truth: literature and other forms of disciplined thinking and imagining sharpen one's hearing, restore one's responses. "The thing about reading and all that," Self realizes, "is—you have to be in a fit state for it. Calm. Not picked on. You have to be able to hear your own thoughts, without interference. On the way back from lunch (I walked it) already the streets felt a little lighter. I could make a little more sense of the watchers and the watched" (130). Besides Freud, Martina has given Self books on Marx, Darwin, Einstein, Hitler, and a book titled *Money* (not the novel but an economic history). By reading the latter, Self almost articulates a recognition that capitalism, and his own greed, go hand in hand with economic and social inequality: "by wanting a lot, you are taking steps to spread it thin elsewhere" (263). But he never pursues the moral implications of this fact. Martina has offered him the lifeline of ideas, and he even recognizes it as such. He simply cannot hold on to it long enough.

Martina is the first woman Self has related to on fully human terms since his mother died during his childhood. Since then, all his relations with women have been mediated by money and pornography. His passion for Selina is spoken in these two voices exclusively, which unite in fetishistic rapture whenever he speaks of the "omniscient underwear" he eagerly purchases for her. When he dreams of her, he dreams of "the arched creature doing what that creature does best—and the thrilling proof, so rich in pornography, that she does all this not for passion, not for comfort, far less for love, the proof that she does all this for *money*. I woke babbling in the night—yes, I heard myself say it, solve it, through the dream-mumble—and I said, *I love it. I love her . . . I love her corruption*" (39–40). Note the significance of the ellipsis points here: Self loves Selina's commodified sexuality, not Selina herself.

Initially, Self has no way at all of relating to Martina; outside the language of pornography, women have no identity for him. "I can't find a voice to summon her with" (114) he says of her at first, before imagining her as a kind of alien (her name is after all an anagram for Martian): "she is a woman of somewhere else" (128). The story of Martina and Self's evolving relationship—ill-fated, interrupted throughout by the shouts of money and pornography—is genuinely moving. When he finally, temporarily wakes from his pornographic stupor, he glimpses the difference between fetishistic desire and human connection:

> I know I'm a slow one and a dull dog but at last I saw what her nakedness was saying. I saw its plain content, which was—Here, I lay it all before you. Yes, gently does it, I thought, with these violent hands . . . And in the morning, as I awoke, Christ (and don't laugh—no, no, don't laugh), I felt like a *flower*: a little parched, of course, a little gone in the neck, and with no real life to come, perhaps, only sham life,

bowl life, easing its petals and lifting its head to start feeding on the day. (310)

By the time Self relates this experience, Martina has taken in a dog she names Shadow, who keeps tugging at his rope when she or Self walk with him near Twenty-third Street, "where everything was unleashed, unmuzzled. . . . He looked baffled and hungry, momentarily wolverine, answering to a sharper nature" (267). Martina says that each night Shadow's desire to return to this region, where he once lived, "gets weaker," but says "sometimes . . . he wants to go." Self reassures her that Shadow "knows what the good life is," that it is with her.

Self's attempted reassurance here is double-voiced: he is speaking of himself as well as Shadow. He wants to stay with Martina, to live in her world of order and contemplation. But part of his nature, or more precisely his mediated desires, pull him in other directions. In response to Self's comforting words about Shadow, Martina frets that "it's his *nature*" to seek that other region. While in America, the land of second chances, Self entertains the possibility of change and reform. But just when Martina seems to have made this possible, Selina arrives from England, where second chances do not come quite so easily. And she stokes the fires of his pornographic desires. His subsequent loss of Martina is accompanied by a symbolic devolution. Selina calls Self while he is exercising, "wiggling my legs in the air like an upended beetle" (312). After Selina has seduced him into bed, Martina appears. Self is on his back, and he describes what Martina sees: "the decked joke, flummoxed, scuppered, and waving his arms" (319). Like Kafka's Gregor Samsa in *The Metamorphosis,* Self has become an insect.

He does not remain one, however. Despite his debasement, Self's radical honesty and capacity for shame raise him above the level of many other characters in the novel. Reformative change remains a (faint) possibility for him, even at the end of his narrative. If anything, the American film actors Self deals with are more debased than he is, and certainly more deluded. In Lorne Guyland, the actor signed to play Gary, Self's father, Amis has created a classic portrait of the aging male narcissist. Self wants his film to accurately echo his own lower-class roots; Lorne wants to rewrite the father's character so that he becomes a "lover, father, husband, athlete, millionaire—but also a man of wide reading, of wide . . . culture, John . . . I see Garfield at a lectern reading aloud from a Shakespeare first edition, bound in unborn calf" (172). The role of Garfield's son in the film has been assigned to Spunk Davis, fresh from his first successful film role and thus in high demand. He was poor before discovering fool's gold in Hollywood, and at one time "never wanted to forget what it was like to be poor" (315). But he has fallen for the actress Butch Beausoleil, who has taught him to deny his past. "I'm through with all that now and I feel good about my money," Spunk says defiantly, which inspires Self, wiser at least than this, to indulge in an observation about American-style self-deception that sounds suspiciously like his creator: "So this philosopher had frowned his way to a conclusion. The pity was that the whole of tabloid and letterhead America had reached it before him" (315–16).

Doubles and Doubling

Throughout the novel, Self's personal life and moral squalor are refracted through the filter of his film project. The project itself is one of Self's many attempts to double himself in the novel. Thus it is not surprising that his life and the film project get constantly entangled. Caduta Massi, approached to play the role of the mother, takes an immediate maternal interest in the motherless Self, and literally succors him at her breast. Butch Beausoleil, sought for the part of the mistress, embarrasses Self sexually in anticipation of Selina's later betrayal. And the revised plot of the film, alternately titled *Good Money* and *Bad Money,* concludes with a scene of Oedipal violence that anticipates Self's violent encounter with his father near the end of the novel. Just as Self seeks to recreate himself on screen, he also doubles himself with some of those associated with the film. In near-perpetual envy of the sleek and suave Fielding (himself a double of Selina), Self imagines going to the West Coast for a complete physical makeover. "When I wing out to Cal for my refit, when I stroll nude into the lab with my cheque, I think I know what I'll say. I'll say, 'Lose the blueprints. Scrap those mock-ups. I'll take a Fielding'" (207). Even Spunk Davis inspires a passing infatuation, causing a brief sexual identity crisis until Self takes his own counsel: "relax, he's just giving you a pang of your younger self" (301).

The most extensive of these doublings involves Self's relationship with the character Martin Amis, hired to rewrite the film script (which is also, of course, Self's story). All four of Amis's previous novels have contained self-reflexive elements; in *Money* he makes this explicit. He does so with a blunt honesty worthy of Self's narrative voice. He creates a protagonist named Self whose life parallels his own to a surprising degree; he embodies himself in the novel as a recurring character; and he doubles this character through the American Martina Twain ("twain" literally means two). He even has Self voice the theme: "people are doubling also, dividing, splitting" (64). The reader is virtually invited to consider Self, Amis, and Martina as aspects of a single consciousness.

The presence of Amis's persona in *Money* has generated much criticism and critical misunderstanding. John Bayley has called the strategy "tiresome," and an "artistic trick."[13] Laura L. Doan, following the lead of earlier critics, claims its sole function is to maintain a satirical distance between Self and his creator: "Amis takes exceptional care to ensure that the narrator-protagonist, so disgusting in his values and lifestyle, cannot be mistaken for the writer by literally putting himself into the text. Martin Amis, the character, is a suave, intelligent, highly educated, comfortably middle-class writer who quite obviously finds Self, and what he represents, unsavory."[14]

Bayley's impatience is hard to credit, given the fact that each appearance by the Amis character is unique to the dramatic situation, and reveals additional facets of his real and symbolic relationship to Self. Furthermore, Amis's existence in the novel is handled with such offhandedness and comic panache that his presence never feels like the self-consciously obtrusive trick it has seemed in other works where it occurs (from John Barth's *Lost in the Funhouse* to John Fowles's *The French Lieutenant's Woman*). Since *Money* is about the way reality is mediated, and features conversations between a filmmaker and the actors who will play his characters, it seems almost natural that the filmmaker's author would converse with *his* main character.

Doan's charge, on the other hand, is seriously misleading—though consistent with her mistaken assumption that Self is punished in the novel for attempting to rise above his "station." Doan's claim that the character Martin Amis finds Self and what he represents "unsavory" is contradicted throughout the novel, but especially by the second meeting between the two. The Amis character, thoroughly familiar with Self's television work, tells Self, "I thought those commercials were bloody funny"—just before ordering what Self calls "a standard yob's breakfast" (165). It is not Self's upward mobility or his downward aesthetic that Amis and his persona object to, but his moral fatigue syndrome. Nowhere does Amis imply that exposure to high culture per se is a sufficient inoculation against this condition.

Self and the Amis character are secret sharers more than antagonists. Many of Self's experiences are, in fact, those of his creator viewed through the distorting lens of an unlikely double.[15] During their first conversation, Self tells Amis he heard that his father is also a writer, adding: "Bet that made it easier." Amis's sarcastic reply: "Oh, sure. It's just like taking over the family pub" (85). This alludes to the difficulties inherent in the actual Amis's quest to establish his own identity and voice in the shadow of his famous literary father. He has experienced both envious accusations of nepotism and favoritism as well as public criticism from Kingsley, who has called his son's novels unreadable.[16] This withholding of paternal support is mirrored in Self's relationship to his father (who owns a pub named after the ultimate literary father: The Shakespeare). Barry Self's interactions with his son in the novel range from cavalier to callous to cruel. Their most emotional encounter is a grotesque parody of familial intimacy, in which Self is invited to share the joy of his stepmother's appearance in a pornographic magazine (this occurs after Self's father has sent him a bill for his upbringing). Under ordinary circumstances, Self might have assumed that he would eventually inherit his father's pub. By the end of the novel, however, his father has denied paternity and disowned him.

Self's career also constitutes a fun-house mirror image of Amis's. Both were shaped by the youth culture of the 1960s, which is reflected in their work; both made professional names for themselves in the 1970s; both sought artistic recognition on the other side of the Atlantic in the 1980s; both have worked in film. "Remember the stir in the flaming summer of 1976?" Self asks. "My nihilistic commercials attracted prizes and writs. The one on nude mags was never shown, except in court" (76). Amis experienced prominence and success in the 1970s for a body of work that generated considerable controversy, including charges of tastelessness and obscenity. Publication of the American edition of his third novel, *Success,* was delayed for nine years— a postponement which Amis has attributed to the novel's sexual explicitness.[17] Self's film project has a similar resonance. Two years before Amis began writing *Money,* he wrote the screenplay for the science fiction movie *Saturn 3,* released in 1980 (like his persona in *Money,* he was hired to adapt someone else's story). An American-British coproduction, *Saturn 3* is a bigbudget space opera featuring one Hollywood legend (Kirk Douglas), one emerging star (Harvey Keitel), and one actress attempting to move from television to film (Farah Fawcett). The movie itself—as ludicrous as those Amis parodies in *Money*—is a triumph of celebrity and special effects over plot and characterization. During his involvement with the film, Amis, like Self, learned firsthand about the unbridled egos of actors.[18]

Self's tribulations with his film project slyly mirror the critical controversies attending Amis's postmodern narratives. When the Amis character agrees to become Self's script doctor, Self spells out his ailments: "We have a hero problem. We have a motivation problem. We have a fight problem. We have a realism problem" (221). Amis's own novels exhibit these "problems" as well. His protagonists are antiheroes;[19] their motivation is seldom fully explained; they are often involved in grotesque violence; and they inhabit fictional worlds that obey a literary but not always a conventionally realistic logic. Self's "aesthetic standards" are driven purely by the conventions of the popular market, so he wants Amis to provide larger than life heroes, clear-cut motivation, and "realism" as defined by current mainstream conventions. The Amis character obliges, since the price is right, all the while schooling Self in his own literary assumptions (and explaining to the attentive reader why *Money* is the kind of novel it is).

In all of his appearances, the Amis character is treated with the same comic irony that is leveled at Self. In the following encounter, Self and Amis talk about how their similar "problems" affect their chosen genres—films and novels. Amis explains why heroes are scarce in modern fiction:

> "The distance between author and narrator corresponds to the degree to which the author finds the narrator wicked, deluded, pitiful or ridiculous. I'm sorry, am I boring you?"
>
> "—Uh?"
>
> "This distance is partly determined by convention. In the epic or heroic frame, the author gives the protagonist everything he has, and more. The hero is god, or has god-like powers or virtues. In the tragic . . . Are you all right?"
>
> "Uh?" I repeated. I had just stabbed a pretzel into my dodgy upper tooth. Rescreening this little mishap in my head, I suppose I must have winced pretty graphically and then given a sluggish, tramplike twitch . . . .
>
> "The further down the scale he is, the more liberties you can take with him. You can do what the hell you like to him, really. The author is not free of sadistic impulses." (229)

Self's complaint about his tooth here comically emphasizes his status as an antihero subject to his author's impulses. But in true dialogic fashion, it has an additional, countervailing effect. By interrupting the Amis character's would-be monologue, Self asserts his autonomy, his refusal to be a mere authorial "gimmick." A few paragraphs later this impression is strengthened. The Amis character claims that "the twentieth century is an ironic age—downward-looking. Even realism, rockbottom realism, is considered a bit grand for the twentieth century." Self's irrepressible, skeptical response: "'Really,' I said, and felt that tooth with my tongue" (231). Self and realism alike emerge triumphant from this encounter.

Self may be the victim of his author's postmodern assumptions about fiction, but he never surrenders his fundamental autonomy within these constraints, nor the freedom of his elemental responses. He retains what the Amis character calls a fictional character's "double innocence" (241)—ignorance of his role in a fiction, ignorance of the reasons why things are happening to him in a particular way. In the final pages of the novel, an italicized section symbolizing Self's escape from his author's surveillance and control, he has one brief, final encounter with the Amis character, curses him, and watches him leave the room, looking "stung, scared" (359). Having survived suicide, Self even survives his author's withdrawal of authorship. As Amis said in an interview after *Money* was published, "I learned very early on that no matter how much you do to forestall it, the reader will believe in the characters and feel concern for them."[20]

Self's relative autonomy, like the many ways in which he is an authorial double, is crucial to the dialogic design of *Money*. While Self is unmistakably represented as less intelligent, educated, and self-aware than the Amis character, he still speaks for him in significant ways. Both, for instance, must make their way in the cultural marketplace. One of the novel's unspoken ironies is that Self's television advertisements and mainstream film project are far more viable commercially than Amis's literary narratives. The relative print space given to Self and the Amis character in *Money* accurately reflects the currency of their chosen genres. One of the novel's running jokes about the Amis character is Self's concern about how much money he makes. When Self notices that he washes his clothes at a Laundromat, he says to the reader, "I don't think they can pay writers that much, do you?" (71). When they converse for the first time, in The Blind Pig pub, Self asks him, "Sold a million yet?" In response, Amis "looked up at me with a flash of paranoia" (85). The Amis character's presence in the novel highlights the predicament of the serious writer in a commodity culture indifferent to traditional artistic values.

In terms of the novel's critique of late capitalism, the Amis character is guilty of false consciousness. He is a naive literary modernist clinging to the fiction that he can protect his art from the influence of the marketplace. When Self learns that Amis makes "enough" yet does not own a video player, he becomes indignant. "You haven't got shit, have you, and how much do you earn? It's immoral. Push out some cash. Buy stuff. Consume, for Christ's sake." Amis's response: "I suppose I'll have to start one day. . . . But I really don't want to join it, the whole money conspiracy" (243). He does so when revising the film script, however, and as the extraliterary Amis knows, it is impossible for any working writer to avoid. His vocation depends on a market for his books—and legal "ownership" of something as personal as his verbal style. After Self asks the Amis character to rewrite his film script, he tells Fielding about it. "Fielding, of course, had heard of Martin Amis—he hadn't read his stuff, but there'd recently been some cases of plagiarism, of text-theft, which had filtered down to the newspapers and magazines. So, I thought. Little Martin got caught with his fingers in the till, then, did he. A word criminal. I would bear that in mind" (218). As in Self's interpretation of *Othello*, just the opposite is true. Jacob Epstein committed "text-theft" on Amis's first novel *The Rachel Papers* in composing *Wild Oats*.[21] Amis needed to draw attention to this plagiarism in order to protect his economic viability as a unique artistic voice.

In other words, both Amises—the author of *Money* and his persona within the narrative—have been shaped by the forces that have shaped Self. So have all the novel's readers. This is made explicit when Self and the Amis character sit down together to watch the wedding of Charles and Diana, and Self describes the face of his secret sharer. "As I twisted in my seat and muttered to myself I found I kept looking Martin's way. The lips were parted, suspended, the eyes heavy and unblinking. If I stare into his face I can make out the areas of waste and fatigue, the moonspots and boneshadow you're bound to get if you hang out in the twentieth century" (243–44). Although Self claims that Martina's moneyed background has protected her from these physical symptoms, her own experience of loss and isolation—represented both in her situation and in her dialogues with Self—mark her as another sharer of the postmodern condition as diagnosed by the novel.

When Self reads *1984*, he is attracted to the world it depicts: "A no-frills setup, run without sentiment, snobbery, or cultural favouritism, Airstrip One seemed like my kind of town. (I saw myself as an idealistic young corporal in the Thought Police)" (207). The reader familiar with Orwell's savage satire will note that Self already lives in a version of Airstrip One. The totalitarian state of Oceania is dedicated to reducing human freedom and choice by steadily narrowing the range of thought. In the mass-mediated commodity culture in which Self has temporarily thrived, advertising and film have engendered a similar effect. Like Winston Smith, the doomed hero of *1984,* Self spends most of his narrative discovering that he is trapped—not by a totalitarian state, but in the prison of a debased private culture. "I sometimes think I am controlled by someone," Self says late in his narrative. "But he's not from out there. He's from in here" (305). Near the end of *1984,* Winston Smith is led away to "Room 101," where he is threatened with torture and loses his last shreds of freedom and dignity. It is no accident that Self's expensive New York hotel room, arranged for him by Fielding, has the same number.[22]

Among other things, *Money* represents a narrative representation of the "shock experience" that Walter Benjamin saw typifying modern urban life. Writing in the 1920s, Benjamin foresaw the destruction of what he called "the space of contemplation" by the forces of modernity, in particular the aggressive, inescapable influence of advertising and its technological ally, film. "The most real, the mercantile gaze into the heart of things is the advertisement. It abolishes the space where contemplation moved and all but hits us between the eyes with things as a car, growing to gigantic proportions, careens at us out of a film screen."[23] John Self, who made himself through advertising, who has a "screening-room inside my head" (304), is the embodiment of modernity as Benjamin conceives it. He careens at the reader from the pages of his narrative, recording the spectacle of his life careening out of control. "At sickening speed I have roared and clattered, I have rocketed through my time, breaking all the limits, time limits, speed limits, city limits, jumping lights and cutting corners, guzzling gas and burning rubber, staring through the foul screen with my fist on the horn" (288). The word "screen" here has a double significance, referring not just to a windshield but to the debased cinema of pornography and money that takes up so much room in Self's imagination. Like modernity, it threatens to crowd out contemplation itself.

CHAPTER 5

Apocalypse Now

Einstein's Monsters; London Fields; Time's Arrow,
or, The Nature of the Offense

In 1985, Martin Amis and his wife had a son. That same year, he published the short story "Bujak and the Strong Force" in the *London Review of Books*. The first event influenced the narrative strategies and themes of his fiction over the next six years; the second previewed them. "Bujak and the Strong Force," which became the first story in *Einstein's Monsters*, is about the horrors of the twentieth century and the dilemma of the writer attempting to confront them. Its narrator is a new father newly sensitized to the "critical fragility" of life, a would-be writer paralyzed by "thought and anxiety" (42). Through his acquaintance with Bujak, whose life "went deep into the century" (34), this narrator takes a crash course in the Second World War, the Nazi Holocaust, the nuclear threat, and the unstable Einsteinian universe which has played host to these plagues. He emerges with greater compassion than Amis's previous narrators, and greater awareness of the world beyond his personal borders. But he also contracts an incurable malaise.

"Bujak and the Strong Force" thus serves as a prelude to another informal trilogy in Amis's career: *Einstein's Monsters, London Fields,* and *Time's Arrow.* Although the first two deal with the nuclear threat and the third with Auschwitz, John Updike's comment in his review of *Time's Arrow* suggests a common thread: "'Holocaust' has taken on two meanings in our time—nuclear war, which hasn't yet happened and we hope never will, and Nazi Germany's systematic murder of six million helpless European captives, most of them Jews. This Holocaust did happen, yet remains, like the other, unthinkable."[1] A determination to think the unthinkable unites all three books, as well as a restless search for narrative forms adequate to the task. Each work reflects Amis's attempt to modify his earlier "art for art's sake" stance and bring his fiction into closer contact with world-historical realities. His guide in this quest is Saul Bellow. "Bellow has made his own experience resonate more memorably than any living writer," Amis has written. "He is also the first to come out on the other side of this process, enormously strengthened to contemplate the given world."[2] This chapter will consider Amis's three "millennial" fictions as part of a similar process.

Einstein's Monsters

Einstein's Monsters (1987), a book about nuclear anxiety, is a transitional work in Amis's career. It is a fascinating, uneven, at times frustrating collection comprising five stories and a polemical introduction titled "Thinkability." The stories are organized sequentially: two are preapocalyptic, and three are postapocalyptic. In the latter three, Amis employs science fiction, a genre he embraced as an adolescent and as a scriptwriter. He takes advantage of its imaginative license to try out new narrative strategies. Ultimately, these experiments lead to the remarkable hybrid, *Time's Arrow,* in which the venerable science fiction convention of time travel is radically revised. In *Einstein's Monsters* the results are mixed, though like everything in the collection they testify to Amis's risk taking and experimental range.

One of the greatest risks Amis takes in *Einstein's Monsters* is comparison with Norman Mailer. In 1981, Amis charged that Mailer "had fallen prey to the novelist's fatal disease: ideas. His naiveté about 'answers,' 'the big illumination,' 'the secret of everything,' persists to this day," Amis wrote.[3] But six years later, Amis exhibits similar symptoms. Consider this passage from "Thinkability": "Soon after I realized I was writing about nuclear weapons (and the realization took quite a while: roughly half of what follows in this book was written in innocence of its common theme), I further realized that in a sense I had been writing about them all along. Our time is different. . . . A new fall, an infinite fall, underlies the usual—indeed traditional—presentiments of decline" (21). Amis claims in the author's note that the stories in *Einstein's Monsters* were written with "no purpose at all—except, I suppose, to give pleasure, various kinds of complicated pleasure" (I). Yet the stories are unmistakably shaped by the ideas in the introduction; they are all about "the deformations and perversities of the modern setting" caused by the omnipresent nuclear threat. "What is the hidden determinant that could explain it *all*?" asks Samson, the narrator of "Bujak and the Strong Force." As John Lanchester has written, "it is a dangerous question for a writer of fiction to be interested in." Amis is attuned to Mailer's naiveté, Lanchester continues, "because he is also prone to it: there's a curious simplemindedness in the idea that there will be a 'hidden determinant' at all, let alone one as concrete as nuclear weapons."[4]

Einstein's Monsters begins with an introductory essay that Amis says can be read "last or later" (I). "Thinkability" is several things at once: a polemical attack on the notion of nuclear deterrence (combined with a call for phased nuclear disarmament); an attack on his father and his father's generation for ignoring the nuclear threat; and an attempt to measure its human toll. Amis's stylistic virtuosity is on display even here, where it is used to intensify the reader's apprehension of geo-political realities. When Amis calls the Star Wars debate a "technophiliac space-opera" (10), and coins the phrase "Necropolis" to describe the post-bomb city, his gothically inflected terms convey the radical destructiveness and perversity of nuclear warfare. "Thinkability" is best in its short bursts of haunting imagery and frank bewilderment; it is less successful as a polemic. Amis conducts his argument for disarmament in semi-isolation, dismissing the tireless antinuclear crusader E. P. Thompson (on the grounds of his anachronistic rhetoric) and ignoring the Campaign for Nuclear Disarmament. He also ignores the women's peace community of Greenham Common. Although this important group held a continuous protest vigil at the American cruise missile base fifty miles southwest of London during the 1980s, the nuclear debate, as Amis describes it, is conducted exclusively by men.[5] Amis does invoke Jonathan Schell, whose seminal antinuclear polemic *The Fate of the Earth* incited his own nuclear imaginings. Yet he does not link Schell's argument, or his own, to such non-weapons issues as nuclear reactors—even though the Chernobyl disaster occurred the same year *Einstein's Monsters* appeared. In addition, Amis's own stridency at times threatens logical consistency. Early on, he claims that "we are slowly learning how to write about [nuclear weapons]" (4), but he later criticizes an earlier genera-tion of writers who "evidently did not find that the subject sug-gested itself naturally" (23). Elsewhere he argues that a nuclear device is "in essence an antibaby device. One is not referring here to the babies who will die but to the babies who will never be born, those that are queueing up in spectral relays until the end of time" (6). As Adam Mars-Jones asked in his review of *Einstein's Monsters*, "would he acknowledge the cogency of such an argument if it was advanced by someone who opposed both contraception and abortion, or is this that worrying development even within single-issue politics, the single-issue argument?"[6]

"Thinkability" is most valuable as a conceptual map of the stories themselves. Among other things, each story dramatizes one or more elements of the essay's argument. "Bujak and the Strong Force," for instance, is about the cruel illusion of nuclear deterrence. "Insight at Flame Lake" features a twelve-year-old narrator driven mad by a nuclear physicist father blind to the moral "malformations" his work spawns. "The Time Disease" is set in a postapocalyptic world in which time itself has been diminished. As Amis articulates midway through the essay: "the past and the future, equally threatened, equally cheapened, now huddle in the present" (22). In "The Little Puppy That Could," a long nuclear winter has led to sex role inversions viewed as aberrant by the patriarchal voice of the introduction. And one significance of "The Immortals" is revealed in a passage from Jonathan Schell's book *The Abolition,* which is quoted in "Thinkability": "The eternal has been placed at stake in the temporal realm, and the infinite has been delivered into the care of finite human beings" (20). Analysis of the individual stories will reveal how they imaginatively elaborate these themes.

"Bujak and the Strong Force" is set in 1985. Its narrator, an American Jew named Samson, has given up writing. "The sense of critical fragility (myself, my wife, my daughter, even the poor planet, baby blue in its shawls), it drove me from my study in the end. The study life is all thought and anxiety and I cannot take the study life anymore" (42). He is now a teacher living in

New York. He has one story left to tell—the one that made him lay down his pen. "This is the only story I'll ever tell, and this story is true" (38). It relates the end of the narrator's innocence, of his sense of safety. Five years earlier, Samson lived in west London, next to a Polish family headed by the formidable patriarch Bujak, a widower who lives with his mother, his daughter Leokadia, and his granddaughter Boguslawa. "Sixty years old, hugely slabbed and seized with muscle and tendon. . . . You slept a lot sounder knowing that Bujak was on your street" (33). Economic distress and racial tension were rife at this time, and the entire neighborhood spoke of Bujak as "the peacekeeper, the vigilante, the rough-justice artist. . . . He was our deterrent" (39, 41). This illusion is shattered when Bujak returns from an overnight trip to find his family senselessly murdered by two Scottish vagrants. Bujak finds the murderers asleep at the scene when he arrives, but refrains from killing them.

While "Bujak and the Strong Force" succeeds as a story of loss and of life's violent unpredictability, it also operates on an allegorical level. All of the story's characters have been marked by the Second World War and its nuclear legacy: Samson is too traumatized to speak of his ancestors killed in the concentration camps; his Japanese wife Michiko lost a relative in the bombings of Nagasaki and Hiroshima; Bujak himself, who fought in the Polish resistance against the Nazis, has been hardened by the "strong force" he was forced to employ. The story itself is saturated with what Samson calls "Einsteinian" metaphors "accelerated particles," "the energy locked in matter," "neutronium," "Big Bang." The allegorical explanation for the murders is locked in this language as well. "All peculiarly modern ills, all fresh distortions and distempers, Bujak attributed to one thing: Einsteinian knowledge, knowledge of the strong force. It was his

central paradox that the greatest—the purest, the most magical
—genius of our time should introduce the earth to such squalor,
profanity and panic" (46). Bujak's explanation is also Amis's;
here is the "hidden determinant" that informs all of *Einstein's
Monsters*.

As the language used to describe him suggests, the Bujak
that Samson meets in 1980 personifies nuclear deterrence: he is
a human Minuteman missile. But his grievous loss convinces
him that deterrence is a sham—the threat of violence does not
deter violence. In the story's final scene, Samson returns to London to ask Bujak why he didn't kill the killers when he discovered them. His short answer is "I had no wish to add to what I
found." He describes the murderers as "terrible mutations, a
disgrace to their human molding" (58)—Einstein's monsters, in
other words, "vivid representatives of the twentieth century"
(51). "If I had killed them then I would still be strong," Bujak
continues. "But you must start somewhere. You must make
a start." Samson's overly schematic response: "And now that
Bujak has laid down his arms, I don't know why, but I am
minutely stronger" (58).

Morally stronger, perhaps, but aesthetically chastened.
Samson is, in part, an authorial alter ego (he believes in unilat-
eral disarmament, he is a recent father, he even reads Saul
Bellow), and his world-weary, word-wary voice announces a
modulation of Amis's narrative tone. In part this represents a
return of the bewildered, pained narrator of *Other People*. But
it also looks ahead. Samson is the prototype of Samson Young,
the terminally ill narrator of *London Fields*, who is also determined to tell a true story—about millennial malaise. In *Einstein's Monsters* Samson learns from Bujak the language of
diminishment that will characterize Samson Young's narration

in *London Fields:* "To paraphrase Bujak, as I understood him. We live in a shameful shadowland. Quietly, our idea of human life has changed, thinned out. We can't help but think less of it now. The human race has declassed itself" (48).

As in *London Fields,* however, this anti-aesthetic coexists uneasily with Amis's verbal inventiveness. In "Thinkability" Amis writes that "nuclear realities are always antithetical or palindromic"; "Bujak and the Strong Force" ends by illustrating this proposition. Samson recalls Bujak's claim that eventually the expanding universe will contract. "At that moment, with the cosmos turning on its hinges, light would begin to travel backward, received by the stars and pouring from our human eyes." Samson continues, spelling out the imaginative physics underlying the trajectory of *Time's Arrow* and anticipating its vertiginous effect:

> If, and I can't believe it, time would also be reversed, as Bujak maintained (will we move backward too? Will we have any say in things?), then this moment as I shake his hand shall be the start of my story, his story, our story, and we will slip downtime of each other's lives, to meet four years from now, when, out of the fiercest grief, Bujak's lost women will reappear, born in blood (and we will have our conversations, too, backing away from the same conclusion), until Boguslawa folds into Leokadia, and Leokadia folds into Monika, and Monika is there to be enfolded by Bujak until it is her turn to recede, kissing her fingertips, backing away over the fields to the distant girl with no time for him (will that be any easier to bear than the other way around?), and then big Bujak shrinks, becoming the weakest thing there is, helpless, indefensible, naked, weeping, blind and tiny, and folding into Rosa. (59)

This unexpected beauty, granted by means of poetic images and cadences, is so at odds with the actual loss recorded by the story that it highlights the gap between the world and the word.

"Insight at Flame Lake" exhibits a similarly wavering commitment to subdued narration. Dan is one of its two narrators, a verbally precocious twelve-year-old schizophrenic whose nuclear physicist father has just committed suicide. The other narrator is his uncle Ned, who has invited his nephew to spend the summer with him, his wife Fran, and their newborn girl Hattie at Flame Lake. Alternating excerpts from Dan's notebook and Ned's diary structure the story. The uncle is notably lacking in imaginative insight; his prose is clichéd and affectless. Shortly after Dan's notebook records that he has stopped taking his medication and is becoming delusional, Ned records this observation: "Dan continues to come on wonderfully well. He has bouts of agitation and gloom—but who doesn't? No, he's much, much happier" (68). Amis does not consistently sustain this voice, however; at times Ned comes off sounding like Martin Amis by way of *Money*'s John Self. Worrying about his daughter, he writes "she's safe here of course, but then there's the crib-death gimmick, dreamed up to ensure that parents get no peace of mind *at all*" (63).

The reader, meanwhile, grows increasingly convinced that Dan poses the greatest threat to Hattie. In his delusional state Dan has decided she, too, is schizophrenic, and that she talks to him: "she told me how—together—we might end our trial by fire. She wants me to take her out into the sleeping warhead of Flame Lake, and so foreclose the great suspense" (77). In terms of the story's nuclear symbolism, Dan has been turned into an "antibaby device." Mentally poisoned by his father's "technophilia," he now seems poised to infect the next generation.

In the end, Dan does not bring death to the baby—just to himself. The story ends with Ned reading his nephew's note-book, realizing that he was blind to the boy's deterioration, and recognizing what triggered his suicide:

Yesterday, at breakfast, Dan was there. As he drank his juice he gazed at the backs of the cereal boxes. What could be more—what could be more natural? I used to do that myself as a kid: toy-aircraft designs, send-in competitions, funnies, waffle and cookie recipes. But now? On the back of the high-fiber bran package there are tips for avoiding cancer. On the back of the half-gallon carton of homogenized, pasteurized, vitamin D-fortified milk there are two mugshots of smiling children, gone, missing. (Have You Seen Them?). Date of birth, 7/7/79. Height, 3'6". Hair, brown. Eyes, blue. Missing, and missed, too, I'll bet—oh, most certainly. Done away with, probably, fucked and thrown over a wall somewhere, fucked and murdered, yeah, that's the most likely thing. I don't know what is wrong. (79)

Here, as at the end of "Bujak and the Strong Force," language is at odds with reality. In this case, Ned's hard-boiled style tries but fails to hold bitter hopelessness at bay.

Language is also used as a protective cloak in "The Time Disease," the first postapocalyptic story in the collection. The limited nuclear exchanges that have ravaged the sky are only one of the proposed explanations for the epidemic that gives the story its name: others include urban life, television, evolutionary change, and the twentieth century itself. Whatever its sources, the disease reverses the aging process, restoring energy and vitality. In the inverted world created by an endless nuclear winter, feeling of any kind causes pain. It is the enemy. Thus a condition that constitutes a fountain of youth is considered a disease. The plot of the story turns on the panic that erupts when the narrator's ex-wife, forty years old and one of the country's leading "Daydrama" stars, comes down with the disease.

The trauma of nuclear disaster has produced a reductio ad absurdum of human responsiveness in this deathly world, a collective numbness reflected in the language of the story's characters. "The Time Disease" is narrated by the TV producer Lou Goldfader, whose straitjacketed prose reaches its limits of expressiveness in the phrases "it's a thing," "it's a situation," "it's a feature." Comic writing is scarce in *Einstein's Monsters,* but it is used to great effect in "The Time Disease." As in *Money,* Amis makes the most of his narrator's narrow obsessions: "Nobody thinks about anything else anymore. Nobody even pretends to think about anything else anymore. Oh yeah, except the sky, of course. The poor sky. . . . It's a thing. It's a situation. We all think about *time,* catching *time,* coming down with *time. I'm* still okay, I think, for the time being" (80). In "Thinkability," Amis claims that "something seems to have gone wrong with time" (21). The result: "the present feels narrower, the present feels straitened, discrepant, as the planet lives from day to day" (22). This precisely describes the phenomenal world Amis so effectively conjures in "The Time Disease."

Amis breaks free of these self-imposed linguistic restraints in "The Little Puppy That Could" by employing the genre of the mythic fable. Specifically, he rewrites the Greek myth of Andromeda, who was about to be sacrificed to a prodigious sea monster when Perseus killed the beast. The main (human) character in "The Little Puppy That Could" is a young girl who embraces the Greek heroic past, in part by rejecting her given name ("Briana") and adopting "Andromeda." She lives in a postapocalyptic world of rampant mutation. The reader first encounters the physical variety: human beings who have devolved into "some uncharted humiliation of webs and pouches, of trotters and beaks" (109–10), a hominivorous dog, eight feet long, four feet high, whose crimson saliva is "capable of entirely dissolving human bones" (110). Then it turns out that traditional gender roles have become reversed in this society, and that Amis views this as another kind of mutation. The females in the unnamed village, with names like Keithette, Kevinia, and Royene, are all "rugged and ruddy and right" (119). They bully their husbands—named Tom, Tim, Tam—who are "drab, effaced, annulled" (120). Amis's overuse of verbal triplets in this story becomes as annoying as his implicitly reactionary sexual politics.

Andromeda alone resists the gender inversion of her community. She takes in a puppy that destroys the mutant dog. Like much else in the story, this puppy seems to have wandered off the pages of a children's story. His simple determination recalls the train engine in "The Little Engine That Could," which Amis's title echoes. In sacrificing himself to purge the village of this evil, the puppy does its part to restore what Amis implies is a more "natural" gender order—a return to the male dominance of the ancient Greeks. At the end of the story, the spirit of the puppy returns to Andromeda, reborn as a boy. "His arms were strong and warlike as he turned and led her into the cool night. They stood together on the hilltop and gazed down at their new world" (134). While the first-person speakers of the other stories in *Einstein's Monsters* express the symptoms of nuclear blight, the omniscient narrator of "The Little Puppy That Could" allows Amis to speak from outside this condition.

But his vision of a remedy is equally limited. It strikes a discordantly anachronistic note.

The last story in *Einstein's Monsters,* "The Immortals," presents the most grandly deluded character in the collection, the most spectacular set of symptoms. It is 2045: the last year of recorded time. The narrator says he has come to New Zealand to be with the last people on earth as they die. He also claims he has been on the earth longer than any living creature, and that he is immortal. His language, like that of Ned in "Insight at Flame Lake," is structured like a shield, though in this case one built by a stand-up comic monologuist. "The first batch of ape-people were just a big drag as far as I was concerned" (138), he says; he later confides that "long-term relationships have always been difficult for me. . . . I've only been married three or four thousand times—I'm not the kind to keep lists—and I shouldn't think my kids are even up there in the five figures" (145–46). The pain of living through so many deaths inspired hundreds of suicide attempts beginning in the Middle Ages, followed a nearly hundred-year alcoholic binge (1945–2039) in an attempt to "find the state where nothing matters. This was how the whole world seemed to be behaving. And you cannot find this state. Because it doesn't exist. Because things do matter. Even here" (144).

The narrator's shield falls in the story's final pages, and we discover that he is in fact mortal—even though, in his deluded state, he imagines that this fact is itself a delusion. "Sometimes I have this weird idea that I am just a second-rate New Zealand schoolmaster who never did anything or went anywhere and is now painfully and noisily dying of solar radiation along with everybody else. It's strange how palpable it is, this fake past, and how human: I feel I can almost reach out and touch it." His next words reveal the hidden emotional heart of his story. "There was a woman, and a child. One woman. One child. . . . But I soon snap out of it" (148). This revelation radiates beyond "The Immortals" to all of *Einstein's Monsters*. Though its ostensible subject is the omnipresent nuclear threat, and the distinctive ways this has (mis)shaped postmodern life, the book's emotional core can be found at a more traditional site of fission: the family fireside.

To quote John Lanchester once more, "the stories in *Einstein's Monsters* are haunted, as is the introduction, by the imagined deaths of children. Often, this death (these deaths) is where the real imaginative weight of the story seems to be placed: the emotional balance is, as in 'The Immortals,' slightly off-centre."[7] The murder of Bujak's granddaughter, the suicide of Dan, the near-deaths of Hattie and Andromeda, the death of all children, all future children, and childhood itself in "The Immortals"—these are the central stories of *Einstein's Monsters*. And while Amis's struggle to imagine them, to expand his art to accommodate them, brings a greater compassion to his writing, it also leads to missteps. For instance, the attempt at unadorned sentiment in "The Little Puppy That Could," the very title of which spells trouble, results in false sentiment, in disingenuousness: "Why do people love children? Why do children love babies? Why do we all love animals? What do animals love, that way?" (115).

In "Thinkability," Amis argues about nuclear weapons with his own father, who considers them an "unbudgeable given" (14), and claims that "in this debate, we are all arguing with our fathers" (13). "They got it hugely wrong," he claims, adding, "perhaps there will be no hope until they are gone" (13). This critique would seem to call for radical rethinking, but aside from his rhetorically extremist tone, Amis's ideas in "Thinkability" are surprisingly traditional. They are rigidly patriarchal, for one thing. Amis presumptuously assumes that he will become the reluctant executioner of his wife and children if London suffers a nuclear attack. Writing in an apartment a mile from his home, he imagines what will happen if he survives the first blasts. "I shall be obliged (and it's the last thing I'll feel like doing) to retrace that long mile home, through the firestorm, the remains of the thousand-mile-an-hour winds, the warped atoms, the groveling dead. Then—God willing, if I still have the strength, and, of course, if they are still alive—I must find my wife and children and I must kill them" (4). The reader is moved to ask: should his wife not have some say in this?

Ultimately, *Einstein's Monsters* is more successful as a set of experiments in fictional technique and tone than as an attempt to locate postmodern malaise exclusively in the nuclear fire zone. Most of the ideas in the collection receive richer, less simplifying treatment in *London Fields* and *Time's Arrow*. In his next book, Amis abandons his single-issue focus—though not his dubious quest for the big illumination.

London Fields

London Fields (1989) is like the monstrous, mutant canine that terrorizes the postapocalyptic villagers in "The Little Puppy That Could." The novel relentlessly pursues a vision of deformation and death, darkening the lives of everyone caught in its force field. Even the two babies in the novel are affected: one is monstrous from birth, the other is deformed by physical abuse. The dog's appetite in "The Little Puppy That Could" is satisfied by the village council, which feeds it one human victim each week; *London Fields* has Nicola Six, a ravenous creature described by the narrator as "a mixture of genres. . . . A mutant." She, too, lives by preying upon other human beings; her goal is to "get to the end of men" (188). The novel is a mutant form as well—an unstable mixture of millennial murder mystery, urban satire, apocalyptic jeremiad, and domestic farce.

Despite its inner darkness, *London Fields* is often wickedly funny. At its core, the novel is a dark comedy about the death of love. As with all of the real and imagined deaths in the novel, nuclear terror is the prime suspect: "Hard to love, when you're bracing yourself for impact" (197). The presiding spirit of this comedy (or "motionless Cause," as she calls herself) is Nicola Six, who shares with the novelist a knowledge of the future. Among other things, she knows that on the night of November 6, 1999—her thirty-fifth birthday—she will be murdered. She knows this because she has planned it. She has come to the end of love, which in the novel's terms means the end of everything, and she is bent on artful suicide. At the beginning of the novel, she is the murderee in search of her murderer. She finds the leading candidates one morning when she walks into the Black Cross Pub (a cross has four points, the narrator reminds us). Here sit the three other major characters comprising the novel's sexual rectangle. They are Guy Clinch, an unhappily married aristocrat and "a good guy—or a nice one, anyway" (27); Keith Talent, a small-time cheat, big-time adulterer, and tabloid and television addict—"a bad guy . . . a very bad guy" (4); and Samson Young, the novel's narrator. Young is an American writer living in London who is terminally ill and suffering from a twenty-year writer's block. He feels "sickly and enraptured" at having met Nicola, who relieves him of the burden of creation by creating the story of *London Fields*, which he can simply

transcribe—although it is the novelist Mark Asprey who ultimately creates the novel by compiling the papers Samson has
left in his apartment.[8]

As the narrator's description of her as a "mixture of genres"
suggests, Nicola is a literary character down to her linguistic
bones. In one of her metafictional incarnations she is an authorial alter ego—an instrument of the author's satirical aims. She
is especially adept at parody. In her relationship with Guy she
enacts a grotesque parody of love; in her relationship with Keith
she performs a grotesque parody of sex; and in her relationship
with Samson, she offers a sly parody of Amis's postmodern narrative habits. Like Amis, she is merciless in her treatment of
the novel's characters, and she takes them down with her in
the end—shaming them all at the end of a shameful century.
Despite, or perhaps because of her hyper-literary status, she
serves as agent of much prescient reporting on late-century
sociosexual realities. This emerges from her relationships with
Guy and Keith, who represent cartoonish extremes of status,
attitude, behavior, and class consciousness familiar to readers of
Amis's previous novels.

Guy Clinch "had a tremendous amount of money, excellent
health, handsomeness, height, a capriciously original mind; and
he was lifeless" (27). This initial description sounds distressingly
pat and final, but it is followed by a pregnant sentence: "He was
wide open." He is wide open to Nicola's designs, wide open
because he and his wife Hope have been pushed apart by the
birth of their son Marmaduke, and because "what had meant
to come closer had simply moved further away" (29). Amis's
depiction of Marmaduke and his effect on Guy's marriage represents another grotesque parody in the novel—a parody of the
effect parenthood can have on a couple's relationship. "When

Hope called his name—'Guy?'—and he replied *Yes?* there was never any answer, because his name meant *Come here.* He appeared, and performed the necessary errand, and disappeared again. Now, with Hope's requests, the first time of asking sounded like the second time of asking, and the second time of asking sounded like the ninth." Guy takes to picking up Marmaduke less and less often, because his "bashfully inquiring face would somehow always invite a powerful eye-poke or a jet of vomit, a savage rake of the nails, or at the very least an explosive sneeze." As a result, "Guy shocked himself by suspecting that Hope kept the infant's nails unclipped the better to repel him. Certainly his face was heavily scored; he sometimes looked like a resolute but talentless rapist. He felt supererogatory" (29). Amis thus gives an accurate, if satirically exaggerated, representation of a male's response to the loss of exclusive attention from his wife.

Marmaduke himself is an unforgettable comic creation. He heralds the death of the myth of childhood innocence in a novel whose pitch-black comedy feeds on the death of all cherished beliefs. "His chaos is strongly sexual, no question. If you enter his nursery you'll usually find him with both hands down the front of his diaper, or behind the reinforced bars of his playpen leering over a swimsuit ad in one of the magazines that some nanny has thrown to him. . . . Yeah, that's it. Marmaduke looks as though he is already contemplating a career in child pornography: he knows it's out there, and he can tell that there's a quick buck in it" (158). At the end of the novel, when Guy returns home after informing his dying mother-in-law of his infidelity (at Nicola's insistence), he has been utterly displaced by a miraculously matured Marmaduke, possessed of speech and expressing distaste at his father's return. Established in his mother's bedroom, dressed in full armor, Marmaduke undresses while his father attempts a reconciliation with Hope. The end of this scene caps a grotesque episode of Oedipal rivalry: "Marmaduke stood there in his underpants. These too he stepped out of. He climbed into bed. 'Mummy?'" (450).

Guy's undoing is facilitated by the cocoon of privilege in which he lives—privilege bought and paid for by his father's money, accumulated by way of "sweatshops, sanctions-busting, slain rainforests, toxic dumping, and munitions, munitions, munitions" (255). Guy's "gentility" and "honor" are luxuries purchased with this tainted money, and he lavishes them on Nicola. She spends them on the equivalent of a gunpowder plot that explodes in her victim's face. Nicola is thirty-five, a former actress, and "magically, uncontrollably attractive" (17). Yet she manages to convince Guy that she is a virgin still waiting for the right man. "I'm dying to do some kissing" (319), she tells him at one point, in a devastating parody of schoolgirl innocence. When their long-delayed coitus finally occurs, Nicola abruptly interrupts it, leaving Guy stunned, permanently frustrated, and hopelessly deceived—though just one page earlier he had called himself "rich in understanding" (414).

To Guy, Nicola is a woman of beauty and breeding in need of his protection; she fires his nostalgia for the passion that has leaked from his marriage. To Keith, whose libido is "all factoid and tabloid" (202), she is the incarnation of his wildest pornographic fantasies. Nicola knows this, and she knowingly exploits it. She satisfies Keith with explicit videos she has taken of herself that he watches while she is out of the room—a significant fact in a novel where the image, the simulacrum, is inexorably supplanting reality. Just as Guy's humiliations climax in an Oedipal nightmare, Keith's end in onanistic squalor. Keith is living proof of Nicola's earlier thought that "if love was dead or gone then the self was just self, and had nothing to do all day but work on sex. Oh, and hate. And death" (298).

Keith's chief talents are cheating and darts. Everyone in the novel is involved in some form of cheating, but it is Keith's sole means of support. He circulates a glossy brochure throughout west London advertising chauffeur services, casino consulting, luxury purchases, and darts lessons. He sells an Italian perfume called *Outrage,* and one day he gets a shipment of five hundred sachets containing water, "a substance not much less expensive than *Outrage,* but harder to sell. Keith was relieved that he had already unloaded half the consignment on Damian Noble in the Portobello Road. Then he held Damian's tenners up to the light: they were crude forgeries. He passed on the notes without much trouble, in return for twenty-four bottles of vodka which, it turned out, contained a misty, faintly scented liquid. *Outrage!* The incident struck Keith as a sign of the times" (113). Keith constitutes the third portrait in Amis's fictional triptych of driven, grasping "super-yobs" (the other two are Terry Service in *Success* and John Self in *Money*), and he is by far the most corrupt. "Modern and reptilian," utterly unreflective, he makes John Self sound like a seasoned philosopher. And he is utterly incapable of love.

As Graham Fuller has written, "Keith himself is damned by class, a victim of cancerous cultural conditioning and forlorn dreams of betterment, the sleaziest excrescence of Thatcherite greed in fiction."[9] Nowhere is this more damningly portrayed than in the scene where Nicola pays him a surprise visit in the cramped council flat where he lives with his wife Kath and their infant daughter Kim. Kath answers the door, and Nicola pretends to be a social worker, wondering aloud what kind of mother would expose her child to the cigarette smoke that clouds the apartment, and asking her if she abuses her daughter. Keith, not knowing it is Nicola, is roused by the insults—but not because they involve his wife. "Keith could stand for this no longer. His protective instincts were stirred. Loyalty: it was a question of loyalty. Nobody talked that way about Keith's dog —or about his cigarettes, which were superking-sized and had international standing" (258).

Amis has an unerring eye for the telling social detail. He enters so fully into Keith's world—where men are proudly misogynistic, pubs are cultural meccas, darts are a world-class sport, and cigarette brands are status symbols—that no matter how cartoonish Keith appears, the reader never doubts the reality of his milieu. "Every pub has its superstar, its hero, its pub athlete, and Keith was the Knight of the Black Cross" (23) the narrator tells us. But his kingdom is stubbornly quotidian. "The place was ruined and innocuous in its northern light: a clutch of dudes and Rastas playing pool over the damp swipe of the baize, the pewtery sickliness of the whites (they looked like war footage), the twittering fruit-machines, the fuming pie-warmer" (35). It is here that Keith regales his cohorts with tales of his cheats, his scams, his conquests on the darts battlefield and in the bedroom (or kitchen, bathroom, stairway, alley). And it is here, not in the upper atmosphere of its apocalyptic allegory, where *London Fields* lives and breathes.

Nonetheless, this other atmosphere is constantly pressing down on the novel's characters. As they experience the "sudden eschatology of the streets" (271) on the eve of the millennium, Samson Young issues frequent apocalyptic weather bulletins. "The winds tear through the city, they tear through the island, as if softening it up for an exponentially greater violence," he reports early in the novel. "In the last week the winds have killed nineteen people, and thirty-three million trees" (43). Later, Guy's knowing brother Richard makes the following predictions: "that at the moment of full eclipse on November 5, as the Chancellor made his speech in Bonn, two very big and very dirty nuclear weapons would be detonated, one over the Palace of Culture in Warsaw, one over Marble Arch. That until the cease of the flow of fissionable materials from Baghdad, the Israelis would be targeting Kiev. . . . That the confluence of perihelion and syzygy would levitate the oceans. That the sky was falling—" (394).

Meanwhile, each of the novel's main characters experiences one or more "little deaths" that anticipate the ultimate end that geopolitical and ecological events continuously portend.

Samson Young, whose father was involved in nuclear weapons research, is slowly dying. Unlike his biblical namesake, he is being robbed of his strength by an unnamed disease whose symptoms suggest radiation poisoning or AIDS. "We are most of us . . . in some kind of agony" (62), he tells Nicola Six, who has cauterized her own nerve endings but whose ever-anticipated death agony propels the novel's plot. Keith Talent suffers from a "bad chest, his curry-torn digestive system, the itchings and burnings of his sedimentary venereal complaints, his darts elbow, his wall-eyed hangovers" (108). Guy Clinch comes down with a permanent case of nausea after meeting Nicola. "She really did a number on him," the narrator notes. "What was that number? It was Six. Six. Six" (97). Pronouncing her name repeatedly in this way yields "sick," a word with special relevance to Nicola's symbolic role in the novel.

Nicola Six carries a heavy symbolic cargo in *London Fields* —a metaphor appropriate to her association with the B-52 bomber that dropped the atomic bomb on Hiroshima. This particular association reveals both the novel's symbolic ambitions and their awkward execution. Early in the novel the reader learns that Nicola had an imaginary childhood friend named Enola Gay, who later had a child named Little Boy. After she meets Guy, Nicola concocts an elaborate story about how Enola and Little Boy are now trapped in Cambodia, victims of "The Proxy War." "Her name is En Lah Gai. I called her Enola. Enola Gay" 124). Guy spends the rest of the novel using his money and his contacts to search for Nicola's nonexistent friends. Finally Nicola gives him a book to read where he learns—and Amis informs the uninformed reader—that Enola Gay was the plane that dropped the first atomic bomb, which was named Little Boy.

Is Nicola herself meant to personify what Freud called *Thanatos,* the death instinct he believed all human beings harbor? More importantly, is she meant to personify the forms this has taken in the twentieth century, which offers "death to everybody . . . by hemlock or hardware" (297)? The metaphors that pile up around her suggest as much. She is a connoisseur of nonprocreative sex. We are asked to "imagine Nicola's loins as ground zero" (195), and late in the novel she is associated with "Venus, wife of Vulcan, lover of Mars, and never brighter than when the darkness of totality played across the earth" (444). She is also linked to the planet Earth, which is exhibiting all the signs of a death wish. She says she identifies with the planet, and several times during the novel men wolf-whistle at her: "Are you Miss World?" Amis himself encouraged this identification in an interview when he suggested that the planet itself is the "murderee" in the novel.[10] Yet there are inconsistencies in the elaboration of these metaphors. Nicola has a conversation with Keith in which she tutors him in the etymology of the word "bikini," for instance. "From Bikini Atoll in the Marshall Islands, Keith, the site of the US weapons tests in 1946 and 1954. . . . I looked it up in Brewer before you came. He chummily suggests a comparison between the devastating effects of the explosion and the devastating effects of the costume" (127). This, the reader might imagine, would be an ideal costume for Nicola—she who embodies mega-sex and megadeath. In truth, though, "Nicola Six disapproved of bikinis. She execrated bikinis" (126).

Nicola is also wrapped in all the metaphors men have used through the ages to express their fear of (and desire to control) female sexuality. Her first name alludes to "Old Nick," the proverbial name for the devil—an association she underscores when she introduces Keith to Keats's poetry with "Lamia," a poem about a female demon lover. Samson Young scrolls through a long list of terms appropriate to Nicola, including "Sack artist," "Mata Hari," "Vamp," "Ballbreaker," and "Femme Fatale." Nicola doesn't reject these terms, she simply responds "I'm a Murderee" (260), which may be Amis's way of suggesting that such metaphors are themselves instruments of a destructive misogyny. She lends support for this interpretation when Samson tells her he is concerned about how readers will respond to her behavior in the story. "I'm worried they're going to say you're a male fantasy figure." Nicola replies: "I *am* a male fantasy figure. I've been one for fifteen years. It really takes it out of a girl" (260). It seems that male objectification of women is another cause of planetary decline, of millennial malaise.

The problem with this additional layer of metaphor lies in the mixed messages Amis gives off in elaborating it. Early in the novel Nicola prepares to attend the funeral of a woman antique dealer for whom she once worked. As she admires her naked form in front of her mirror, Amis writes that she "stood side-ways with a hand flat on her stomach feeling everything that a woman would hope to feel at such a moment" (20). This decla-ration is followed by Nicola's memory of a previous weekend's torrid encounter with "some new man of the moment" (20). The passage as a whole implies that sexual desirability is the be-all and end-all of a woman's existence, that "female" and "car-nal" are synonymous terms. Moreover, the novel immerses the reader in Nicola's sexual expertise, from her underwear philos-ophy to her "concordance of kisses." This results in ambiguity concerning Amis's point of view. As Graham Fuller has written: "if *London Fields* inevitably fails as an indictment of social malaise rooted in the man-made image of a promiscuous woman, it is because Amis himself is unable to resist Nicola's pornographic promise or the lascivious lexicon of sexism— which alone should offend many women readers."[11]

Unlike some of Amis's critics, Fuller understands that while Amis is implicated in the sexism he represents, "that doesn't mean Amis endorses sexism as a cultural given, any more than he endorses child abuse (a tangential theme of *London Fields*), or the misanthropy which leaves most of the characters in his books dead. He is a novelist wallowing in the spiritual bank-ruptcy of the late 20th century; his methods may make you feel increasingly queasy, but there is always a moral beneath the miasma."[12] If this miasma is thicker in *London Fields* than in any of Amis's previous novels, that is because at the allegorical level the novel is an apocalyptic jeremiad about the world's decadence and exhaustion at the end of the century.

Exhaustion is, in fact, the unifying theme of the novel's alle-gory. "Over the gardens and the mansion-block rooftops, over the window boxes and TV aerials, over Nicola's skylight and

Keith's dark tower (looming like a calipered leg dropped from heaven), the air gave an exhausted and chastened sigh" (229). The sun itself is no longer able to mount the sky ("quite uncanny, the sun's new trajectory, and getting lower all the time" (309). Under its weakening light, moral energies are flagging. Sympathy, tenderness, belief, meaning, and, of course, love are all collapsing. This exhaustion extends right down to the low comedy of Keith's petty criminality. Consider this description of what he and his cohorts discover when they enter a house they intend to rob: "it was all burgled out. Indeed, burgling, when viewed in Darwinian terms, was clearly approaching a crisis. Burglars were finding that almost everywhere had been burgled" (248). When Nicola, noting that she has been a male fantasy figure for fifteen years, says "it really takes it out of a girl," she is contributing her voice to this theme as well.

Amis links all this exhaustion to modern physics, which not only unlocked the destructive power of the atom, but also a scientific concept—entropy—that informs many contemporary visions of disorder. Based on the second law of thermodynamics, entropy describes the tendency of all systems toward randomness or chaos. Borrowing a page from Thomas Pynchon's short story "Entropy," Amis describes the way Guy Clinch's house descends into disorder. "Each day the doublefronted dishwasher, the water softener, the carrot peeler, the pasta patterner got closer and closer to machine death, hurtling towards chaos. Each day the cleaning-lady went home tireder, older, iller. A citadel of order, the house hurried along much entropy elsewhere. With so much needed to keep it together, the house must deep down be dying to collapse or fall apart" (276). Amis views nuclear weapons as the technological handmaidens of entropy; Guy reads a newspaper column noting "that there were man-made devices—pushbutton, fingertip—which could cause equivalent havoc" (276). Guy recognizes that he is implicated in this destructiveness, that his desire for Nicola is itself entropic and "could turn the house into a bomb" (278). In fact, he imaginatively welcomes a nuclear attack on London, which would transform his house into a "thrumming edifice of negative entropy." Then "everything would be allowed," even coupling with Nicola, which he envisions as "an act of love performed among the splinters" (277).

If the nuclear threat effects Guy's imagination in this way, imagine its effect on a novelist. Samson Young implicitly invites us to do so. Samson's twenty-year writer's block is Amis's way of saying that literature, too, is suffering from exhaustion. The problem, Samson says, is that "writers always lag behind the contemporary formlessness. They write about an old reality, in a language that's even older. It's not the words: it's the rhythms of thought. In this sense all novels are historical novels. Not really a writer, maybe I see it clearer. But I do it too. An example: I still go on as if people felt well" (237–38). For this reason, Samson distrusts fiction itself. "In fiction (rightly so called), people become coherent and intelligible—and they aren't like that. We all know they aren't. We all know it from personal experience. We've been there." So what are people like? "People are chaotic quiddities living in one cave each. They pass the hours in amorous grudge and playback and thought-experiment" (240). They are, in other words, like entropy.

Despite its futuristic setting, there is nothing new about Amis in *London Fields;* the novel's themes are overfamiliar, just as its author's tone is overly knowing. In expanding to panoramic breadth the nuclear-age anxieties of *Einstein's Monsters,* Amis has created a pastiche assembled from his own six previous works of fiction. The plot of *London Fields* recycles and combines elements from *Success* and *Other People*. As in *Success,* the reader follows the crossing paths of a falling aristocrat and a rising yob, both involved with the same doomed female. And like *Other People, London Fields* focuses on a woman who is more symbol than character, a woman who is fatefully, synergistically involved with her narrator. In terms of characterization, too, *London Fields* revisits old ground. It maximizes Amis's preference for caricatures over characters, extremes over complexities. Nicola is the ultimate male fantasy, Guy is the ultimate dupe, Keith is the lowest lowlife, Marmaduke the most destructive of babies, Kim the most innocent of victims, and so on. Samson's summary description of Keith's girlfriends, meant to mock Keith's "way with women," encapsulates this tendency: "One was drunk, one was nuts, and one was fifteen. The ladykiller. These, then, were Keith's birds" (52). Samson himself is a metafictional device in *London Fields,* allowing Amis to pose questions about the status and purpose of fiction, but these questions were posed more subtly in *Other People,* and to greater effect in *Money.*

In terms of its own narrative devices, then, *London Fields* itself exhibits signs of exhaustion. In a novel about coming to the end of things, this may be intentional. *London Fields* marks an important end point in Amis's career. Through his two authorial alter egos, Amis conveys a dissatisfaction with the narrative forms the novel employs. Samson is, after all, incapable— not to mention ethically wary—of creating fiction. So he relies on Nicola's darkly satirical plotting. Like many of the characters in Amis's previous novels, Nicola is merciless in exposing human weakness, and adept at creating scenes of comic misery. But she has come to the end of desire, and since desire drives all plots, she decides to end it all. Her chosen murderer is Samson, who first appeared in *Einstein's Monsters*, the herald of a new emphasis in Amis's fiction. He also dies in the end, but not without gesturing toward the future. In a suicide note to Kim Talent, the innocent child he has tried to protect and nurture, he says "I failed, in love and art."[13] But he adds: "Nevertheless, I ask you to survive me" (469).[14] Amis's next novel, *Time's Arrow*, is narrated by a childlike being who survives the death of its host. It represents a radical departure from the sociosexual satire of Amis's other novels, and a radical artistic response to the endgame of *London Fields*. To the extent that Kim symbolizes artistic renewal, *Time's Arrow* grants Samson's request.

Time's Arrow

Schindler's List (1993), Steven Spielberg's film about the Holocaust, contains a much discussed sequence that might have been taken from the pages of *Time's Arrow* (1991). Three hundred women on a train bound for Oskar Schindler's new factory in Czechoslovakia end up instead at the Nazi death camp at Auschwitz-Birkenau. They are stripped, shaved, and herded into the showers, and the viewer follows them, horribly aware of what happened to hundreds of thousands like them. The women look up at the shower heads, the lights go out, and a collective scream erupts. Then, in defiance of viewer expectation, the sound of water is heard: this is not the moment of death but a decontamination process. Momentarily relieved, the viewer braces for the next horror, but it does not come. Schindler learns that his train was misrouted, rushes to the camp, bribes the commandant, and takes the women to his factory—back to jobs they held before they were first sent to the camps. It is almost as if the film were suddenly running backwards: the women enter the gas chamber, the lights go out—then life-giving water showers down on them, and they return to the trains, to their jobs, to their husbands and loved ones. The viewer knows this exception is just that, knows from the film itself that systematic terror and extermination were the norm. But in the midst of this knowledge, Spielberg creates a brief sequence that is the filmic equivalent of poetic justice, imagining what it might look like if history were reversed, if the genocidal horror were undone.

Time's Arrow is also about the Holocaust. In the midst of imagining both the bureaucracy and the psychology of genocidal evil, it also offers poetic justice—on a grand historical scale. It does so by means of an audacious variation on the folk wisdom that just before death individuals see their entire lives flash before them. At the moment of his death in an American hospital, onetime Nazi doctor Odilo Unverdorben "gives birth" to a doppelgänger (literally, "double-goer"), a childlike innocent who relives Unverdorben's life—in reverse. He inhabits Unverdorben, who is unaware of his presence, like a "passenger or parasite" (8). Though he lacks access to his host's thoughts, he is "awash with his emotions" (7). He also possesses a rudimentary conscience—most notably an aversion to human suffering. Fortunately for the narrative, this narrator is "equipped with a fair amount of value-free information, or general knowledge," and a "superb vocabulary" (8, 9). But he is unaware that his backward trajectory through time violates ordinary chronology. He is also utterly ignorant of history.

During his time in America, where Unverdorben works as a surgeon, the narrator witnesses Unverdorben inflict terrible wounds on his patients and send them home in agony. He concludes that doctors "demolish the human body" (74). When he finally arrives at Auschwitz-Birkenau, however, "the world . . . has a new habit. It makes sense" (129). Here he and Odilo create life, heal wounds, and send inmates to freedom. "Our preternatural purpose? To dream a race. To make a people from the weather. From thunder and from lightning. With gas, with electricity, with shit, with fire" (120). In his descriptions of breathing life back into the victims of Nazi genocide the narrator effects a poetic undoing of the Holocaust, all the more poignant for the reader's knowledge that it never *can* be undone. "You present it as a miracle, but the reader is supplying all the tragedy," Amis has said of the narrative perspective he employs in *Time's Arrow*. "It was that kind of double-edged effect that I wanted."[15] As in Jonathan Swift's "A Modest Proposal," the narrator never registers horror at the systematic human cruelty occurring around him—which *increases* the reader's horror. The result is a short novel with what M. John Harrison has called "a long ironic reach."[16]

Time's Arrow is a remarkable imaginative achievement, and it places special demands on the reader. Disorientation is one's initial response to a world in which time moves in reverse and effect always precedes cause. A simple process like gardening becomes a bizarre ritual of uglification when it takes place in reverse: "all the tulips and roses he patiently drained and crushed, then sealed their exhumed corpses and took them in the paper bag to the store for money. All the weeds and nettles he screwed into the soil—and the earth took this ugliness, snatched at it with a sudden grip" (18–19). Everything in *Time's Arrow* is narrated backwards: old people become younger and more vigorous, children grow smaller and eventually enter hospitals from which they never return. Eating, drinking, lovemaking, even an abortion are all described in reverse. Early on, Amis even reverses words and sentences so that "how are you today?" becomes "Aid ut oo y'rrah?" (7)—though after this initial demonstration the narrator helpfully translates.

Faced with this confusion, the reader develops coping mechanisms. Conversations in *Time's Arrow* always run in reverse sequence, for instance, and the reader soon learns to read them from finish to start. Before long, this inverted world becomes comprehensible, because it follows predictable rules. In adapting to its crazy logic, the reader is also preparing to confront another inverted world: Auschwitz and its obscene logic. Although other fiction can be cited in which time is reversed —the Dresden firebombing sequence in Kurt Vonnegut's *Slaughterhouse Five* is perhaps the best known example[17]—the narrative conceit of *Time's Arrow* is placed wholly in the service of a grim moral reckoning. Even passages which may smack of verbal showmanship when quoted in isolation are part of this larger purpose, like the narrator's bewildered response to the world he inhabits: "it's all strange to me. I know I live on a fierce and magical planet, which sheds or surrenders rain or even flings it off in whipstroke after whipstroke, which fires out bolts of electric gold into the firmament at 186,000 miles per second, which with a single shrug of its tectonic plates can erect a city in half an hour" (15). In the actual world, of course, it is destruction that is easy, creation that is difficult—a fact which this ironic reversal forces us to confront. In so doing, it prepares the reader to confront Auschwitz.[18]

Writing about Spielberg's use of "close research" in making *Schindler's List,* Amis revealed his own concern with historical authenticity in *Time's Arrow:* "nearing the Holocaust, a trespasser finds that his imagination is decently absenting itself, and reaches for documentation and technique. The last thing he wants to do, once there, is make anything up."[19] In his brief afterword to *Time's Arrow,* Amis acknowledges several documentary sources, including the writings of Primo Levi (himself a survivor of the death camps). But he singles out one book in particular: *The Nazi Doctors,* by his friend Robert Jay Lifton. Lifton, a psychologist, interviewed survivors of the Nazi death camps as well as surviving Nazi doctors. *The Nazi Doctors* is simultaneously a history of "medicalized killing"[20] during the Nazi regime, which began with eugenics and ended in the Final Solution; a series of portraits of individual Nazi doctors, including the notorious Joseph Mengele; and a theory of psychological "doubling" that attempts to explain how men sworn to uphold the Hippocratic oath could dedicate themselves to mass murder. In his afterword Amis says of *The Nazi Doctors* "my novel would not and could not have been written without it" (167), and it is easy to see why.[21]

When the novel's trajectory is reversed, and Odilo Unverdorben's life and career is summarized using ordinary chronology, for instance, it becomes apparent that he is typical of the Nazi doctors Lifton studied. Unverdorben is born in 1916 in Solingen, the birthplace of Adolf Eichmann. When he comes of age he enters medical school, marries, and joins the Reserve Medical Corps. He is posted to Schloss Hartheim, the notorious medical facility where "impaired" children and adults were put to death ("above its archways and gables the evening sky is full of our unmentionable mistakes," the narrators says, "hydrocephalic clouds and the wrongly curved palate of the west, and the cinders of our fires" [146]). It was here that Hitler experimented with various means of medical killing, rehearsing the systematic eugenics he would soon pursue against entire populations. "National Socialism is nothing more than applied biology" (151), the narrator notes—a claim originally made by National Socialist Deputy Party Leader Rudolf Hess in 1934 (Lifton, 31).

After Schloss Hartheim, Unverdorben works with the SS forcing the Jews into ghettos. His wife Herta becomes pregnant. Soon after, he is transferred to Auschwitz. He kills inmates with injections of phenol and assists Mengele (fictionalized here as "Uncle Pepi") with his gruesome experiments (*The Nazi Doctors* contains a long chapter on Mengele, whom the Gypsy children in the camps called "Uncle Mengele"). Herta gives birth but the baby dies soon after. She writes her husband letters questioning his actions; they grow more and more estranged. He defends his work by noting "I am famed for my quiet dedication" (133). Soon he is assisting the mass exterminations by inserting pellets of Zyklon B into the gas chambers. Lifton writes that "no individual self is inherently evil, murderous, genocidal. Yet under certain conditions virtually any self is capable of becoming all of these" (497). The narrator echoes this when he concludes that "Odilo Unverdorben, as a moral being, is absolutely unexceptional, liable to do what everybody else does, good or bad, with no limit, once under the cover of numbers" (157).

At war's end Unverdorben flees to escape prosecution, first to the Vatican, then to Portugal (where he takes on the first of his aliases—"Hamilton de Souza"), and finally to America. Once in America, Unverdorben takes the name "John Young" and goes to work as a surgeon, first in a New York hospital, then for American Medical Services on a commercial strip somewhere in New England. He follows the path of many of the doctors Lifton interviewed, reconnecting with the Hippocratic sphere and attempting to reclaim his pre-Nazi self (Lifton,

456–57). But, of course, he can never be whole again; as the narrator observes, he "can't feel, won't connect, never opens up, always holds something back" (52). In the late 1950s, Unverdorben is in danger of being discovered once again, and he changes his name one last time. He becomes "Tod T. Friendly" ("Tod" means "death" in German) and loses himself in "affable, melting-pot, primary-color, You're-okay-I'm-okay *America*" (6). As presented in *Time's Arrow*, America is a good hiding place for a war criminal—a Lotus-like land of attenuated memory where no one inquires about Unverdorben's past, and few care about history. Here Unverdorben ages and dies in obscurity—but not in peace. "His dreams are full of figures who scatter in the wind like leaves," the narrator observes, "full of souls who form constellations like the stars I hate to see" (29).

When viewed in relation to Lifton's theory of psychological "doubling," the narrator of *Time's Arrow* can be seen as that part of Unverdorben that Unverdorben disavowed at the moment he began performing euthanasia at Schloss Hartheim. Unverdorben's name is significant in this regard: the definitions of "verdorben" in German include "tainted," "rotten," "depraved," and "corrupt," while "unverdorben" signifies the opposite of these, and also "innocent" and "unsophisticated." His surname contains both himself and his double, in other words.[22] In Lifton's theory, "doubling" involves the creation of a "second self" that exists *alongside* the original self. In extreme situations, he argues, this second self "can become the usurper from within and replace the original self until it 'speaks' for the entire person" (420). The Nazi doctor, Lifton continues, struck a Faustian bargain with Auschwitz and the regime: "to do the killing, he offered an opposing self (the evolving Auschwitz self)—a self that, in violating his own prior moral standards, met with no effective resistance and in fact made use of his original skills (in this case, medical-scientific)" (420–21).

This description applies precisely to Unverdorben, who struck *his* bargain before Auschwitz, at Schloss Hartheim. Significantly, when the narrator returns to the period in Unverdorben's history before his host embraced the ideology of "medical killing," he emerges from his dungeon of suppression to hover in the higher regions, like a soul or conscience. "I who have no name and no body—I have slipped out from under him and am now scattered above like flakes of ash-blonde human hair" (147). A terrible irony is embedded in this image, which associates the ghostly narrator with the Jews whose ashes will soon float through the skies of Auschwitz.

Like the relationship between Unverdorben and his double, the relationship between the two "halves" of *Time's Arrow*—the Auschwitz and pre-Auschwitz sections—is an uncanny one. Freud explained the uncanny as a return of the repressed, a moment when something in the individual's psychic past emerges unbidden, and the familiar suddenly turns strange.[23] The narrator's reverse-time observations of postwar American hospitals, doctors, and doctoring in the first half of *Time's Arrow* function in this way, eerily anticipating his eventual immersion in Auschwitz and intimating the terrible secret of his host's past. For the narrator, they constitute moments of precognition (which replaces memory in his time-reversed world), anticipating the appalling future his narrative will reveal.

From the narrator's reverse-time perspective, Unverdorben's medical work in America involves an endless fight "against health, against life and love" (93). Borrowing a phrase Lifton uses to describe the Auschwitz environment (426), the narrator calls the hospital "an atrocity-producing situation" (92). It is easy to see why: "Some guy comes in with a bandage around his head. We don't mess about. We'll soon have that off. He's got a hole in his head. So what do we do? We stick a nail in it. Get the nail—a good rusty one—from the trash or wherever. And lead him out to the Waiting Room where he's allowed to linger and holler for a while before we ferry him back to the night" (76). Well before Auschwitz, then, the narrator has looked directly into the face of human suffering. "Its face is fierce and distant and ancient" (93).

As for the doctors themselves, "it is abruptly open to question, this idea the doctors hold in secret, that they must wield the special power; because if the power remains unused, then it will become unmoored, and turn back against their own lives" (80–81). Although he is describing surgeons in a New York hospital here, there is something eerie about this passage, which becomes fully apparent when we come to the end of the novel; it could stand as a description of the Auschwitz doctors themselves. Similarly, the narrator's description of hospital patients surrendering autonomy and control intimates the radical victimization the Auschwitz inmates suffered at the hands of Unverdorben: "all the intelligent pain of the victims, all the dreams of the unlistened to, all the entreating eyes: all this is swept up in the fierce rhythm of the hospital" (88). By the time the reader reaches Auschwitz with the narrator and enters the medical experimentation rooms with "Uncle Pepi" (Dr. Mengele), his earlier perceptions echo through the years with new and shattering relevance: "Meanwhile, on their beds and trolleys, the victims look on with anxious faces" (90).

There is more to Amis's method here than rendering the ways in which Unverdorben's past continues to haunt his present. M. John Harrison has written that the narrator's description of the doctors' exercise of power "approaches one of the deep political underpinnings of every society: the assumption of authority over other people's bodies, other people's most internal processes."[24] This assumed monstrous proportions under the Nazi regime, but it persists in "free" societies as well. It is also not confined to those invested with institutional authority—as the continuing scourge of sexual violence attests. Early in the novel, the narrator describes the fate of women in crisis centers. It is a haunting reversal, all the more so because only the reader recognizes the source of the women's pain—the assumption of authority over their bodies by individual men: "the women at the crisis centres and the refuges are all hiding from their redeemers. . . . The welts, the abrasions and the black eyes get starker, more livid, until it is time for the women to return, in an ecstasy of distress, to the men who will suddenly heal them. Some require more specialised treatment. They stagger off and go and lie in a park or a basement or wherever, until men come along and rape them, and then they're okay again" (31).

Yet in the midst of these assaults on the body, which begin with individual acts of violence and proceed through Unverdorben's regress to the extermination camps, Amis's benighted narrator maintains his childlike, life affirming innocence. "Skin is soft. Touch it. It gives. It gives to the touch" (36). He also possesses an unconditional love for others that is the only antidote for the horrors the novel unsparingly records. Near the end of the novel, when to his mind the Jews who died in the camps have been restored to life, the narrator says "I love them as a parent should, which is to say that I don't love them for their qualities (remarkable as these seem to me to be, naturally), and only wish them to exist, and to flourish, and to have their right to life and love" (152). As Frank Kermode has written, the "image of inhumanity" contained in *Time's Arrow* "mirrors a notion of humanity, a tenderness for fragile flesh, not extinct though always rare and difficult of access."[25]

In the trilogy that begins with *Einstein's Monsters,* Amis explores the geopolitical developments that have recently threatened this image of humanity as never before. But amidst his savage indignation at these developments, a voice of tender innocence can be heard, all the more poignant for the despair that finally overcomes it: "I within, who came at the wrong time —either too soon, or after it was all too late" (165).

CHAPTER 6

Amis Agonistes

The Information

Agonistes, Greek for "in struggle" or "under trial," aptly describes Richard Tull, the long suffering protagonist of *The Information* (1995). But it also applies—in two senses—to his creator. As in *Dead Babies* and *Other People,* Martin Amis appears throughout the novel as an omniscient but personalized narrator, presiding over what he calls an "anti-comedy" of rancor and thwarted revenge. He speaks in a voice of male midlife angst, brooding on innocence lost, dreams deferred, fears not allayed. The novel's opening lines are characteristic: "Cities at night, I feel, contain men who cry in their sleep and then say Nothing. . . . Swing low in your weep ship, with your tear scans and your sob probes, and you would mark them" (9). Like Richard himself, this narrator views individual miseries as chapters in a much longer story of cosmic abasement. In Richard's words, "the history of astronomy is the history of increasing humiliation. First the geocentric universe, then the heliocentric universe. Then the eccentric universe—the one we're living in. Every century we get smaller" (129).

While these words were working their way toward print, a parallel narrative was being written in the British press, one in which Martin Amis, not Richard Tull, found himself "under trial." Reports began circulating in November 1994 that Amis had directed his literary agent to seek a £500,000 advance from his longtime publisher Jonathan Cape for *The Information.* At the time, this was a large advance for what the British call "literary novels," although early-twenty-first-century advances have made it seem like small change.[1] Howls of indignation erupted from some quarters, most notably from the novelist A. S. Byatt, whose aesthetic and political allegiances are the antithesis of Amis's.

In her public comments, Byatt seemed intent on turning Amis into his fictional creation John Self, the vulgar, promiscuous, superficial, and unscrupulous entrepreneur of *Money.* She reduced Amis's painful 1993 separation from his wife to a financial inconvenience, and his surgery to treat a serious dental problem to an expression of vanity. "I always earn out my advances and I don't see why I should subsidize his greed, simply because he has a divorce to pay for and has just had all his teeth redone," Byatt fumed. "He must believe that his name is so extraordinary that anyone will pay an extra £250,000 simply to have him on their list. It's *folie de grandeur.*" Byatt also put a gendered spin on her wrath, calling Amis's behavior "male turkey cocking."[2]

The irony of this public Amis-bashing will not be lost on readers of *The Information,* a novel about literary competition, envy, and malice which regards writers and writing with deep suspicion. During the six months preceding publication of his eighth novel, Amis's life imitated his art—a fact underscored when the March 6, 1995 *New Yorker* published a long account of the Amis controversy followed by an excerpt from *The Information.* In addition to its publicity value, the press coverage in Britain and America provided much important information about the contemporary Anglo-American literary scene and Amis's place in it—all of it relevant to *The Information,* which is about the contemporary Anglo-American literary scene and (obliquely) Amis's place in it. Interested observers learned that when Cape responded to Amis's demand of £500,000 with a counteroffer of £350,000, and an additional £110,000 for a collection of short stories, Amis changed agents and publishers. He left Pat Kavanagh, the wife of his old friend and fellow novelist Julian Barnes, for the American Andrew Wylie, and moved from Cape, a division of Random House U.K., to the Rupert Murdoch–owned Harper Collins (he returned to Cape in 1997). They also learned that although *The Information* failed to make the best-seller list, it had sold over 116,000 copies within six months of its release, making Amis one of Britain's most widely read "literary" novelists.[3]

More importantly, it became clear that for a writer who attains celebrity status, public reception of his work often has little to do with genuine questions of literary value. For Amis's friend and fellow novelist Salman Rushdie, the press treatment of Amis and *The Information* had less to do with money than with envy. "It's just 'This guy has had it too good for too long —let's murder him.'" Amis admitted to being shaken by the animus, but also acknowledged that "my novels have violent effects on people" and that these reactions often blur the distinction between art and life. "My stuff and my personality, up to a point, go to something invidious in people. I write about invidiousness, about injustices, about one-upping."[4]

In *The Information,* it is Gwyn Barry who has it too good, and incites murderous thoughts in his chief rival. Gwyn is Richard Tull's longtime friend and mortal enemy, a fellow writer who feeds the public's desire for fictions of hope, comfort, and multicultural utopia. His novel *Amelior* (the title is the root word of ameliorate, meaning to make better) is in its eleventh printing, and he has just switched agents, "controversially taking his custom from Harley, Dexter, Fielding to Gal Aplanalp" (59). Opposites in terms of worldly success, Richard and Gwyn are similar in many ways, like the rancorous near-twins Greg and Terry in *Success*. Born a day apart, both Oxford graduates, both turning forty as the novel opens, Richard and Gwyn offer complementary portraits, one of midlife misery, one of midlife complacency.

Gwyn's phenomenal success has incited Richard's literary envy, which in turn fuels the revenge plot of *The Information* (in the narrator's words, Richard "was a revenger, in what was probably intended to be a comedy" [133]). Richard hires the drug dealer Steve Cousins to break into the Barry house, gather information on Gwyn and his wife Demeter, and harass them both. Richard's rage is murderous. He "wants to do to Gwyn what Gwyn has done to him. He wants to assassinate his sleep. He wants to inform the sleeping man: an I for an I." (91). Like Amis's enemies in the press, and like all novelists, Richard knows the power that comes from possessing intimate knowledge of others. When he uncovers damaging details about Demeter, he knows "he had information on her now, which always meant the vulnerable, the hidden, the intimate, the shame-steeped" (168).

In terms of celebrity and literary status, Gwyn is Amis's fictional double in *The Information*, garnering large advances, jetting across the Atlantic for readings, interviews, and signings. But Amis has never identified with the successful in his novels. *The Information* invests Richard Tull with whatever literary virtue is to be found in its fallen world of falling standards. In this world, his very failure as a writer grants him a perverse kind of integrity.[5] His perspective may be a "tortured squint," a phrase Amis has used to describe *Lolita*'s Humbert Humbert,[6] but he can still spot the spurious through the haze of his envy: "he cackled and yodeled his way through *Amelior:* its cuteness, its blandness, its naively pompous semi-colons, its freedom from humour and incident, its hand-me-down imagery, the almost endearing transparency of its little colour schemes, its tinkertoy symmetries" (43).

Richard knows all about "trex," his term for that which is subliterary: he is the Fiction and Poetry Editor at the Tantalus Press. In Greek mythology, Tantalus was consigned to an eternity of unfulfilled desire, of satisfaction proffered, then withdrawn. Tantalus Press offers publication to any author with a checkbook, but never wins the writer an audience. "'Private' publishing was not organized crime exactly, but it had close links with prostitution," Richard muses, describing the manuscripts he receives as "anti-literature. Propaganda, aimed at the self" (75, 77). Although Gwyn publishes with a commercial press and has a wide readership, his novels are similarly subliterary. The difference—and the reason for Gwyn's success—is that they are designed to massage his readers' egos as well as his own.

Amis's satiric design in *The Information,* on the other hand, is anti-egoistic. In this sense he is more like the criminal Steve Cousins, whom Richard calls the "scourge of hubris," than any of the novel's other characters. The very title of the novel plays a role in this design, leading the reader to expect some specific, ultimately clarifying revelation which never in fact materializes. In the post-Hubble universe, where "astronomically, everything is always getting further away from everything else" (65), stable meaning is an illusion. So is the idea of a stable center of self. *The Information* is Amis's most deconstructive novel; Richard's failed plotting, and his failures of interpretation, point toward an unsettling indeterminacy. So does the novel's dark ending, an emotionally charged "pregnant arrest" that abandons the generic stability of satire and leaves the reader stranded in the realm of nightmare.[7]

Ironically, this ending is preceded (and foreshadowed) by some of Amis's most impressive and resonant comic writing. Although much of the novel's action takes place in the familiar West End London of *Success, Other People,* and *London Fields,* all of part three (the novel is divided into four parts) is taken up with Richard's trip to America. He and Gwyn take a jet-hop tour of seven American cities, arranged to promote Gwyn's new novel, *Amelior Regained.*[8] Richard accompanies his rival because he has been hired to write his profile by Gal Aplanalp, the literary agent whose palindromic last name suggests she has a plan for every contingency. She has also taken on Richard as her client and arranged for the publication of his novel, *Untitled,* by the fledgling American publisher Bold Agenda.

During the flight from London to New York, Richard walks from his seat in coach to visit Gwyn in first class—a "journey within a journey" (288) as he calls it. "His progress through the plane described a diagonal of shocking decline. In Coach the laptop literature was pluralistic, liberal and humane: *Daniel Deronda,* trigonometry, Lebanon, World War I, Homer, Diderot, *Anna Karenina.* As for Business World. . . . they were reading outright junk. Fat financial thrillers, chunky chillers and tublike tinglers: escape from the pressures facing the contemporary entrepreneur." Worse awaits. Richard discovers that the captains of industry in First Class are napping and have ceased reading altogether—"the few books lying unregarded on softly swelling stomachs were jacketed with hunting scenes or ripe young couples in mid swirl or swoon" (288–89). Amis's love of comic lists is evident as Richard makes the return trip and observes another series of titles that describe similar divisions of status and lived experience. "He made his way back, past *Magenta Rhapsody* and *Of Kingly Blood,* past *Cartel* and *Avarice* and *The Usurers,* and into the multitudinousness of *Hard Times, La Peste, Amerika, Despair, The Moonstone, Labyrinths*" (291).

After arriving in New York, Gwyn and Richard fly to Miami, and here begins a memorable series of urban portraits. Miami is a city of "raked and watered sands," and Gwyn's South Beach hotel is a "regency spaceship of fishtanks and startling energy bills" (320). Chicago, which "awaited them in its vapours and grey medium, deeply massed and square-shouldered on the vague horizon," is "the cradle, or the ancient assembly point, of the American political machine" (332). In Denver visitors are taken on tours "of male-pride Sweat Lodges and Reservation casinos" (342). The last stop on the swing west is Los Angeles—at the end of the continent, near the end of the century—its apocalyptic aura evoked when Gwyn discusses a movie deal "on a sofa in a luxurious prefab within the Millennium precinct of Endo Studios, Culver City, in Greater Los Angeles" (351). The return flight to New York takes the travelers over Manhattan, which "looked like a coda to the urban-erotic, the garter and stocking-top patterning of its loops and bridges now doing service as spinal supports and braces, hernia frames. Above it all, the poised hypodermic of the Empire State" (386).

During his initial stop in New York, Richard discovers that his publisher has no plans to promote his book. Instead, he is given eighteen copies in a tattered mailbag and asked to sell them himself. "What could he do? *Untitled* was his youngest, and probably his last born. The sack looked ragged, frayed, at the end of its tether. But Richard swung it up on to his shoulder" (304). Richard drags this sack all across America, a comic Ancient Mariner condemned to suffer repeated humiliations for committing the sin of literary modernism. As a writer, Richard stands for "the not-so-worldly, the contorted, the difficult" (364), but in America he learns that "if you do the arts, if you try the delirious profession, then don't be a flake, and offer people something—tell them something they might reasonably want to hear" (388). Like that of his fictional predecessor, Dickens's Martin Chuzzlewit, Richard's encounter with America leaves him deeply chastened—though not reformed.

Like *Other People, Money,* and *London Fields, The Information* is a multilayered narrative, as its multivalent title suggests. Within its symbolic web Richard's tragicomic misery comes to represent male midlife crisis generally, and the decline of a literary culture exists in a metonymic relationship to other forms of cultural decay—from the widening gap between rich and poor to the erosion of childhood innocence. Richard's story is the unstable center of a series of symbolically concentric circles in *The Information,* a fact which Amis alludes to midway through the novel. Richard has been thinking about "The Aleph," a story by the Argentinean writer Jorge Luis Borges that "everything always reminded him of" ("aleph" is the first letter of the Hebrew alphabet). The story is "about a magical device, the aleph, that knew everything. . . . About a terrible poet, who wins a big prize, a big requital, for his terrible poem" (224).

Ironic parallels to Richard's situation abound. He is famed at his local pub, The Warlock, for his skill at Wise Money, a video game that tests the player's cultural knowledge.[9] In reality, Richard is like Tantalus, constantly striving for a cultural mastery that always exceeds his grasp, despite his wide reading and the endless book reviews he writes for *The Little Magazine*.[10] "Who was said to be the last man to have read everything? Coleridge. . . . Two hundred years on, nobody had read a millionth of everything, and the fraction was getting smaller every day" (242). Moreover, Richard's rival is a terrible novelist who is nonetheless about to win a prestigious literary award called "The Profundity Requital."

The significance of "The Aleph" does not stop here. In Borges's story, the aleph is "a sphere whose center is everywhere and whose circumference is nowhere. . . . one of the points in space that contains all other points."[11] It is a paradox, in other words: a center without a center. For Borges, it symbolizes the nothingness of the individual ego, and the corresponding idea that the one is the all—that the microcosm contains the macrocosm. Both symbolic associations are relevant to *The Information*. So is the image of the sphere itself, which Amis evokes through repeated references to the sun and solar system, and through a web of mythological allusions (readers of *The Information* will benefit from regularly consulting a handbook of classical literature, as well as a copy of Milton's *Paradise Lost*). Richard's trials are one long lesson in his insignificance, from his literary humiliations to his interpretation of literary and cosmic history (like his walk from Coach to World Class, both describe "shocking decline") to "the information," which comes to him during the night, whispering its existential message of dissolution and death. These hard lessons are not for Richard alone; his story is the human story, the story of lost innocence, what Richard calls "the journey from Narcissus to Philoctetes" (197). The final sentence of the novel borrows the cadences and evokes the tone of Philip Larkin's poem "High Windows," which begins by imagining a kind of paradise and ends with a vision of "the deep blue air, that shows / Nothing, and is nowhere, and is endless": "And then there is the information, which is nothing, and comes at night" (374).[12]

The underlying vision may be bleak, but Amis's method of linking the comic to the cosmic—the microcosm to the macrocosm—is often exhilarating. Consider his symbolic rendering of Richard's plane flights. Before leaving, Richard announces to his wife Gina that "America will kill me" (287). Earlier, in an imaginative effort to "solarsystematize his immediate circle," Richard describes himself as Pluto, adding "Charon was his art" (230–31). Pluto is the god of the dead in Greek mythology, and Charon is the ferryman who conveys the dead to Hades. When Richard and Gwyn fly to New York, Richard has several brushes with death, beginning with an epic nosebleed that erupts soon after takeoff. Later, while he is visiting Gwyn in First Class, Richard notes that "the light was coming in sideways, and everything looked combustible or already white-hot, close to burn-out or heat death" (290). On his way back to his seat, he notices several women crying and confronts death in more intimate terms. "Women on planes are crying because someone they love or loved is dead or dying. Every plane has them. . . . Death can do this. . . . Death, which sends women hurrying to the end of the street, to bus stops, which makes them run under the clocks of railway stations, which lifts them five miles high and fires them weeping through the air at the speed of death, all over the world" (292).

These intimations of mortality serve as a prelude to Richard's near-death experience in the small plane he and Gwyn board in Boston on their way back to New York. As they take off late in the day, during a storm, Richard looks through his porthole (another illuminating sphere, like the aleph and the sun). He likens the end of the day to the end of life. "The storm was there, like a gothic cathedral, with all its glaring gargoyles . . . Diurnal time was a figure for the human span: waking, innocent morning, full midday and the pomp of the afternoon, then loss of colour, then weariness, then mortal weariness and certainty of sleep, then nightmare, then dreamlessness" (378–79). Once in the eye of the storm, Richard comes closer to a religious experience than any other character in Amis's fiction: "The gods had put aside their bullwhips and their elemental rodeo and were now at play with their bowling balls clattering down the gutters of spacetime. Within were the mortals, starfished from white knuckle to white toejoint, stretched like Christs, like Joans in her fire. Richard looked and now felt love for the publicity boy, his sleek, shaking, tear-washed face" (381). Richard survives this battering, only to return to a different kind of nightmare back in England when the revenge plot he has set in motion goes spinning out of his control.

Another symbolic circle within the widening sphere of Richard's story is an autobiographical one. While it is misleadingly reductive to claim, as some have, that *The Information* is a roman à clef about Amis's relationship with Julian Barnes (author of the acclaimed novels *Flaubert's Parrot* and *A History of the World in 10 1/2 Chapters*),[13] or the breakup of his marriage, there is no question that Richard's story tells important truths about Amis's life as a writer. Richard embodies Amis's reputation for personal and literary "difficulty," his famed erudition, his overreaching ambition to capture modern consciousness between the covers of a novel. One of the best running jokes in *The Information*, for instance—the fact that except for the criminal Steve Cousins, every person who attempts to read *Untitled* comes down with a debilitating illness by page nine—

has a precise autobiographical source. Amis's father publically reported that he cannot finish his son's novels, and Martin Amis told an interviewer in 1984 that "my wife-to-be felt completely exhausted and had to go to bed after reading the first twenty pages of *Money*."[14]

Certainly Richard's literary values will sound familiar to careful readers of Amis's fiction:

> Essentially Richard was a marooned modernist. If prompted, Gwyn Barry would probably agree with Herman Melville: that the art lay in pleasing the readers. Modernism was a brief divagation into difficulty; but Richard was still out there, in difficulty. He didn't want to please the readers. He wanted to stretch them until they twanged. *Afterthought* was first person, *Dreams Don't Mean Anything* strictly localized third; both nameless, the I and the he were author surrogates and the novels comprised their more or less uninterrupted and indistinguishable *monologues interieurs*. (170)[15]

The Rachel Papers is narrated in first person; *Dead Babies* in third; these and Amis's subsequent novels all contain author surrogates. In *The Information*, the affinities between Richard Tull and Amis's personalized third-person narrator are so strong that many readers will consider the narrator's interventions redundant.

Of all the author surrogates in *The Information*, Richard's son Marco is the most haunting. Like Richard and Gwyn, Marco and his brother Marius were born one day apart (they are twins, but emerged on either side of a midnight divide).[16] From the first Marco is identified with Richard and with novelists generally. His learning disability, for instance, is suspiciously similar to the "stupefaction by first principles" to which Richard says all artists are reduced: "If you told Marco why the chicken crossed the road, Marco would ask you what the chicken did next. Where did it go? What was its name? Was it a boy or a girl? Did it have a husband—and, perhaps, a brood of chicks? How Many?" (11, 70). As this passage also suggests, Marco loves narrative. He often cries inconsolably in the night when he awakes in the middle of a dream, because "he never wanted any story to end" (225). Marco bears the emotional brunt of his father's anger at Gwyn's successes, and he is more sensitive than his brother to the widening rift between his parents. "All this had made Marco more vigilant, more sensibly watchful, than a six-year-old would normally have need or reason to be" (220). He is losing his innocence, in other words, while developing the mental habits of a novelist.

Amis's rendering of Richard's relationship to his sons is realistically compelling in ways that most of the rest of the novel is not. Compared with the portrayal of Richard's marriage to Gina, for instance, which relies on crude gender stereotypes, it is a marvel of engaging realism. Despite Amis's emphasis on Richard's self-pitying self-absorption, he cannot help investing his absurd alter ego with his own parental love, care, and anxiety (*The Information* is dedicated to Amis's two sons, and to his cousin Lucy Partington, who was murdered by the serial killer Fred West).[17] The scenes of Richard at home and at play with his sons are the most touching in the novel, vividly capturing the boys' distinct speech patterns, their skewed insights, and their love of toys and television, parks and zoos. Moreover, Marco and Marius inspire their father's most lyrical language: "Richard contemplated his sons, their motive bodies reluctantly arrested in sleep, and reef-knotted to their bedware, and he thought, as an artist might: but the young sleep in another country, at once very dangerous and out of harm's way, perennially humid with innocuous libido" (11).

Amis wrote *The Information* during a national uproar in Britain over two brutal child murders.[18] Anxiety about children and childhood itself is central to the novel's plot and its painful ending. The depth of Richard's downward spiral ("it seemed to him that all the time he used to spend writing he now spent dying" [446]) is marked by a reversal of parent-child roles. As his miseries mount, he begins telling Marco and Marius "Twins stories." He told these stories "while the boys lay on their backs, clutching their boyhoods, with drugged eyes." The last story he is reported telling his sons is one "in which they bravely rescued their daddy—rescued him, and then tended to his wounds" (475).[19] Richard had earlier thought of the day when his wife Gina will ask him to leave, and "the children will have to come to love us separately" (448); now, as he leaves the sleeping boys, they "looked like figures on a battlefield, arrested, abandoned" (476).

Abandonment is the disturbing note on which *The Information* ends. While Richard drinks in a below-street bar, hatching one final plot against Gwyn, Marco is aboveground, with Steve Cousins's criminal coterie. He has been left there by his babysitter, and he is tempted into Steve's van—horribly entangled in the web of revenge his father has spun. Earlier the reader learned of Steve's psychopathic impulses: "What he wanted to hurt had something to do with himself. Not himself *now*. But himself. Himself *then*" (478). *Then* refers to childhood, which explains why he singles out Marco for a kind of harm all the more disturbing because it is never specified. When Richard emerges from the bar, he spots his son, who has just come out of the van. He is walking with a "brittle and defeatist stride. There was something terribly wrong with Marco: there was nobody at his side. And yet the child's solitude, his isolation, unlike the father's, was due to an unforgivable error not his own. . . . Richard had never seen him looking so unhappy" (492).[20]

Richard himself is an absurd sight in this scene, literally entangled in the hoses of the vacuum cleaner he is carrying back from the repair shop. "Richard was still Laocoon, engulfed in coils and loops" (492). Laocoon was a priest of Apollo, who along with his two sons was killed by serpents after warning the Trojans not to bring the wooden horse into their city. The serpents were sent by the gods, who wanted Troy destroyed so that Aeneas would leave the city and found Rome. The gods of contemporary culture in *The Information* embrace Gwyn's imagined new world order and reject Richard's vision of diffi- culty and asceticism. "The universe was definitely through with him" (485), the narrator says of Richard just before the final chapter. This does not mean that Amis absolves Richard of responsibility for the harm done to his son and family. Unlike Laocoon, Richard is morally culpable, too blinded by envy to see that he has invited chaos into his domestic Troy.

In an earlier chapter, Richard concluded that "writers are nightmares. Writers are nightmares from which you cannot awake. Most alive when alone, they make living hard to do for those around them" (418). There are enough grains of harsh truth in this assessment to apply to many writers—including Richard, Gwyn Barry, and Martin Amis. When he first announced his plan for *The Information,* in 1990, Amis said "it feels at the moment like a light novel about literary envy."[21] Instead, he wrote a dark and self-lacerating one.

CHAPTER 7

Thiz Zdrange Resizdanze
Night Train; Heavy Water and Other Stories

The midlife crisis that is both the source and the subject of *The Information* engendered an artistic reevaluation as well. Amis did not publish another novel for eight years, concentrating instead on nonfiction (two memoirs and a collection of literary essays and reviews). His fictional output during this period was quite small: the novella *Night Train* (1997), extending to just 145 pages in hardback, and four post-1995 short stories published along with five pre-1995 stories in the collection *Heavy Water and Other Stories* (1998). One clue to Amis's partial retreat from fiction writing during this period can be found in "What Happened to Me on My Holiday" (1997), the story that closes out *Heavy Water*. It is narrated by an eleven-year-old boy, a thinly fictionalized version of Amis's son Louis, whose summer holiday on Cape Cod is shattered by the death of his stepbrother Eliaz (based on Elias Fawcett, the son of Amis's first wife Antonia Philips, who died at seventeen).[1] Amis represents Louis's response to this loss by means of a highly stylized phonetic speech (part "sarcastic Americanese," part British diction) that is the verbal equivalent of the estrangement and stupefaction death leaves in its wake: "I dell id thiz way—in zargazdig Ameriganese—begaz I don'd wand id do be glear: do be all grizb and glear. There is thiz zdrange resizdanze. There is thiz zdrange resizdanze" (223). Reading the story aloud, the reader feels Louis's grief as a physical presence—thick, hard, unyielding.

The story's language embodies its recognition that the hard facts of life and death resist the most artful attempts to make sense of them.

This recognition is also the philosophical engine of *Night Train*, Amis's most somber fiction to date, and it emerges even in the most audaciously comic stories in *Heavy Water*. Unsurprisingly, these short fictions were followed by two long memoirs (*Experience* and *Koba the Dread*) in which Amis directly confronted the personal losses he suffered in mid-career—losses that, among other things, caused him to reevaluate his fictional methods and motives. This chapter will focus on *Night Train* and four of the stories in *Heavy Water*—the title story (revised in 1997), "State of England," "The Coincidence of the Arts," and "What Happened to Me on My Holiday." These fictions are full of interest in their own right (*Night Train* audaciously appropriates the detective genre to address existential questions, while the stories are simultaneously brilliant contrivances and masterpieces of realism); they also illuminate the nature and implications of Amis's mid-career realignment.

Satire is always multi-voiced. Even when muffled, accents of affirmation and empathy often sound alongside those of negation. Amis's satirical manipulation of his most vividly appalling characters, for instance—John Self, Keith Talent, Richard Tull—often vies with or resembles a skewed form of love. In many of the short fictions of the late 1990s, satire gives way to imaginative sympathy as it confronts loss. The autobiographical matrix of this impulse is summarized in a passage from *Experience* describing Amis's response to the events of 1995, which begins with this tellingly mechanistic metaphor linking grief with (male) loss of power: "I was structurally weakened . . . by the partings and separations from my wife and two children over the summer and autumn. The theme is clear: partings, sunderings, severances, with the great depth charge of my cousin Lucy" (198).

While Amis's pursuit of the cultural zeitgeist remains undiminished in these fictions, they register an increasingly sympathetic identification with the all too human frailties and failings of his characters. This shift is evident even in the hyper-dyspeptic science fiction story "The Janitor on Mars," the title character of which is a dead ringer for Amis the satirist ("the weakness of the janitor's—for harsh language and harsh sarcasm—was the focus of much terrestrial discussion, and much disquiet" [166]). Despite this janitor's nihilistic conviction that the universe is ruled by one desire on the part of all sentient creatures—"the superimposition of will" (187)—his multi-millennium study of human life has elicited something resembling empathy: "Forgive me. My immersion in your story, particularly over these last ten thousand years, while often poisoned by an unavoidable—an obligatory—contempt, has caused me to . . . Why do I say that: 'Forgive me'?" (188). A similar wonderment in the face of human suffering characterizes Amis's fiction during this period.

Night Train

Many readers were surprised at Amis's creation of a female protagonist narrator for his neo-noir detective novella *Night Train*. They wondered if the bard of butch had gone feminine, if the mythographer of misogyny had been transmogrified. Creating another "rigorous dramatic monologue," Amis imaginatively inhabits a tough but tender police detective with the unlikely name of Mike Hoolihan, whose investigation of a mysterious suicide stirs her to depths of imaginative sympathy reminiscent of a George Eliot novel. Yet it is no surprise that Amis would create a female character whose voice, attitude, and behavior raise questions about the very meaning of gender. For all the press about Amis's testosterone poisoned prose, his fictions have always come to anatomize masculinity, not to praise it.

In his very first sentence of published fiction, Amis gave voice to a callow youth whose words pair braggadocio with insecurity: "My name is Charles Highway, though you wouldn't think it to look at me. It's such a rangy, well-travelled, big-cocked name, and, to look at, I'm none of these" (*The Rachel Papers*, 3). Insecurity often turns to terror for Terry Service, the lower-middle-class orphan who narrates one half of *Success*, and who helps give frenzied voice to the most emotionally naked of Amis's novels: "I want to *scream,* much of the time, or quiver like a damaged animal. I sit about the place here fizzing with rabies" (52). Even John Self, who strides through *Money* like a grotesque colossus of male appetite, undergoes a momentary gender-bending transformation under the influence of Martina Twain, who makes him feel, fleetingly, "like a *flower;* a little parched, perhaps, a little gone in the neck, and with no real life to come, perhaps, only sham life, bowl life, easing its petals and lifting its head to start feeding on the day" (310). In this sense *Night Train* extends a longstanding preoccupation.

Gender, however, is not the only concern in *Night Train*, which employs the detective genre to produce a haunting rumination on the mystery of human motive and the emotional whirlpool suicide leaves in its wake. *Night Train* enacts this mystery at the most basic level of plot and structure, purposefully frustrating the reader's desire for a satisfactory ending, even at the syntactical level. Like *Time's Arrow*, it is a palindromic narrative, the ending of which drives the reader back to its beginning in search of clues that may or may not be embedded in its narrator's bruised and bruising voice. Its very first sentence, in fact, announces that satisfactory endings will be withheld: "I am a police" (11). Confronted with this defiant fragment—this idiosyncratic rhythm—the reader feels a vague unease, a sense of thwarted expectation and, to employ one of the book's own section headings, an existential desire for a "sense of an ending" (93). These initial responses are entirely appropriate to the novella's themes, and to suicide itself, which Hoolihan calls "uniquely incoherent, . . . without shape and without form" (94). The book's initial fragment obeys a poetic logic by opening its story of endings with a sentence that lacks one.

For most of *Night Train's* first paragraph, this "police" is defined solely by the peculiar argot of a bureaucratic order: "it's a parlance we have. Among ourselves, we would never say I am a policeman or I am a policewoman or I am a police officer. We would just say I am a police" (11). Absent a name, absent the accents of gender and race, this voice seems to speak of and for a system—a mode of seeing and operating—rather than for an individual (*Night Train* is preoccupied with the ways in which conventions of thought, language, and imagery shield us from the pain of what the novella calls "naked-eye seeing"). A name comes next, but even here the syntax emphasizes a role: "I am a police and my name is Detective Mike Hoolihan." Then, almost as an afterthought, the paragraph ends by supplying the noun that seemed to be missing from the fragmentary first sentence, and again thwarting the reader's expectations: "I am a police, and a woman, also" (11). Like bookends, the words "police" and "woman" frame this paragraph—and Hoolihan's identity. These terms, and the discordant structure of their presentation, also encompass the novella's central concerns—with the mystery of other people, with the conditional nature of identity, with the manifold implications of "policing."[2]

But before these ideas crowd in, the reader is brought under the spell of Hoolihan's voice, her idiomatic American speech. Not only is Hoolihan's language appropriately chopped and elliptical, she slums her vocabulary in a convincingly American way, as in "I was fostered some, but basically I'm state-raised" (104), or "Too, I'd washed my hair the night before" (130). The following paragraph offers many more examples like these (note the redundant—and distinctively American—adverb "totally" in the fifth sentence), but it also reveals the tones of need, affection, vulnerability, and pathos that leak through the shell of her hard-boiled prose:

> What with AA, golf, the Discuss Group on Mondays, and the night-class on Thursdays at Pete (together with countless and endless correspondence courses), plus the Tuesday nightshift, and Saturdays, when I tend to hang with my bunkies in the Forty-Four—what with all this, my boyfriend says I don't have time for a boyfriend and maybe my boyfriend is right. But I do have a boyfriend: Tobe. He's a dear guy and I value him and I need him. One thing about Tobe—he sure knows how to make a woman feel slender. Tobe's totally enormous. He fills the room. When he comes in late, he's worse than the night train: Every beam in the building wakes up and moans. I find love difficult. (31)

Amis's literary accents can be heard here as well; Hoolihan loves repetition with variation, as does her author. Tobe has made a tape for her containing eight versions of the blues standard

"Night Train"; her favorite is Oscar Peterson's reading, full of "passion and muscle." In his own *Night Train,* Amis is striving to marry the angular muscularity of his prose to a wider emotional range—and to do so, paradoxically, within a genre dedicated to muffling the sounds of feeling.[3]

Hoolihan lives on the edge of a kind of domestic and personal entropy, which is one reason she is stunned by Jennifer Rockwell's death. A scientist at the Department of Terrestrial Magnetism at the Institute of Physical Problems, Jennifer is "an embarrassment of perfection. Brilliant, beautiful" (17–18). If she takes her own life, what does that imply about Hoolihan's? The case is personal, too; Jennifer was the daughter of Colonel Tom Rockwell, who was Hoolihan's squad supervisor when her life spiraled out of control at the end of eight years in the homicide division. He took her into his home, where Jennifer read to her at night. "I never felt judged by her," Hoolihan writes. "As gifted as she was, she never glassed herself off from you. If you ran into her, at a party, say, or downtown, she wouldn't say hi and move on. She'd always be particular with you. She'd always leave you with something" (32, 51).

Hoolihan, like Amis, is a shrewd reader of clues and character. She is vexed in her investigation of Jennifer's death by questions of cause and effect, and their increasingly problematic relationship; she distrusts conventional motive explanations (unlike homicide, suicide raises questions about what actually constitutes a motive). In this sense, *Night Train* is part of a long tradition. Historically, the novel as a genre emerged in part to satisfy the social needs of the emergent middle class. The former gave the latter a collective voice, a distinctive literary form, but also a guide to manners. The novel, in other words, contributed to the self-policing of an entire social body. In its social function, the novel is *like a police,* to adopt Hoolihan's (and Amis's) parlance. Charles Dickens literalized this connection in his 1851 novel *Bleak House* by virtually giving over the end of his novel to police inspector Bucket, simultaneously creating what is arguably the first detective novel in English literature and locating one solution to increasing social fragmentation in the regulatory procedures and rules of his society's emergent state bureaucracy.

In *Night Train,* Amis slyly winks at Dickens by giving the name Hi Tulkinghorn to Jennifer's physician; in *Bleak House,* Mr. Tulkinghorn is the urbane and sinister lawyer who prides himself on knowing more secrets than anyone else. Amis's fictions, for all their vile and violent energies, are informed by a lordly intelligence that invades the privacy of their characters, subjects them to chastening forms of discipline and punishment. Like Hoolihan, Amis may be deeply suspicious of motive, may value tolerance as the highest human virtue ("I don't judge," Hoolihan repeats like a mantra), but his satirical fictions arrest us with the spectacle of human misdoing, invoke our own tendencies to judge, to sentence, to correct. They invite us to become police. In *Night Train,* however, the emphasis is on internal discipline.

From the beginning of her self-description, it is clear that Hoolihan is policing herself as much as she is policing the "second-echelon" American city in which she works. A survivor of childhood sexual abuse, Hoolihan became a ward of the state at age ten. "And as a child I always tried to love the state the way you'd love a parent, and I gave it a hundred per cent," she explains (104). After working homicide for eight years, she fell into an alcoholic spiral, and following her recovery she was assigned to "Asset Forfeiture," a subdivision of Organized Crime.

Taking psychic comfort in all the internal and external regulations of her job, she has maintained her equilibrium through work discipline, a rigid adherence to procedural rules, and a will to believe. "A police works a suspicion into a conviction: that's the external process. But it's the internal process also. It is for me. It's the only way I can do it. I have to work suspicion into conviction" (62).

Night Train reverses this trajectory. Jennifer's suicide is a case in which the solution, Hoolihan realizes, "only points toward further complexity. I have taken a good firm knot and reduced it to a mess of loose ends" (164), she despairs near the end of her narrative. As Adam Phillips has written, self-awareness in *Night Train* is "experienced as an obscure punishment."[4] "I have no idea what I'm feeling," Hoolihan says late in the book, but she experiences "random stabs of love and hate" (168). It is her sensitivity, her feelings, that are killing her, "as though she is committing suicide whether she likes it or not," in Phillips's words.[5]

Experience reveals the autobiographical sources of Amis's rumination on suicide in *Night Train*. Meeting and getting to know his daughter Delilah Seale in 1995 revived memories of his affair with her mother Lamorna Seale, who hanged herself in 1978 when Delilah was two (*Experience*, 275–80). Then, in 1996, Aschel Rothschild, an Israeli friend Amis had consulted about his description of firearms in *Night Train*, also hanged himself. Amis writes in *Experience* that novel writing comes "from the back of your mind," from "silent anxiety" (280). Suicide appeared in his fiction well before *Night Train*, from Ursula Riding's destruction in *Success* to John Self's botched suicide attempt in *Money*, a novel which is subtitled *A Suicide Note*. "I find I have written a great deal about and around suicide," Amis writes in *Experience,* adding "it awakens terror and pity in me, yet it compels me, compels my writing hand. Perhaps because what I do all day and what they do, the suicides, in an instant, are so close to being antithetical" (281).

"Heavy Water"

An attempted suicide ends "Heavy Water," a short story Amis originally wrote in 1978, the year Lamorna Seale hanged herself. It was originally published in the Christmas 1978 issue of the *New Statesman* and was revised in 1997 for the collection *Heavy Water and Other Stories.*[6] "Heavy Water" looks forward to *Night Train* in several ways—in its sympathetic portrayal of a female character, in its melancholy tone, and in its undercurrent of compassion. The story is about a mother (called simply "Mother") and her forty-three-year-old retarded son John who take a Mediterranean cruise on a ship loaded with working-class British vacationers, including many Labour Party members and bosses. Her husband is gone; in the original, he died when John was eighteen months old, but in the more symbolically freighted revision he "walked away, one Christmas Eve. John was fourteen when that happened, and apparently a normal little boy. But then his panics started; and Mother's life became the kind of tired riddle that wounding dreams set you to unlock" (132).[7]

If John's literal retardation has resulted from the breakup of this family, a kind of moral idiocy has followed upon the decline of British working-class culture, typified in the story by the union man, Mr. Brine, and his wife. The former is drunk every day from mid-morning onwards ("pickled," as his last name suggests) and spews clichés by the boatload, even when they are hideously inappropriate to the recipient. He does not inspire confidence in the Labour Party's vaunted concern for the disadvantaged: "Mr. Brine took the sopping cigar out of his mouth and said, 'What's his name. *John*? How are you, John? Enjoying your cruise, are you John? Whoop. Look. He's at it again. Cheer up, John, cheer up!'" (128).[8] Amis was Literary Editor of the *New Statesman* when he published this story, working alongside the committed socialists James Fenton and Christopher Hitchens, and he reserves special scorn for trade union leaders who betray their party's principles.[9]

In light of the forced and brittle merrymaking of the ship's other passengers, John's mother—with her uncomplaining loyalty to her son and her stoic response to the slings and arrows of outrageous fortune—emerges as an island of empathy. Virtually joined at the hip to a mentally and physically retarded son who "looked like the Artful Dodger with rickets" (129)—and whose frequent atavistic outbursts require her constant interventions (including frequent feedings from a gin-laced baby bottle)—she nonetheless loves him "with all her heart" (140). Admittedly, both her heart and her head are simple organs, and there is also something insidious in her use of alcohol to quell her son's restlessness. Yet she is spared the mockery Amis usually reserves for such characters. Instead, like the glassy water that sometimes surrounds the ship, she and her son serve as mirrors, reflecting the moral crudities of the ship's other passengers.

John's suicide attempt at the end of the story comes after he, his mother, and several other passengers have taken a day trip to the dilapidated Municipal Aquarium in Iberia. Here "Mother fairly beamed" as she gazed at the "sea-anemones that looked just like Mrs. Brine's smart new bathing cap with its tufted green locks," and at the "flounced, refracted tiddlers" that "waltzed among the dunce's-hat shells and the pitted coral" like "the ladies on Ballroom Night" (138). While John's mother is buoyed from witnessing this magical diminishment of her con-descending shipmates, John is horrified by what seems to be his recognition of solidarity with a lone turtle apathetically wallow-ing in a "baby's swimming pool in the center of the room" (138). Momentarily separated from her son, John's mother approaches him and notices that he is staring fixedly at "the heavy shadow of the turtle: with all its appendages retracted, the humped animal extended to the very perimeter of its confines" (139). She pulls him away, he becomes violently ill, and the next day he tries to hurl himself from the ship.

The passage associating John with the trapped turtle is one of many revisions Amis made to "Heavy Water" for its 1997 reappearance between hard covers. Many changes replace expo-sition with dialogue, and represent improvements in dramatic economy. The more substantial modifications, however, reflect Amis's ambitions as a cultural sage, and the ways in which his journalism often serves this impulse. In October 1977 Amis attended the Tory Party conference in Blackpool and wrote a column for the *New Statesman* analyzing the party's anti-union, anti-Labour maneuvers.[10] A year later, he spent two weeks aboard the British cruise ship *Oriana* on a tour of the Mediter-ranean, and published an account of the trip for the *Sunday Telegraph Magazine,* blending standard travel article reportage with commentary emphasizing the ways in which the ship and its passengers represented a microcosm of English society in the late 1970s. The original "Heavy Water" drew from both of these experiences to create its floating signifier of a cruise ship; in revising it twenty years later, Amis imported additional observations and details from his travel article so that the story's allegorical dimension is unmistakable.

In "Action at Sea," for instance, he writes that the attraction of such cruises is that they allow passengers to see foreign countries without ever leaving home: "That edge of anxiety which is part of all genuine travel has been cleanly and painlessly removed. The ship remains a capsule of England, basking in unfamiliar seas."[11] One of the new passages in the revised version of "Heavy Water" adapts this last sentence: "The ship was a pub afloat, a bingo hall on ice. This way you went abroad on a lurching chunk of England, your terror numbed by English barmen serving duty-frees" (130). If the ship symbolizes Great Britain, it has become a nation without a clear identity or purpose. If the passengers symbolize the British, they are in decline, clinging to an illusion of national tradition while drifting aimlessly. Commodity capitalism has the same effect on them as gin does on John, lulling them into quiescence.

At the beginning of "Action at Sea," Amis notes:

In the early 1970s, P & O cruises abolished the distinction between first and second class: after a fortnight on one of their ships (Southampton to Southampton, via Italy, Greece, Sicily and Portugal), I am beginning to suspect that England did too. "A mega-Butlins on ice" would be too sweeping a description of life on the *quite* good ship *Oriana*. Here, however, is the sort of thing that could happen you in the course of an average day.[12]

In the revised story, this becomes part of a longer passage emphasizing the political culture of 1977:

Mr. Brine was a union man. There were many such on board. It was 1977: the National Front, the IMF, Mr. Jenkins's Europe; Jim Callaghan meets Jimmy Carter; the Provos, Rhodesia, Windscale. This year, according to Mother's morning news sheet, the cruise operators had finally abandoned the distinction between first and second class. A deck and B deck still cost the same amount more than C deck or D deck. But the actual distinction had finally been abandoned. (130–31)[13]

The ship is a great leveler—anyone with enough disposable income can come aboard—but instead of having a salutary, democratizing effect, it only serves to reduce all the passengers to a level of shared cultural infantilism. In this passage describing their guided tour through the streets of Iberia, John rather too obviously serves as the outward and visible sign of a more general diminution: "Mother felt herself obscurely demoted. Language had sent them all to the bottom of the class, had expelled them. They were all like children, all like John, never knowing what on earth they were expected to do. At the restaurant everyone absolutely fell on the wine, and then sat back, rolling their eyes" (137).

Ironically, passages like this one, which appears only in the revised version of "Heavy Water," weaken the emotional resonance of the story by forcing John and his mother to serve a generalized critique of working-class culture. They bring to mind John Lanchester's claim that since *Money*, Amis's fiction has "tended to have a mix of superbly good writing with false notes and a straining for effect or largeness."[14] At the center of "Heavy Water," unchanged by subsequent revision, stand a damaged mother and son, isolated, suffering, and mutually dependent. The best imagery in the story, retained in both versions, represents this precisely, as in the description of John's mother after being asked if her son always cries ("her nicked mouth was like the crimp at the bottom of a toothpaste tube" [128]), or in this account of John's attempted suicide: "Alone in the thin rain John faced the evening at the very stern of the ship, a hundred feet from the writhing furrows of its wake. Spreading his arms, he received the bloody javelin hurled at him by the sun" (139). Here the experiences of two individuals subtly speak to Amis's larger concerns: the way the world handicaps the individual, and the way the individual's fate is bound up with that of the larger culture. By the end of the story, John and his Mother are prisoners on a ship that has come to resemble a Titanic churning toward an iceberg.

"State of England"

As its brazenly ambitious title suggests, "State of England" (1996) is also centrally concerned with what Hamlet called "the form and pressure of the times." This story is more successful than "Heavy Water," however, in marrying the individual to the cultural. Set on an athletic field rather than a cruise ship, the story concerns Big Mal, nightclub bouncer and bumbling lout of a father ("built like a brick khazi: five feet nine in all directions" [38]), whose son Jet is participating in "Sports Day." Their story captures the social realities of English life in the roaring 1990s, while the narrative itself demonstrates that Amis is the only author since Dickens able to encompass contemporary London and provide a cold-eyed analysis of English class relations.

Mal's class, profession, education, and East End address make him a near-relative of Keith Talent, the small-time thief in

London Fields. But the social landscape has changed since Keith walked the same London streets in the 1980s. England has become a classless, multicultural society obsessed with sports, children, cell phones, and the profit motive. "Now that prejudice was gone everyone could relax and concentrate on money," the narrator observes, adding sardonically, in the concluding sentence and paragraph of the section, "which was fine if you had some" (61). Mal's communication skills, never highly developed, are barely adequate in this new milieu. "Most of the foreign dads—the Nusrats, the Fardouses, the Paratoshes—spoke better English than Mal. Much better English. While presumably also being pretty good at Farsi, Urdu, Hindi, or whatever. And he had to wonder: how could that be?" (42). When they do communicate, Mal and his estranged wife Sheilagh ("She" for short) do so via cell phone—even when they are standing only yards away from one another. "With a mobile riding on your jaw you could enter the arena enclosed in your own concerns, your own preoccupation, your own business" (42).

Unlike "Heavy Water," "State of England" employs comedy to achieve its ends, but it elicits more than laughter. Mal's desperate moneymaking schemes are hilariously unsuccessful, as is his affair with his "Asian babe" Linzi ("he sensed that he was a cliché—and sensed further that he'd even fucked *that* up" [41]). In the midst of this comedy of personal, social, linguistic errors, however, Mal's rough-and-ready paternal tenderness remains constant. In the course of the story he discovers that his turf has turned artificial, and that the goalposts are constantly moving, yet he ultimately achieves a separate peace with his son that is credible and moving. Amis's use of the athletic field as metaphor for Mal's shifting personal and social milieu is subtly handled throughout, as exemplified in the final paragraph, where comedy and pathos combine in a description of Mal and the other middle-aged fathers competing in the "dad's race":

> After five stumbling bounds the pain barrier was on him and wouldn't get out of the way. But the big man raced on, as you've got to do. The dads raced on, with heavy ardour, and thundering, their feet stockinged or gym-shoed but all in the wooden clogs of their years. Their heads bent back, their chests outthrust, they gasped and slavered for the turn in the track and the post at the end of the straight. (70–71)

"State of England" contains many comic surprises; the last of these occurs when it turns surprisingly poignant.

"The Coincidence of the Arts"

In his 1983 profile of Saul Bellow, Amis describes walking the streets of Chicago and noticing a sign in an art supply shop "prominently offering 'Art Material—for the artist in everyone.'"[15] "The Coincidence of the Arts," originally published in the *New Yorker* in 1997, uses this detail as the basis of an extended comic riff on life in late-twentieth-century New York City, where "everyone was already an artist. The coffee-shop waiters and waitresses were, of course, actors and actresses; and the people they served were all librettists and scenarists, harpists, pointillists, ceramicists, caricaturists, contrapuntalists. . . . The AC installers were all installationists. The construction workers were all constructivists" (89). The story is both an unconventional love letter to America, which Amis described in a 1996 interview as a more "dynamic and vibrant" place than England,[16] and an homage to Saul Bellow. Like so much of Bellow's fiction, it features sexual double-dealing, social climbing, and racial anxiety, all intensified by the superheated atmosphere that characterizes American cities.

In a 1992 essay on the singer Madonna and her book *Sex*, Amis wrote that "Madonna tells America that fame comes from wanting it badly enough. And everyone is terribly good at badly wanting things."[17] This precisely defines Pharsin Courier, the slightly unhinged black chess hustler in "The Coincidence of the Arts," who is convinced he is a literary genius. He will become an artist because he desires it—not because, like the failed painter-turned-portraitist Sir Rodney Peel, he inherited it from the peerage. Pharsin presses an enormous manuscript on Rodney, a deracinated English aristocrat who, "after many soggy years of artistic and sexual failure, in London, . . . was now savoring their opposites, in New York" (89). Unbeknownst to both men, Rodney's greatest sexual success is with the would-be-novelist's wife (a professional mime), who turns out to be English—a fact she hid from Rodney by remaining silent during their trysts. The story turns into a kind of revenger's comedy, with Rodney paying both literally and figuratively for his complacency and presumption. It is a measure of the imaginative sympathy infusing Amis's fiction from this period, however, that even after Rodney suffers his much deserved comeuppance, his fate elicits pity along with the sense that poetic justice has been done.

Amis knows all too well how the old world looks when set against the new, and this contrast generates much of the sharpest satire in the story. He is also fearless here in writing frankly about race, class, and sex. One evening Rodney and Rock, a fellow expatriate, meet in an Irish restaurant on Lexington Avenue, and Rock discovers Rodney's current lover is black (or "bleck," as they both pronounce the word, busy as they are "recultivating" their "class signatures" after two years spent shedding them). Over drinks the two indulge in the worst sort of imperialist condescension, racial stereotyping, and objectification. When Rock asks if Rodney's lover is what he calls "American-African," Rodney speculates on her origins as if he were guessing the province of a gourmet coffee: "I taste Africa in her. One of the French bits, probably. Senegal, perhaps. Sierra Leone. Guineau-Bissau" (98). The two trade appalling thought clichés for several pages, Rodney at one point claiming that "English blacks are posher than their American cousins" before Rodney concludes that they are all from the "same stock" (98–99).

This exchange is followed by a single paragraph that carries a multivalent historical and satirical significance, encompassing the colonial depredations and slave economy that have empowered the Rocks and Rodneys of the world and engendered the moral bankruptcy their dialogue has just laid bare. It does so by delving into the roots of their own "stock":

Rod and Rock: their family trees stood tall. Their family trees stood tall and proud. But what kind of trees were they—weeping willow, sallow, mahogany, ash? And something ailed or cankered them, shaping their branches all arthritic and aghast. . . . The Peels had been among the beneficiaries when, on a single day in 1661, Charles II created thirteen baronetcies on the plantation island of Barbados. Rock's lot, the Robvilles, rather disappointingly (from Rodney's point of view), didn't go back quite so far. But the Peels and the Robvilles alike had flourished at a time when every English adult with cash or credit owned a piece of it: a piece of slavery. The place where Rock's dad lived had been assembled by massive shipwright profits out of Liverpool, *circa* 1750. (99)

This paragraph lends deadly serious weight to the story's far-cical plot, which hinges on Rodney's increasingly desperate at-tempts to avoid discussing Pharsin's unread manuscript (at the moment of potentially violent reckoning, Rodney feels "the spasms of unused muscles: his lits, his crits" [119]). Pharsin des-perately desires the kind of cultural capital Rodney was born with—capital he was denied, and Rodney inherited, because of the enslavement of Pharsin's ancestors. "The Coincidence of the Arts" deftly demonstrates the intricate ways in which the per-sonal and the political always coincide.

"What Happened to Me on My Holiday"

Originally published in the July 21, 1997 *New Yorker,* "What Happened to Me on Holiday" closes *Heavy Water* as well as an important chapter in Amis's career. It also looks ahead to Amis's next book, *Experience,* inhabiting an intimate domestic sphere where relationships are messy, primal, and indispensable —and where verbal virtuosity is married to emotional vulner-ability. Wordsworth's "still, sad music of humanity" sounds throughout the story, preserved in a meticulously crafted fugue-like structure in which the voices of other characters and nature itself contribute to the theme of loss. Louis plays with his younger brother and his four-year-old cousin, catching crabs and minnows, understanding all too well (as his cousin does not) that a dead sprat will never return to life. He sees in the natural world intimations of the mortality he is now struggling to understand, observing the "gloud of grey" he sees rising from a pond on the day he hears that his stepbrother Eliaz has died back in London: "nat mizd [mist], nat vag [fog], but the grey haze of ziddies and of zdreeds [cities and streets] . . . and nothing was glear" (201).

Eliaz now inhabits the distant land of memory, where Louis imagines him hurrying about "with bags and bundles . . . jaggeds and hads [jackets and hats], gayadig, vestive [chaotic, festive]" (204). Meanwhile, another of Louis's cousins goes into the pool without his water wings and must be rescued. At the end of his holiday, in the car on the way to the airport, the word "grey" returns again, like a haunting melody—the melody of mortality: "Greynezz is zeebing ubwards vram the band. And nothing is glear. And then zuddenly the grey brighdens, giving you a deeb thrab in the middle of your zgull" (207). Now all the notes of the story converge, all the deaths come together, and Louis realizes that someday his brother, too, will die: "one vine day you gan loob ub vram your billow and zee no brother in the dwin bed. You go around the houze, bud your brother is nowhere do be vound" (207–8). "What Happened to Me on My Holiday" radiates what Kingsley Amis would have called a "terrible compulsive *vividness*" of style. But in this case, style is feeling as well as morality—the morality of imaginative sympathy.

In a chapter that has emphasized a new emotional emphasis in Amis's fiction, it is worth acknowledging that *Heavy Water* also contains several outrageous comic fantasies. Each proceeds from an imaginative conceit involving a singular change in the status quo. In "Straight Fiction," for instance: what if heterosexual people were an oppressed minority and homosexuality was the cultural and sexual norm? ("In the Castro, it seemed, everyone was straight. The whole community. They had straight greengrocers, straight bank tellers, straight mailmen. They even had straight cops" [184]). In "Career Move": what if screenwriting were the occupation of shabby losers, and poets basked in heated pools of money, glamour, and celebrity? ("'I always thought of "Sonnet" as an art poem,' said Joe. 'But sonnets are so hot now I've started thinking more commercially'"[31]). In "The Janitor on Mars": what if we discovered a robot on the red planet who knew how and when the world would end? ("Among the countless trillions of type-y worlds so far catalogued, none, I can confidently divulge, presents a picture of such agonizing retardation as Mother Earth"[168]). And in "Let Me Count the Times": what if a married businessman became sexually obsessed with—himself?

Some readers will reject stories like these as exercises in bad taste. But as A. O. Scott has written, "brazen insouciance, and the defiance not only of literary convention but of plain common sense, are the hallmarks of Amis's mature style."[18] Indeed, it is Amis's verbal extremism that lifts him above the role of storyteller or mere chronicler of times and tastes. He is a master of language, and will constantly expand it, play with it, and find new ways of making it new. This impulse unifies a group of stories whose composition spans three decades, whose settings span several literal and imaginative planets, and whose emotional range spans half a lifetime of experience.

CHAPTER 8

Patriarchy and Its Discontents

Experience: A Memoir; Koba the Dread:
Laughter and the Twenty Million

> She was a victim of my father's power and pres-
> ence, perhaps, but only in the saddest way. Kings-
> ley always worried that when he died Sally would
> lose her *raison d'etre*. It's only now that I realise
> how prescient the remark was.
> —Martin Amis, on his sister Sally Amis

> If you want to know how a man felt about his
> wives then you look at how he treated his children.
> —Martin Amis, on Stalin, *Koba the Dread* (134)

In his memoirs, as in his fiction, Martin Amis has a great deal to
say about men—as fathers, mentors, friends, rivals, domestic or
world-historical tyrants. He has so much to say, in fact, that
women are often crowded off the page. Nowhere is this more
apparent than in *Koba the Dread: Laughter and the Twenty
Million* (2002), where the death of Amis's sister Sally,
announced in prepublication reports as one of the book's central subjects, is relegated to several sentences, most of them part
of an afterword titled "Letter to My Father's Ghost."[1] These
sentences—primarily concerned with Sally's relationship to
Kingsley, and with Martin's attempt to soothe his father's spirit
by reporting on Sally's "quiet" last years and peaceful death—

reinforce the perception that in Amis's world, the primary purpose of women is to delineate relationships between men.[2] Like *Experience: A Memoir* (2000), *Koba the Dread* is a hybrid—part memoir, part history, part statement of political and literary principles. The explicit emphasis of each is distinct: autobiography dominates in the first, history and historiography dominate the second. Yet both books are united by their focus on male power, privilege, and perverse impulse. And *Koba the Dread* is, in many ways, a coda to *Experience,* since Amis's preoccupation with the evil of Stalin emerges from his desire to understand why his father "believed, and believed in, Soviet Communism for fifteen years" (272). As this chapter will argue, both works constitute extended conversations about and with Kingsley, and both implicitly function to chart Martin Amis's emergence as ruling patriarch of what he calls, in *Koba the Dread,* "our clan" (275).[3]

Father(s) and Son: *Experience*

Experience begins with a single word of dialogue, an interrogative, spoken by Amis's eleven-year-old son Louis: "Dad." This is followed by the father's response—"Yes?"—which is itself followed by a long paragraph describing how *his* father would have responded: "'Yeeeess?' with a dip in it, to signal mild but invariable irritation" (3). This opening precisely establishes the patriarchal focus and preoccupation of the memoir that follows. Like many of Amis's novels—most notably *London Fields* and *The Information*—*Experience* is a digressive book, encompassing everything from F. R. Leavis and the function of literary criticism to Auschwitz. Yet its most compelling pages are those devoted to Kingsley. Like Edmund Gosse's classic memoir *Father and Son* (1907), *Experience* paints an unforgettable portrait of a powerful patriarch raging against the dying of his power and influence. In the case of *Experience,* this portrait is enriched and complicated by the fact that the son has chosen to follow in his father's footsteps—a decision that both deepened the bond between them and intensified their father-son rivalry.

Experience grew out of a surfeit of experiences between 1993 and 1995. Amis's ten-year marriage to Antonia Phillips broke up, in part because of his relationship with Isabel Fonseca (whom he married in 1998); he discovered that his cousin Lucy Partington, missing since Christmas 1973, was a victim of the serial murderer Frederick West; he met his first daughter, Delilah, who had only been told of his relation to her at age nineteen; he parted from his longtime agent Pat Kavanagh over the much-publicized negotiations for a large advance on his novel *The Information* (which also resulted in the dissolution of his close friendship with Kavanagh's husband, the novelist Julian Barnes); he underwent a series of protracted and painful dental treatments and oral surgeries; his father Kingsley died following a slow and painful decline; his literary hero and mentor Saul Bellow contracted a nearly fatal illness.

One of the central quests of *Experience* is the struggle to preserve or recapture in adulthood some version of one's childhood innocence (the poet William Blake, whose spirit presides over this memoir, called it "organized innocence") in the face of inevitable loss, pain, and betrayal. One of the many surprises of *Experience* is that both book and writer do achieve "organized innocence"—through repeated moments and acts of commemoration, intimacy, and love. *Experience* is a profoundly literary book; eschewing chronology, it employs the poetry of recurrence and return to deepen its themes.[4] Joan Acocella has aptly described the effect:

What happens, chapter by chapter, is that a subject is let out of the bag—dentistry, women, whatever—and, like a bird, wheels and flies, picking up this and that bit of material, from whatever point in time, and then at last alights, with a quiet little plop. The great points are made not symphonically but by accumulation, as in a Symbolist poem.[5]

Readers familiar only with the corrosive fires of Amis's novels will experience a different kind of baptism in *Experience*. And those who only knew of their public disagreements about novels, novelists, and novel writing will be struck by Martin Amis's generosity toward and abiding love for his father, who repeatedly dismissed his son's novels as unreadable and referred to him in his letters to the poet Philip Larkin as "the little shit."[6] One source of this generosity is the younger Amis's recognition of the many ties that bind him to his father. Martin followed in his father's footsteps not only as a novelist but as someone who left his family for another woman.

Kingsley abandoned his first wife Hilly for the novelist Elizabeth Jane Howard when Martin was twelve. As *Experience* makes clear, this event was an emotional watershed in Martin's life, as decisive for the future novelist as Charles Dickens's consignment to the blacking warehouse at age thirteen. So when he left his wife Antonia Phillips for Isabel Fonseca, he was acutely aware of the emotional toll of his departure: "I said to myself, Look at it: Look at what you've done. There is the rented car . . . in which you will drive alone to Logan. There is your wife, crying in the drive. Beyond her are your boys on the patch of grass, with that zoo of theirs—the frogs, the turtles" (269). Unlike his father, he is capable of acute self-criticism in the face of his decision: after noting that he left his first wife and family "for love," he unsparingly asks "how does it look, the love ledger, by the time you're done? Because you are also the enemy of love and—for your children—its despoiler" (256).

Within the structural economy of *Experience*, however which devotes precious little space to Martin Amis's first marriage or the reasons for its dissolution—the emphasis falls (unintentionally but decisively) on the ways this breakup strengthened the Kingsley-Martin relationship. It deepens Martin's bond with his father, whom he quotes in this passage:

> "Stopping being married to someone," he had written, ten yeas earlier, "is an incredibly violent thing to happen to you, not easy to take in completely, ever." He knew I was now absorbing the truth and the force of this. And he knew also that the process could not be softened or hastened. All you could do was survive it. That surviving was a possibility he showed me, by example. But he did more. He roused himself and did more. "Talk as much as you want about it or as little as you want": these words sounded like civilization to me, in my barbarous state, so disheveled in body and mind. Talk as much or as little . . . I talked much. Only to him could I confess how terrible I felt, how physically terrible, bemused, subnormalised, stupefied from within, and always about to flinch or tremble from the effort of making my face look honest, kind, sane. Only to him could I talk about what I was doing to my children. Because he had done it to me. (99)

Father and son bonded in other ways as well. Kingsley could be tenderhearted to his children, and unostentatiously loving. Jokes, joking, and comedy were second nature to him; the author of *Lucky Jim* and *The Old Devils* was, as Martin observes, an "engine of comedy" presiding over a household whose daylight hours often thrummed with humor and high spirits. Martin's own considerable comic gifts owe a great deal to his example, as does his passionate and curatorial relationship to the English language. One of the most telling details in *Experience* is this description of Kingsley's intimacy with the *Concise Oxford Dictionary*: "he would sometimes pat and even stroke the squat black book, as if it were one of his cats" (285).

Amis works hard in *Experience* to reclaim his father from the mere caricature of reactionary opinions he became—or posed as—in his last decade. He does so without ever resorting to the airbrush. Kingsley's phobias, compulsions, and failures of tolerance are all made manifest, but sympathetic understanding replaces rancor. Charting Kingsley's descent into obesity, physical infirmity, alcoholic stupor, and reactionary politics in his later years, Martin relates a memorably miserable Thursday lunch and its aftermath, featuring dangerous quantities of alcohol. After a rancorous argument about Nelson Mandela (whom Kingsley absurdly characterized as a terrorist who murdered women and children), Kingsley experiences "an exponential alcoholic kick-in of trouncing efficacy" (338). After Martin carries him out of the restaurant and onto Edgware Road:

> Kingsley fell over. And this was no brisk trip or tumble. It was a work of colossal administration. First came a kind of slow-leak effect, giving me the immediate worry that Kingsley, when fully deflated, would spread out into the street on both sides of the island, where there were cars, trucks, sneezing buses. Next, as I grabbed and tugged, he felt like a great ship settling on its side: would it right itself, or go under? Then came an impression of overall dissolution and the loss of basic physical coherence. I groped around him, looking for

places to shore him up, but every bit of him was falling, drop-
ping, seeking the lowest level, like a mudslide. (339)

This is a symbolically charged anecdote, resonating with the
weight of the demands Kingsley placed on his family, foreshad-
owing his final fall into infirmity and oblivion.

As noted in the introduction, Martin's relationship to Kingsley illuminates the psychic wellspring of the son's imaginative
preoccupations, including the intimate knowledge of masculine
compulsion that informs his novels and the paternal anxieties
that have increasingly marked them. In addition, Kingsley's
behavior and attitude toward females helps explain why the
son, who has repeatedly emphasized his progressive gender
politics, suffers from an imaginative diminution when writing
about women. Martin registers his dismay and distress over his
father's repudiation of women in the 1980s, after his second
wife left him ("he tried to rewrite the past, to unperson, to
unlove; and you can't do that, or so I believed" [186]). But he
never convinces us that his father—a serial adulterer—experienced mature, devoted love toward either of his wives. Instead,
Kingsley's *cri de coeur* to his son in 1984—"you know it's only
half a life without a woman" (28)—laments the loss of support
and care that he depended on women to provide (and regained
by effectively hiring his first wife and her third husband to set
up house with him and tend to his needs during the last fifteen
years of his life). Elizabeth Jane Howard's assessment of Kingsley, expressed twenty years after she left him, is more revealing
than Martin's in this regard: "He loved lunching and drinking
with men, and I knew by now [1976] that he had little use for
women. He regarded them as intellectually inferior, and often as
'pests,' hanging about, getting in the way, and interrupting men.

Women were for bed and board, and he'd ceased to be interested in either."[7]

In addition to the emotional trials endured by Martin's mother Hillary Bardwell at the hands of Kingsley, the sufferings of two women are centrally evoked in *Experience:* Martin Amis's first wife Antonia Phillips, and his cousin Lucy Partington, whose 1973 abduction and murder was not discovered for more than twenty years.[8] Significantly, Partington claims the most space in *Experience,* even though Amis had precious little personal contact with her. Not surprisingly, his portrayal of her short life suffers from stereotyping and sentimentality: "Lucy Partington understood the innocence and mystery of animals" (148); "her presence was somehow infinitely self-sufficient and self-determining" (149); "the death of Lucy Partington . . . is what happens when darkness meets light"(172). One of Amis's primary aims in writing about Lucy is a paternalistic one—as an influential writer, he seeks to refute the scurrilous reports that circulated about his cousin after the Fred West interrogation tapes were released. Lucy's sister Marian campaigned for and won a public rebuttal, but Amis seeks to "confirm, solidify and perpetuate" it in *Experience.* Soon after the book was published, however, Marian publicly accused Amis of exploiting his relationship to her sister. She claimed that he only saw her a few times before her disappearance and did not have the close relationship he claims in the memoir. "Her aspirations were towards knowing God, spirituality, poetry and medieval art. She was modest—the very opposite of self-aggrandisement, which is what Martin is doing to her."[9]

Deference to his family partly explains the fact that almost nothing is said about the breakup of Amis's marriage to Phillips, aside from a description of her crying in the driveway as he leaves her. But this would not have prevented a fuller depiction of Phillips herself, including her influence on one of Amis's most important novels. Readers of *Money* will be understandably disappointed that no mention is made of the conversations about aesthetics Amis must have had with Phillips, a professor of philosophy, and how these influenced the conversation about fictional aesthetics between the characters John Self and Martina Twain. Despite (or perhaps because of) its ironic context and comic charge, this conversation is one of the most significant passages about postmodern fiction in the contemporary novel, and *Experience* might have shed light on its autobiographical matrix. Here, as elsewhere, *Experience* has little to say about what goes into the writing of Amis's novels.

Readers seeking traces of the anguish attending Amis's divorce are advised to consider another source of pain essayed in *Experience:* dental trauma. After thirty years of suffering from terrible teeth, Amis had them all pulled out and replaced with implants—after a tumor was removed from his chin and his lower jaw was rebuilt. As he narrates this nightmare in all its visceral intensity, the reader of his novels understands why Amis so convincingly inhabits the minds and voices of such desperate characters as Terry Service in *Success,* who describes himself as a "quivering condom of neurosis and ineptitude" (42). Consider this account of dentist Mike Szabatura extracting Amis's uppers:

> I cannot control my tongue which dances up to meet the dangling bridge. Something light drops on it—a piece of severed root—and slithers off sideways. The aromatic hands of Mike Szabatura are now exerting decisive force. And it is gone— the gory remnant whisked from sight like some terrible misadventure from the Delivery Room. (84)

Recalling that when his mother told an old friend that she had lost all her teeth she added "I know what I'm going to look like when I'm dead," Amis waxes existential: "This was not yet my case. Hopelessly compromised and contingent, my lower teeth were still there. But in the new space above them, impossible to misidentify, was a darkness, a void, a tunnel that led all the way to my extinction" (85).

Joan Acocella has described the "symbolic force" of these passages, noting that they stand for what the memoir itself never addresses directly—how his first marriage came apart, and what his boys thought of him as a result of his departure. "The dental cavalry is . . . his symbol for that," Acocella writes. "The pain, the disfigurement, the shame, the way, when he had a temporary plate, his sons turned away from him, because he looked different to them: here, if I'm not mistaken, we find out what the divorce was like." Acknowledging that it might seem "strange" that severed roots and bloody tissues would represent the anguish of a family's dissolution, Acocella astutely notes that this is "Amis's world—its irony, its grotesquerie, its emotional indirection."[10]

Kingsley's Ghost: *Koba the Dread*

Emotional indirection also marks *Koba the Dread: Laughter and the Twenty Million* (2002). "Koba the Dread" refers to Joseph Stalin, who adopted the nickname "Koba" in childhood after the hero of a popular Russian novel titled *The Patricide*. "Twenty million" is the number of victims who died in his purges, his gulag, his famines, his slave ships, and his forced collectivization. "Laughter" identifies the literary paradigm that organizes—and strains the reader's patience with—Amis's analysis of Stalin's evil. In Amis's hands, Stalin comes to resemble an outsized, world-historical version of the grotesque villains that populate his novels, from Quentin Villiers in *Dead Babies* to Steve Cousins in *The Information* ("Stalin was all caught up in the thrills and heaves of the prospect of prepotence" [110]). Moreover, Amis consistently employs literary tropes and categories to explain the effects of Stalin's evil. Late in the book, Amis assigns the Russian nightmare to a subgenre of comedy, sounding as if he has just returned from one of the 1971 seminars with the literary critic Northrop Frye he reported attending at Oxford in 1969 (*Experience*, 232): "Russia, 1917–53: what is its genre? It is not a tragedy, like Lear, not an anti-comedy, like *Troilus and Cressida*, nor yet a problem comedy, like *Measure for Measure*. It is a black farce, like *Titus Andronicus*" (258). Like Amis's earlier comparison of Stalin to Lear, which grossly distorts Shakespeare's greatest tragedy ("*Lear* remains the central visionary meditation on the totalitarian mind" [232]), these comparisons trivialize both literature and history. Appearing after several hundred pages in which Amis paraphrases and quotes from the vast literature on Stalin's murderous policies, including classic first-person accounts by the likes of Aleksandr Solzhenitsyn, Eugenia Ginzurg, and Nadezhda Mandelstam, they seem both glib and unseemly.

Koba the Dread extends the preoccupation with Kingsley that informs *Experience*. But here the emphasis shifts to Kingsley's political history—both to Martin's astonishment that Kingsley could have "believed, and believed in, Soviet Communism for fifteen years" (272) and his newfound respect for Kingsley's subsequent hard-right turn. Kingsley's case is emblematic of a larger pattern, what Amis calls the "chief lacuna" of the twentieth century: the failure of western intellectuals to condemn the grotesque horrors perpetrated in the USSR even as they were happening, and their reluctance to fully repudiate some of their communist sympathies since. The book begins with a brief overview of the disastrous Soviet experiment before considering the early devotion to and subsequent rejection of that experiment by his father's generation (Kingsley wrote an essay called "Why Lucky Jim Turned Right" in 1967, and his friend Robert Conquest published several books on the Soviet terror—on which *Koba* relies). It then turns to Martin's generation and their embrace of all things leftist during the revolutionary years of the Vietnam War and Paris Rouge, a time when, to quote Amis's reductivist rhetoric, "policemen and even parking wardens were called fascists" (10).

Here Amis rewrites his own political history. He claims that while his *New Statesman* colleagues and friends Christopher Hitchens and James Fenton were committed "Trotskyists," and Julian Barnes was "broadly Labour," he remained "quietist and unaligned" (22). He echoes this claim at the end of the book in his "Letter to My Father's Ghost," writing that "you were ideological and I am not" (272). The first assertion is rendered suspect by the record of Amis's journalism from the 1970s and 1980s,[11] while the second is both false on its face (no human being is free from the grip of ideology in its broadest sense, though many artists like to claim they are) and refuted by the explicitly ideological argument Amis conducted with his father in the polemical introduction to *Einstein's Monsters*. The intention of this revisionist personal history may have something to do with Amis's belief that serious writers transcend ideology, but the often unfortunate effect is to imply that he has achieved a state of wisdom that his father only arrived at after years of ignorance, and that Christopher Hitchens, to whom he addresses a partly scolding letter at the end of *Koba the Dread,* has not yet fully attained. In the most egregious passage of the letter, Amis writes: "An admiration for Lenin and Trotsky is meaningless without an admiration for terror. . . . Do you admire terror?" (249).[12]

The main narrative of *Koba the Dread* details the appalling suffering Stalin (and Lenin before him) visited on his own people. This chronicle of horrors is based on Amis's reading of "several yards of books about the Soviet experiment" (4), including *The Great Terror* and *The Harvest of Sorrow* by his father's friend Robert Conquest; *Stalin in Power: The Revolution From Above* by Robert C. Tucker; and *A People's Tragedy: The Russian Revolution, 1891–1924* by Orlando Figes. As one would expect, Amis the stylist and master of narrative crafts a compelling story from the mountainous historiography on Bolshevism, and for those still harboring illusions about the Soviet experiment, *Koba the Dread* serves a useful purpose in presenting a condensed and vivid account of the profound suffering experienced by the Russian people during the first half of the twentieth century.

Given the preoccupation with fathers and fatherhood that characterizes *Experience,* it is not surprising that Amis consistently links Stalin's cruelty to the Fatherland to his cruelty as a husband and father. He describes the terrible fate that befell Stalin's second wife, Nadezhda (Nadya) Alliluyeva:

After the Revolution, at the age of sixteen, she became Stalin's secretary, and then, a year later, his wife. Vasily was born in 1921, Svetlana in 1926. Nadya shot herself in the head after a party in the Kremlin to celebrate the fifteenth anniversary of the Revolution. November 1932: in a sense, as we shall see, she was just another victim of Collectivization. While he contemplated her open coffin Stalin was seen to make a gesture of dismissal and heard to mutter, "She left me as an enemy." (131)[13]

He also quotes Khrushchev's telling description of Stalin's feelings toward his daughter Svetlana as "those of a cat for a mouse" (163).

In his fiction, Amis favors comic pairs and exaggerated contrasts (Terry Service and Gregory Riding in *Success,* Keith Talent and Guy Clinch in *London Fields,* Richard Tull and Gwynn Barry in *The Information*). He employs a similar procedure in *Koba the Dread*—typically expressed using literary references or categories—to measure the historical and moral differences between the evils of Hitler and Stalin. He does so without seeming to recognize its inappropriateness. After noting that "Nazi terror strove for precision, while Stalinist terror was deliberately random" (85), for instance, Amis employs this allusion to the witches' chant in Shakespeare's *Macbeth* to compare the two leaders: "Ideology brings about a disastrous fusion: that of violence and righteousness—a savagery without stain. Hitler's ideology was foul, Lenin's fair-seeming" (86). Later, striving to explain why, unlike the Holocaust, the Soviet disaster is capable of eliciting laughter, Amis finds the answer in utopian yearning —an idea he expresses with allusions to *Dr. Faustus* and Milan Kundera's *The Book of Laughter and Forgetting:*

Is *that* the difference between the little mustache and the big mustache, between Stalin and Beelzebub? One elicits spontaneous fury, and the other elicits spontaneous laughter? And what kind of laughter is it? It is, of course, the laughter of

universal fondness for that old, old idea about the perfect
society. It is also the laughter of forgetting. It forgets the
demonic energy embedded in that hope. It forgets the Twenty
Million. (256–57)

Since few observers of the Soviet experiment experience "spontaneous laughter" when contemplating Stalin, this comparison
seems forced and false—appropriate to a "black farce," perhaps,
but not to a serious historical study.

Less than a year before *Koba the Dread* was published,
Amis described the book in terms that suggested his sister Sally's
death would be its focus: "Stalin always claimed that one death
was a tragedy and twenty million deaths were a statistic. . . . He
was utterly wrong, of course: twenty million deaths are twenty
million tragedies. That's the idea I'm exploring, by looking at
one individual death."[14] But instead of framing and informing
the entire narrative, Sally Amis is relegated to a few paragraphs
at its end. Paul Berman has suggested that *Koba* does contain an
extended expression of grief over Sally's death (and the death of
Kingsley), albeit a submerged one, in its long cry of outrage over
Stalin's depredations: "from behind his pile of books on Soviet
themes he allows himself, as any grieving person might do, to
vent and rave."[15] Yet this oblique expression of personal grief
does not constitute a memorial to a lost sister.

In fact, the reader learns far more about Sally from *Experience* than from *Koba the Dread*. In the earlier book we learn
that in her last years she lived in a "tiny" flat that made Martin's Notting Hill apartment seem "an edifice the size of Har-
rod's" (352); that this flat contained a "shrine to Kingsley"
featuring "signed copies of his books, photographs, memora-
bilia" (352); that she was with Kingsley when he died (and for
ten hours preceding his death), while Martin and his brother

Philip smoked outside the hospital gates; and that when the brothers arrived to find Kingsley dead she "stood, electrified, as if italicized—as if so many urgent tasks awaited her that she couldn't for the life of her think where to begin" (354). Most tellingly, we learn that four years after Kingsley's death, Sally would call Martin in tears "when she is having a 'bad Dad day'" (365–66). After recording this fact, Martin notes that "it goes all right for me, pretty much, because the books are still here and, therefore, so is his presence: sleeplessly available" (366). This observation comes several pages after he has figuratively limited the meaning of Sally's life to her attendance on Kingsley, and equated Kingsley's death with hers: "Sally, I'm sorry, but no urgent tasks await you. He has finished his work and you have finished yours" (355).

Six months after these words were published, Sally Amis died. This is from *Koba the Dread:*

> In November 2000 it fell to me to help arrange my younger sister's funeral. My father, in the last year of his life, told me that in his most defenseless insomnias he tended to worry about Sally and what it would be like for her when he was dead: the loss of general support, the loss of purpose, of *raison*. And so it proved. A long depression was followed by a sudden illness. (268)

In October 2001, journalist Allan Brown published a feature containing additional details about Sally Amis, cast in the harsh language of journalese:

> Sally Amis, the writer's younger sister, died last November at the age of 46. She was a manic-depressive, an alcoholic and had never recovered from the death of Kingsley. . . . Her

marriage in the 1980s to a wine merchant twice her age lasted six months, after which the first signs of instability manifested themselves and she ended up living in a church hostel. She had a baby daughter following a one-night stand with an Irish alcoholic and the child was later adopted. In 1994, at the age of 40, she suffered a stroke. When she died of an unspecified infection she was living on disability benefit in a council flat in Kentish Town.[16]

In *Koba the Dread* the emphasis is quite different. Consider this passage from the "Letter to My Father's Ghost":

> Her last years were quiet, and quietly comfortable (she managed your legacy with care). . . . Her last days were peaceful, and there was no pain. . . . Rest, rest perturbed spirit.
>
> Anonymously present at Sally's funeral was Sally's daughter. Remember, you and I saw her when she was a baby (in the summer of 1979), just before her adoption. The baby, who was perfect, was called Heidi, named after Sally's very unencouraging new mentor. She is not called Heidi any longer. Sally, then, was twenty-four. Catherine, now, is twenty-two.
>
> She had never met her mother. (271, 275)

As the admonition to Kingsley's ghost indicates ("rest, rest perturbed spirit") the primary purpose of these words is to soothe what Martin imagines to be the paternally anxious spirit of Kingsley. Even in death, Sally Amis facilitates communion between men.

Most readers will finish *Koba the Dread* with unanswered questions about Sally Amis, wondering why none of them were raised, let alone answered. What was her life like, both in and outside the Amis family? Why was her child put up for adoption? Why was this daughter not adopted by any members of the Amis family? Why did Martin, or Philip, or their mother Hillary not notice Sally's decline following Kingsley's death, and intervene? After telling journalist Allan Brown that the family did not realize how much Sally suffered following Kingsley's death, Amis added:

> She adored him, she loved to make herself useful to him but she was physically weakened by his death, though not necessarily in an alarming way. . . . She would visit my mother in Spain, she lived up the road from me, I'd see her. . . . She seemed alert and prosperous. I just didn't realise how diminished she was. She was a victim of my father's power and presence, perhaps, but only in the saddest way.[17]

On the last page of his "Letter to My Father's Ghost" in *Koba the Dread* Martin Amis expresses the depth of his grief over losing both his father and his only sister in a sentence where the deliberate repetition of pronouns (with telling variation) also hints at the emotional costs of a family dynamic that diminished the life of a daughter unaccountably dependent on and devoted to a wayward father: "Remembering her, and you, and you and her, has filled me with an exhaustion that no amount of sleep can seem to reach" (275).

CHAPTER 9

The Novelist as Critic

The Moronic Inferno; Visiting Mrs. Nabokov;
The War against Cliché; Uncollected Essays
and Reviews

> All artist-critics are to some extent secret prosely-
> tizers for their own work; they are all secret agents.
> —Martin Amis

The titles of Amis's three collections of essays and reviews say a great deal about the stylistic influences and preoccupations that have shaped the most distinctive voice in contemporary British writing. *The Moronic Inferno and Other Visits to America* (1986), which begins and ends with pieces on Saul Bellow, takes its title from Bellow himself, whose own prose has left a lasting mark on his most impassioned celebrant. As James Wood has written, it is from Bellow that Amis gets his fondness for "streaming syntax and parenthetical interruptions; for fabulous plurals; . . . for adjectival massing, often in triplicate." Wood concludes that "Bellow taught Amis how to exaggerate, how to stretch, how to linger."[1] *Visiting Mrs. Nabokov and Other Excursions* (1993) evokes the spirit of Vladimir Nabokov, another demigod in Amis's literary pantheon. Just as Bellow's social engagement and panoptic reach appeal to one side of Amis's literary sensibility, Nabokov speaks directly to Amis's militant aestheticism, his willingness to "sacrifice any psychological or realistic truth for a phrase, for a paragraph that has a spin on it."[2] *The War against Cliché: Essays and Reviews, 1971–2000* (2001) makes this militancy explicit, containing close to one hundred reviews and literary essays that constitute a campaign against "inherited, ready-made formulations, fossilized metaphors" (444)—as well as against the stultifying habits of mind and thought that such formulations foster. Amis emerges victorious from this campaign by brandishing a prose that is "half wand, half weapon" (443), critically demolishing the cliché-ridden while celebrating "freshness, energy and reverberation of voice" (xv).

The Moronic Inferno

The Moronic Inferno is a collection of twenty-seven essays and reviews. All but one were originally written for British periodicals (the exception is a profile of filmmaker Brian DePalma that originally appeared in *Vanity Fair*). Most have been reprinted as they appeared, although Amis has added postscripts to several. None of them was originally written as part of a projected book on America, but the demands of the literary marketplace, and perhaps the nudging of the publisher, led Amis to package them in this way. In a sometimes glib, sometimes portentous introduction, Amis claims that when sifting his fifteen years worth of journalism for a collection of occasional pieces, he discovered that "I had already written a book about America—unpremeditated, accidental, and in installments" (10). He writes that he got the book's title—the phrase "moronic inferno"—from Saul Bellow, who borrowed it from Wyndham Lewis; then he acknowledges that it could apply to any time and place, not just America. "It is . . . primarily a metaphor . . . for human infamy: mass, gross, ever-distracting human infamy" (x–xi). Strain is evident here: the strain of forcing a collection of disparate essays to fit a conceptual scheme imposed retrospectively by a writer with a reputation as a satirist.

Such pigeonholing is as unnecessary as it is irrelevant, since *The Moronic Inferno* stands on its own as a superb collection of journalism. Jason Cowley, who has repeatedly faulted Amis's fiction in the *New Statesman,* is zealous in his praise for *The Moronic Inferno*—and for Amis's journalism generally:

> In journalistic mode, Amis is without peer: when he writes about writers—indeed, when he writes at length about any-one, such as Hugh Hefner—the long profile becomes, in his hands, a capacious, infinitely flexible form in which to com-bine reportage, criticism, humour, exalted phrase-making, and a clear-eyed, penetrating sense of purpose.[3]

The Moronic Inferno combines literary reviews (most origi-nally published in the *New Statesman* or the *Observer*), essays on popular culture, and profiles of writers and other celebrities. Among the essays are several on politics and religion, where Amis's leftist sympathies are most clearly in evidence. He is alternately amused and appalled by the unholy alliance of tele-vision, evangelical religion, and politics that characterized the American scene in the early to mid 1980s. Writing about Rea-gan's first bid for the presidency, Amis notes that "Reagan in California showed steady indifference to the poor, the sick, the dissident—and to the tragic mess of the inner cities" (95). When he turns to the evangelical movement that helped elect Reagan, the result is a nuanced analysis of the phenomenon, including its class dimensions. He calls the evangelical right wing the "most proletarian and anti-intellectual of the many mansions of Ameri-can religion" (111), but he eschews outright scorn. "To dismiss the beliefs of the Evangelicals is to disdain the intimate thoughts of ordinary people" (118). On the other hand he is clear-eyed about the dangerous irrationalism of the movement, which makes it "wide-open, . . . abjectly vulnerable, to authoritarian thought" (119).

"Double Jeopardy: Making Sense of AIDS," originally published in 1985, deserves special mention, both for its intrinsic merits and because Amis's voice here contrasts so sharply with the voices in his novels. It stands as a reminder that behind the frenzied, cruel, hard-edged, self-obsessed characters that populate his fiction is an author possessing a fully human—and humane—range of emotional and moral responses. The entire essay is an example of sustained imaginative sympathy. Amis begins by inviting the reader to walk in the shoes of a gay male, verbally assaulted not only for being gay but because he is now perceived as a threat to public health. Such attacks weaken the defenses of those already suffering from AIDS, Amis writes; they also spread their own kind of moral sickness. Faced with a medical insurance system that is "a shambles of pedantry and expediency," AIDS sufferers are soon caught in a "double bind, the double jeopardy" (188). When one AIDS patient was refused insurance, he was sent to a city hospital. "Here he will encounter the suspicion and contempt that America traditionally accords the poor" (189). "In the end," Amis writes, "one cannot avoid the conclusion that AIDS unites certain human themes—homosexuality, sexual disease, and death—about which society actively resists enlightenment" (190).

Amis himself resists this resistance: "the straight world expects the gay man to follow its own sexual master-mould. And he doesn't. Homosexuality isn't a *version* of heterosexuality. It is something else again" (191). Amis's essay contains a detailed explanation of the ways in which the AIDS virus spreads that was rare for the mainstream press in 1985, especially in Britain (the essay originally appeared in the *Observer*). "Why this resistance to corporeal truth?" Amis asks in a postscript written especially for *The Moronic Inferno*. "Even in a near-impeccably enlightened institution like the *Observer* I glimpsed a measure of the intransigence, the reluctance to know, felt by society at large" (196). He concludes the postscript with an unsentimental note of hope: "people are now infinitesimally more receptive to the truth, and this is a start. But it will be a long and wretched road" (198).[4]

The profiles of contemporary writers gathered in *The Moronic Inferno* manage to be several things at once: acute assessments of the writers' achievements; penetrating analyses of their critical reception; and oblique commentaries on Amis's own writerly tendencies. In some cases (the two essays on Saul Bellow that frame the entire collection, for example) they celebrate achievements to which Amis himself aspires. In a 1984 *Observer* review of a collected edition of Bellow's works (inexplicably omitted from *The War against Cliché*), Amis analyzed the "assortment of voices" in Bellow's short stories, noting "this is a large part of what writers are really up to: finding the right voice, the right line, the right instrument."[5] The two *Moronic Inferno* essays continue this self-reflective process. Praising Bellow's inventive character names in "Saul Bellow and the Moronic Inferno," Amis observes that "the way a writer names his characters provides a good index to the way he sees the world—to his reality-level, his responsiveness to the accidental humour and freakish poetry of life" (1). The last piece in the collection, "Saul Bellow in Chicago," concludes with a passage that speaks to the moral dimensions of Amis's novels as well as

Bellow's: "Many times in Bellow's novels we are reminded that 'being human' isn't the automatic condition of every human being. Like freedom or sanity, it is not a given but a gift, a talent, an accomplishment, an objective. In achieving it, some will need more time or thought or help. And, put that way, it doesn't sound too hard a lesson to learn" (208).

More often, the mixed feelings inspired by such writers as Philip Roth, Kurt Vonnegut, Norman Mailer, John Updike, and William Burroughs (all of whom are also represented by multiple reviews in *The War against Cliché*) produce wickedly sharp barbs of wit that simultaneously skewer the author's excesses and reveal Amis's anxieties about his own fiction.[6] In this way, as in others, these profiles complement the reviews. Take his brief assessment of Burroughs, for instance. Amis has been criticized for insufficient attention to plot in his novels, a deficiency that assumes extreme proportions in Burroughs. "Like many novelists whose modernity we indulge, William Burroughs is essentially a writer of 'good bits.' These good bits don't work out or add up to anything; they have nothing to do with the no-good bits; and they needn't be in the particular books they happen to be in" (144). Because of their shapelessness, in other words, Burroughs books do not even deserve the label "novels." Amis concludes that "no living writer has so perfidiously denies his own gifts—most of which are, incidentally, comic and exuberant rather than admonitory and bleak" (146).

Three separate *Observer* pieces on Norman Mailer are juxtaposed in *The Moronic Inferno* (three more appear in *The War against Cliché*), and they constitute a moral and aesthetic evaluation of the man and his works that is at once comic, critical, and self-reflexively admiring. "For thirty years Mailer has been the cosseted superbrat of American letters," writes Amis, who was himself labeled "Britain's Brat of Letters" in one profile after he had become a literary celebrity.[7] Amis quotes a reviewer of Mailer's *Barbary Shore,* who claims Mailer's intention here "is to debauch as many readers as possible"—a charge leveled against some of Amis's own novels. Finally, though, Amis attempts to distance himself from a writer whose hard-boiled stance and unflinching prose once influenced his own. "His name is Norman Mailer, king of kings: look on his works, ye Mighty, and—what—Despair? Burst out laughing? In secure retrospect, Mailer's life and times seem mostly ridiculous: incorrigibly ridiculous" (73).

Amis's essay on John Updike's *Rabbit* trilogy, written two years before the publication of *Money,* is more moderate. It speaks of the advantages and difficulties inherent in the kind of comedy Amis himself often practices: "at its best the narrative is a rollicking comedy of ironic omission, as author and reader collude in their enjoyment of Rabbit's pitiable constriction. Conversely—and this is the difficult part—the empty corners and hollow spaces of the story fill with pathos, the more poignant for being unremarked" (156). Both these points apply to *Money,* in which the protagonist John Self shares certain family resemblances with Rabbit Angstrom. Amis's tart assessment of Updike's style likewise reflects an acute awareness of his own tendencies: "in every sense it constitutes an embarrassment of riches—alert, funny and sensuous, yet also garrulous, mawkish and cranky. Updike often seems wantonly, uncontrollably fertile, like a polygamous Mormon" (157).

Amis has been reviewing Philip Roth since 1973. *The Moronic Inferno* contains two reviews of the Zuckerman novels; like the four reviews collected in *The War against Cliché,* they demonstrate Amis's ongoing fascination with a writer whose energy, fearlessness, "novelistic ear" (45), and celebrity status have offered inspiration and object lessons in equal measure. In light of the intense media scrutiny Amis experienced in the 1990s—and the complex effects this has had on his career—this observation from his 1984 review of *The Anatomy Lesson* reads like prophecy: "it is an awkward and recent truth that most contemporary novelists are deeply influenced by their own lives, and not least by the amount of praise, fame and money their work attracts" (46).

Visiting Mrs. Nabokov

Published seven years after *The Moronic Inferno, Visiting Mrs. Nabokov and Other Excursions* (1993) is a similarly eclectic collection of thirty-three prose pieces, featuring eleven essays on writers, six on sports, and two on political topics (America's nuclear strategists, the 1988 Republican Convention). The remainder encompass celebrities (Madonna, Roman Polanski), places and events (Cannes, St. Lucia), games (chess, tennis, poker, snooker), and personal experiences (being expelled from grammar school, surviving an emergency landing on a jetliner). Two book reviews are also reprinted—of Saul Bellow's *More Die of Heartbreak* and V. S. Naipaul's *India: A Wounded Civilization*. The title essay recounts Amis's sentimental journey to the home of Vera Nabokov, Vladimir Nabokov's widow and a zealous guardian of his literary legacy. Most pieces in the collection were written between the mid 1980s and early 1990s, although several from the 1970s and early 1980s left out of the first collection are also included. *Visiting Mrs. Nabokov* is the most purely "journalistic" of Amis's three essay collections, a fact which seems to cause him some discomfort. "Writing journalism never feels like writing in the proper sense," he writes in the introduction. "It is essentially collaborative: both your subject and your audience are hopelessly specific" (ix).

This is an oddly dismissive claim from one of the best non-fiction writers of his generation, but the tone is in keeping with many pieces in the collection. There is something wistful, world-weary, and elegiac about much of *Visiting Mrs. Nabokov,* as if the spirit of Philip Larkin, who Amis eulogizes in one of the essays collected here, were presiding over the entire enterprise. The tone may in part reflect Amis's increasing confrontations with mortality as he himself aged (he turned forty in 1989) and witnessed the deaths of writers and acquaintances he treasured. Consider the first several sentences of the introduction. "Warily looking back through these pieces, I glimpse a series of altered or vanished worlds, including those of my younger and much younger selves. Things change. Graham Greene is dead. Vera Nabokov is dead. Salman Rushdie is still alive, and still in hiding; if writing fiction is, among other things, an act of spiritual freedom, then Rushdie is a man who has been imprisoned for the crime of being free" (vii). The first three pieces in the collection concern, respectively, a dead novelist ("Graham Greene"), a brush with death on an airliner ("Emergency Landing"), and the possibility of death on a mass scale ("Nuclear City: The Megadeath Intellectuals"). John Updike makes another appearance in this collection, only now Amis visits him in the hospital, where Updike was scheduled to have a potentially cancerous growth removed. Ronald Reagan is also back, this time presiding over George Bush's ascendancy at the 1988 Republican Convention, and looking like "a gorgeous old opera-phantom shot full of novocaine" (103). A eulogy for John Lennon originally published in the *Observer* in 1980 appears here as well, along with the 1985 obituary essay on Philip Larkin that Amis wrote for *Vanity Fair*.

The short Larkin essay is a penetrating assessment of Larkin's poetic vision and a reminder that Amis's own comically bleak outlook derives in part from England's unofficial laureate of diminishment. In a later essay published in the *New Yorker* (and reprinted in *The War against Cliché*), Amis analyzes the waxing and waning of Larkin's literary reputation; this shorter piece, written the year of Larkin's death, is a concise elegy. Even here, Amis's gift for comic surprise comes into play:

> Philip Larkin was not an inescapable presence in America, as he was in England; and to some extent you can see America's point. His Englishness was so desolate and inhospitable that even the English were scandalised by it. Certainly, you won't find his work on the Personal Growth or Self-Improvement shelves in your local bookstore. "Get out as early as you can," as he once put it. "And don't have any kids yourself."
>
> All his values and attitudes were utterly, even fanatically "negative." He really was "anti-life"—a condition that many are accused of but few achieve. To put it at its harshest, you could say that there is in his ethos a vein of spiritual poverty, almost of spiritual squalor. Along with John Betjeman, he was England's best-loved postwar poet; but he didn't love postwar England, or anything else. He didn't love—end of story—because love seemed derisory when set against death. "The past is past and the future neuter"; "Life is first bore-dom, then fear" . . . That these elements should have pro-duced a corpus full of truth, beauty, instruction, delight—and much wincing humour—is one of the many great retrievals

wrought by irony. Everything about Larkin rests on irony,
that English specialty and vice. (201)

As these paragraphs suggest, another implicit theme
informing many of the essays in *Visiting Mrs. Nabokov* is the
postwar, postmodern condition itself. Discussing Benn Crader,
one of the characters in Bellow's *More Die of Heartbreak,* Amis
says that "Benn . . . has innocence, and we all know what
modernity will do with that. Innocence is a claim to immunity,
and there is no immunity any more; modernity makes no exceptions" (137). For Amis, the ever-present nuclear threat is one
source of this chronic immunodeficiency. In "Nuclear City: The
Megadeath Intellectuals," published the same year as *Einstein's
Monsters* (a mostly fictional confrontation with nuclear anxiety)
Amis insists that nuclear terror is here to stay, regardless of
changes in the balance of power. "When nuclear weapons become real to you, when they stop buzzing around your ears and
actually move into your head, hardly an hour passes without
some throb or flash, some heavy pulse of imagined supercata-
strophe. Staring at the many-eyed helmet of the Capitol, you see
the clouds above on fire, the winter sky ignited, taken out" (13).

Amis's revulsion at the cold calculus of technology links this
essay on nuclear strategy with two of the book's strongest essays
on popular culture. One of these describes Amis's visit to the set
of *RoboCop II,* which turns into an analysis of the prophetic
satire of the first two *RoboCop* films. Of the original, Amis
writes that "it wasn't just state-of-the-art. It was also state-of-
the-science: when you see its twirling rivets and burnished heat-
exchangers, when you hear its venomous shunts and succulent
fizzes, you suspect that the future really might feel like this—that
it will act this way on your very nerve-ends. Technology is god

in *RoboCop,* but it is also the villain, with its triumphant humourlessness, its puerile ingenuity, its dumb glamour" (164).

Not coincidentally, Amis's profile of Madonna, written as her book *Sex* was about to appear, discovers in the singer's carefully constructed series of personae a similar technology at work. "From the start Madonna has included pornography in her unique array of cultural weaponry—because she understands its modern, industrial nature." Like RoboCop itself, "the elements of popular culture she has melded together . . . could have been assembled by a corporate computer" (263). Both the *RoboCop* films and the Madonna phenomenon speak directly to the postmodern condition as Amis conceives it, in which the self is part product, part victim of the technologies that increasingly structure life and consciousness. The concluding paragraph of his Madonna profile speaks to the gap produced by the consequent abandonment of and nostalgia for an imagined, autonomous "self": "Alone among celebrities, she seldom talks about the real or private self that she supposedly reverts to when out of the public eye. A good deal of superstar neurosis is probably caused by such futile quests for the innocent original (though a psychotherapist has recently joined Madonna's entourage, maybe with the brief to root out this tiny phantom). Otherwise she is the self-sufficient post-modern phenomenon . . . a masterpiece of controlled illusion" (264).

Not everything in *Visiting Mrs. Nabokov* is postmodern angst. Amis's fleet and fluid prose is a consistent source of delight, for one thing, no matter how much brooding it is asked to do. Also, the collection features several essays on the world of games and sports that are brimming with human comedy. Amis brings to his pieces on chess, tennis, poker, darts, and snooker (the British version of billiards) the wit of a bemused spectator and the expertise of a participant. Amis places the reader inside these artificial worlds, creating miniature comedies of manners the appeal of which extends far beyond sports journalism.

The War against Cliché

Experience: A Memoir provides a useful starting point for analyzing *The War against Cliché,* winner of the 2002 National Book Critics Circle Award for Criticism. Blending personal anecdote with passages of poetry and prose, bursting with adamant judgments (Shakespeare is peerless, Samuel Beckett hopeless, the latter novels of Kingsley represent a return to form), and festooned with footnotes, *Experience* amounts to an informal declaration of aesthetic principles. Reviewers called this book a memoir, and they concentrated on its autobiographical revelations, especially its remarkable portrait of Martin's relationship to his novelist father. But it is also worth attending to the voice of the Oxford don that echoes throughout *Experience*—a voice reminding us that Amis's original career plan was to follow in the footsteps of his tutor Jonathan Wordsworth. In 1970, Amis planned to stay at Oxford for his doctorate in literature, but Wordsworth challenged him to spend a year trying to write a novel.[8] Nine novels later, it is easy to overlook the fact that during his career as a fiction writer, Amis continued his postgraduate education by writing a series of literary essays and book reviews (over two hundred and counting) in the leading English and American newspapers and magazines.[9] *The War against Cliché* is one result of that process.

In one of the reviews collected in *The War against Cliché* Amis writes that "every reader must find his personal great tradition" (78), an allusion to the critic F. R. Leavis, who Amis claims inaugurated "the Age of Criticism" (xii) with his 1948 work *The Great Tradition.*[10] Inevitably, Amis was influenced by Leavis, whose influence on Anglo-American criticism was once pervasive. In January 1969 Amis signed one submission to the *New Statesman* "M. L. Amis," and in *Experience* he claims, erroneously but suggestively, that he signed his first review with the same name (193).[11] As early as 1993 Amis publicly aligned himself with the "Leavisites" as opposed to the Bloomsbury aesthetes: "At lunch, long ago, I asked the company to choose sides between F. R. Leavis and Bloomsbury—to say which they would have gravitated to, back then: Bloomsbury or Leavisland. Everyone except me chose Bloomsbury."[12]

One key to this filiation is expressed in Amis's review of Angus Wilson's *Diversity and Depth in Fiction,* reprinted in *The War against Cliché:* "The ascendancy of Leavis himself might be seen as a reaction against the Bloomsbury establishment—against the snobbery, the leisure culture, the moneyed dilettantism of High Bohemia" (78). As he makes clear in the foreword to *The War against Cliché,* Amis's literary sensibility was fundamentally shaped by the Leavis legacy, both at Oxford and in his early days at the *Times Literary Supplement* and the *New Statesman* (xi). From Leavis he imbibed the belief that literature and literary criticism "are essential to civilization" (xii) as well as the rage to judge and rank literature according to rigorous standards. Amis was consistently critical of Leavis's dictatorial rigidity; in the three reviews of books by Leavis he wrote in the 1970s (omitted from *The War against Cliché*) he attacks Leavis's "stultifying humourlessness, . . . lack of any sense of irony or self-doubt" and his "authoritarian" and "inflexible" mind.[13] And yet, like Leavis, Amis believes fiercely in literary hierarchies, from what he calls the "talent elite" (xii) to the ranking of writers and books (in *Experience*, he records an argument with Salman Rushdie about the merits of Samuel Beckett that nearly ended in a fistfight). He also believes in the moral imperative of literature, although he is always quick to deny that literature has any direct moral influence. "Style is morality," as he insists in the longest piece in *The War against Cliché*, an essay on Saul Bellow's *The Adventures of Augie March*. "Style, of course, is not something grappled on to regular prose; it is intrinsic to perception. We are fond of separating style and content (for the purposes of analysis, and so on), but they aren't separable: they come from the same place. And style is morality. Style judges" (467).

For Amis, reviewing is simultaneously "the lowest and noblest literary form." Although his reviews often give the impression of effortlessness, the form is a demanding one. "I find journalism only marginally easier than fiction," he has written, "and book reviewing slightly harder." One reason for this is that Amis takes reviewing very seriously. "The thousand-word book review seems to me far more clearly an art form (however minor) than any of the excursions of the New Journalism, some of which are as long as *Middlemarch*."[14] This is consistent with Amis's belief that literature, like other arts, represents "the best that humans can do."[15] Like Richard Tull in *The Information*, Amis comes across in these essays as a "marooned modernist" in his attitude toward art, despite his postmodern view of the world and the self. It is clear from his repeated references to Leavis, I. A. Richards, and Northrop Frye in *The War against Cliché* that his critical sensibility was formed before the ascendancy of post-structuralist theory. Along with this earlier generation of critics, Amis believes that literature occupies a privileged status, of but not entirely bound to the historical moment from which it emerges (in the foreword to *The War against Cliché* he calls literature "the great garden that is always there . . . Eden" [xiv]). Reviewing Iris Murdoch's *The Sacred and Profane Love Machine,* Amis charges that it lacks "a linguistic centre of gravity, and without it the book sprawls. Serious literature is, among other things, a pattern of words, and an author's more general procedures will always be reflected in its verbal surface."[16]

"Readers should always be wrestling with writers who feel intimate to them" (96), Amis writes in one of several pieces on J. G. Ballard in *The War against Cliché.* This collection, like *The Moronic Inferno,* testifies to Amis's career-long fascination with specific writers and how their work has evolved and matured. His engagement with the careers of these writers—ranging from J. G. Ballard and Iris Murdoch to John Updike and Gore Vidal —provides evidence of the aesthetic values, themes, and formal strategies that inform his own work, from his fiction to his criticism to his memoirs. His multiple reviews of J. G. Ballard and William Burroughs, for example, written in the 1970s and 1980s (six reviews of Ballard and three of Burroughs appear in *The War against Cliché*) illuminate his novel *Dead Babies* as well as his general interest "in the subject of perversion in our 'post-Warhol era'" (95). His several reviews of John Updike's own critical essays clarify Amis's own militant aestheticism, especially when he indicts Updike for "that vein of folksy uplift which underlies his novels as well as his criticism" (372).[17] And his praise for Gore Vidal's memoir *Palimpsest,* originally published in 1995, helps explain his own formal and thematic procedures in *Experience:* "with its elaborate double-time scheme, its cunning rearrangements and realignments of the past, its blend of impetuous candour and decent reticence, *Palimpsest* is a work of considerable artistry" (282). Correspondences like these abound in both *The Moronic Inferno* and *The War against Cliché,* their discovery awaiting the careful reader.

The British novelist and critic Angus Wilson inspires some of Amis's most self-revealing commentary. Amis's review of Wilson's novel *As If By Magic,* published the same year as *The Rachel Papers,* could serve as a defense of Amis's own fictional territory. "[Wilson's] fictional world, as he himself seems to acknowledge via Margaret in *No Laughing Matter,* is a nasty world, but this doesn't stop him being a great novelist. No writer can determine what may appeal to his imagination and it is simply philistine to arraign him for the things he happens to write about best" (74). Reviewing Wilson's essay collection *Diversity and Depth in Fiction* in 1984, Amis offers a pithy description of his own postmodern art of fiction. "The contexts, the great forms of the eighteenth- and nineteenth-century sagas, have been exhausted; realism and experimentation have come and gone without seeming to point to a way ahead. The contemporary writer, therefore, must combine these veins, calling on the strengths of the Victorian novel together with the alienations of post-modernism" (78–79). Behind these words can be heard the voice of one of the most influential postmodern theorists, Jean-François Lyotard, who in the same year proclaimed that the "postmodern condition" could be described as one in which synthesizing forms and patterns—his "great" or "meta-narratives"—had gradually become exhausted, losing their organizing powers.[18]

In addition to reviews *The War against Cliché* gathers together the series of essays on classic novels Amis wrote for the *Atlantic* between 1986 and 1995 (*Don Quixote, Pride and*

Prejudice, Ulysses, Lolita, The Adventures of Augie March).
Like Virginia Woolf's *Common Reader* analyses of novels and
novelists, these essays are engaging, unpretentious, and consistently illuminating. They are animated by the idealistic belief
that great literature still has a life outside the academy—that it
is always waiting to be discovered by the willing general reader.
They also demonstrate the evergreen nature of classic books—
their power to reveal new facets to successive generations of
readers. Explaining how Nabokov is able to wrest beauty and
significance from the warped mind of his narrator Humbert
Humbert in *Lolita,* "an honest-to-God, open-and-shut sexual
deviant, displaying classic ruthlessness, guile, and (above all)
attention to detail" (472), Amis once again reveals something
about his own motives in employing blinkered first-person
narrators. "Nabokov finds an uncovenanted freedom in Humbert's dark confinement, and writes with the freshness of
discovery about parenthood, marriage, jealousy, America, art,
and love. The angle is a tortured squint, but the vistas are
boundless" (479).

The essay on *Lolita* is one of the best analyses of Nabokov's
masterpiece yet written, and as a bonus it provides a map for
readers of Amis's own dramatic monologues. When Amis calls
Lolita "a cruel book about cruelty" (473), he is describing not
only his own novel *Success,* but also the way all his novels marry
affect and theme. His extended analysis of Nabokov's relationship to his perverse, perverted narrator Humbert Humbert also
helps guide the reader of any of his first-person narratives.[19] In
addition, the essay contains a discussion of laughter that illuminates the uses to which Amis puts his own comic gift. "Human
beings laugh, if you notice, to express relief, exasperation, sto-
icism, hysteria, embarrassment, disgust, and cruelty. *Lolita* is

perhaps the funniest novel in the language, because it allows laughter its full complexity and range" (488).

By far the best known and most discussed of Amis's literary essays is "Don Juan in Hull," originally published in the July 12, 1993, issue of the *New Yorker*. Ostensibly a review of Andrew Motion's biography *Philip Larkin: A Writer's Life,* it constitutes an extended rumination on the politics of literary reputation. Amis begins by noting that in less than ten years, from his death in 1985 to 1993, Philip Larkin went from being England's "best-loved" poet to "something like a pariah." "In the early eighties, the common mind imagined Larkin as a reclusive yet twinkly drudge—bald, bespectacled, bicycle-clipped, slumped in a shabby library gaslit against the dusk. In the early nineties, we see a fuddled Scrooge and bigot, his singlet-clad form barely visible through a mephitis of alcohol, anality, and spank magazines" (153).

Amis calls the "racial hatred—and fear—in the *Selected Letters* . . . insistent . . . and very ugly" (164). But letters are "soundless cries and whispers; 'gouts of bile,' as Larkin characterized his political opinions . . . never your *last* word on any subject" (163). Although in Larkin's writings on jazz (collected in *All What Jazz*) admiration and nostalgia for black musicians are sometimes tinged with condescension, there is no public side to Larkin's prejudices." (163). The term "racism," which constitutes a subject heading in the index to Motion's biography, "suggests a system of thought, rather than an absence of thought, which would be closer to the reality—closer to the jolts and twitches of stock response. Like mood-clichés, Larkin's racial snarls were inherited propositions, shamefully unexamined, humiliatingly average. These were his 'spots of commonness,' in George Eliot's sense. He failed to shed them" (164).

Amis argues that the "unprecedentedly violent" reaction against Larkin "does not—could not—derive from literature: it derives from ideology, or from the vaguer promptings of a new ethos" (153). This ethos, which Amis's own writing at least partially embraces, is a product of progressive liberalism, derided by the reactionary press under the label "political correctness" or the diminutive abbreviation "P.C." Amis defends the impulses behind the negatively-charged phrase.

> P.C. begins with the very American—and attractive and honorable—idea that no one should feel ashamed of what he was born as, of what he is. Of what he does, of what he says, yes; but not ashamed of what he is. Viewed at its grandest, P.C. is an attempt to accelerate evolution. To speak truthfully, while that's still O.K., everybody is "racist," or has racial prejudices. This is because human beings tend to like the similar, the familiar, the familial. I am a racist; I am not as racist as my parents; my children will not be as racist as I am. (Larkin was less racist than his parents; his children would have been less racist than he.) Freedom from racial prejudice is what we hope for, down the line. Impatient with this hope, this process, P.C. seeks to get the thing done right now—in a generation. To achieve this, it will need a busy executive wing, and much invigilation. What it will actually entrain is another ton of false consciousness, to add to the megatons of false consciousness already aboard, and then a backlash. (164–65)

Only in the last three sentences here does Amis adopt the tendency of his opponents. Several times in the essay Amis's critique of the anti-Larkin campaign strikes a similarly strident note, but it never rests there.

Amis has two major aims in this essay. The first reflects his modernist/New Critical aesthetic principles: Larkin's poetry, like any artist's work, should be judged on its own merits, not on the basis of extra-artistic considerations. In light of this, the controversy surrounding Larkin's personal life is insignificant, "because only the poems matter." Nonetheless, "the spectacle holds the attention" (153), and since the spectacle has produced spectacular distortions, Amis also seeks to expose them. For most of the essay, he does so by analyzing the rhetoric of righteous sensationalism adopted by Larkin's attackers. He concludes this portion of his argument by quoting from two of Larkin's poems ("If, My Darling" and "Toads"), showing that "the recent attempts, by Motion and others, to pass judgment on Larkin look awfully green and pale compared with the self-examination of the poetry. He judges them. His indivisibility judges their hedging and trimming" (169).

Amis wisely withholds his own long acquaintance with Larkin until the final paragraphs of the essay. The poet was his father's best friend, his brother's godfather, and a frequent visitor to "the series of flats and houses where I spent my first ten years, in Swansea, South Wales" (70). It was the custom then for godfathers to give money to their godsons when they visited, and since Larkin was "a genuine miser," his performance of this ritual was always solemn ("the tip . . . would be doled out in priestly silence"). Amis writes that when he readdresses his "eager, timid, childish feelings in [Larkin's] presence, I find solidity as well as oddity, and tolerant humor (held in reserve, in case it was needed) as well as the given melancholy" (82). Like Larkin's humor, Amis's biographical evidence is held in reserve until needed. It serves as a coda to an essay that restores some measure of balance to the debate about Larkin's life and legacy.

When Amis turns his attention to the subliterary in *The War against Cliché,* his satirical demolitions provide far more pleasure per word than the books under review. His essays on Hillary Clinton, Michael Crichton, Thomas Harris, Bill McKibben, Michael Medved, Robert Parker, Richard Rhodes, Andy Warhol, and Robert Bly are bonfires of the literary vanities, in which clichéd prose goes up in flames along with the cultural delusions it embodies and reproduces. Reviewing Michael Crichton's dinosaur thriller *The Lost World,* the basis for Steven Spielberg's film *Jurassic Park II,* Amis quotes examples of egregious diction and dialogue before observing: "out there, beyond the foliage, you see herds of clichés, roaming free" (222). *The Andy Warhol Diaries* elicits near-admiration for its "virtuoso triviality" (40), but the "virtuoso vulgarity" of Harris's novel *Hannibal* earns Amis's wrath, since Harris once wrote prose that was "hard and sober and decently sad" (236). Now, however, "Harris has become a serial murderer of English sentences, and *Hannibal* is a necropolis of prose" (240).

Robert Bly's *Iron John: A Book About Men* generates the largest comic conflagration in *The War against Cliché.* Following a wickedly funny demolition of Bly's mythopoeic machismo ("it sounds like a marvellously elemental excuse for getting away with everything"), Amis turns to the feminist critique of male privilege. "Feminists have often claimed a moral equivalence for sexual and racial prejudice," he writes, adding that "there are certain affinities." He continues: "sexism is like racism: we all feel such impulses. Our parents feel them more strongly than we feel them. Our children, we hope, will feel them less strongly than we feel them." He concludes the review by noting that feminism is one important manifestation of our social evolution toward greater gender equity, "intensified by the contemporary search for role and guise and form" (9). *The War against Cliché* begins with this essay, the first review in a section titled "On Masculinity and Related Questions." Amis's placement of this section is strategic, designed to highlight his critical perspective on some of the gendered assumptions he has been accused of reproducing in his fiction.

Uncollected Essays and Reviews

Possessed of Amis's three collections of essays, profiles, and reviews, readers may believe they command a comprehensive collection of his journalism from 1971 to 2000. Indeed, the subtitle of *The War against Cliché* suggests that those literary essays and reviews not gathered in *The Moronic Inferno* will be found within its 500 pages. But as the bibliography at the end of this book makes clear, two additional volumes would be required to contain the more than fifty essays, more than sixty book reviews, and more than forty film and television review columns from this period that remain uncollected. Throughout this study I have selectively cited this material when it has been relevant to specific fictions; the remainder of this chapter can only hint at the additional bounty awaiting the interested reader.

All of the novelists that have engaged Amis's imagination over the past three decades are discussed in important essays and reviews omitted from the collections analyzed above: Ballard, Bellow, Burroughs, Joseph Heller, Nabokov, Updike, Vidal, Vonnegut, Tom Wolfe. In addition, reviews of significant nineteenth-century novels (*Bleak House, Middlemarch*) as well as twentieth-century works by major figures (W. H. Auden, Franz Kafka, Jorge Luis Borges, Yevgeny Zamyatin) are tucked away in the pages of the *Times,* the *Times Educational Supplement,* the

TLS, and the *Observer.* In some cases, these uncollected pieces reveal significant and overlooked literary affinities. Joseph Heller, for instance, whose novel *God Knows* Amis reviewed for the *Observer* in 1984 (and reprinted in *The Moronic Inferno*) held Amis's attention for twelve years, from his review of *Something Happened* in Ian Hamilton's *New Review* (1974) and an interview with Heller in the same journal (1975) to a profile of the author in the *Observer* (1979) and a review, also in the *Observer,* of *No Laughing Matter* (1986).[20] In other cases— reviews of Bellow (a uniform edition of his works up to 1984), Burroughs (*Exterminator, The Place of Dead Roads*), Nabokov (*Transparent Things, Look at the Harlequins!*)—they supplement acknowledged filiations.

Some of the omissions may have resulted from Amis's claim in the foreword to *The War against Cliché* that "enjoying being insulting is a youthful corruption of power" and that he is now surprised at how hard he could be on certain writers, especially those he felt "were trying to influence me: Roth, Mailer, Ballard" (xiv). He might have added Updike, whose 1984 collection of essays and reviews *Hugging the Shore* (which itself contains a dismissive assessment of Kingsley Amis) elicits a withering judgment. Amis quotes Updike's reference to Hemingway's quest for "a language as clean as dawn air" as a way of indicating

Updike's worst vein: the rhapsodic, sub-Lawrentian, super-sensual goo that so memorably coagulated in his worst novel, *Couples.* In the extraneous matter included in the present book, the note of hick whimsy puts in several appearances: "the dear small excited scent" of a "little blue" toy train he owned as a child; . . .[21]

Amis may now want to let such sweeping digs lie, but making this review in particular available to a wider audience would help readers account for the special animus Updike displayed toward Amis's fiction in the 1990s.[22]

Other omissions—Ballard's *Vermillion Sands* and *Low-Flying Aircraft*, Vonnegut's *Welcome to the Monkey House*—are explained by Amis's reluctance to highlight his five-year stint (1972–77) reviewing science fiction for the *Observer* (the three aforementioned books were reviewed in this column). He wrote the first twelve columns using the pseudonym "Henry Tilney" (taken from a character in Jane Austen's *Northanger Abbey*) before "coming out" in August 1974 and writing the next four-teen columns under his own name. While these columns speak to an early love of science fiction that Amis may no longer wish to acknowledge, they also help explain (and reveal sources for) his apocalyptic imagination, evident from *Dead Babies* onward. This sensibility is especially evident when Amis writes of histor-ical crises, from the nuclear threat (*Einstein's Monsters*) to the Holocaust (*Time's Arrow*) to the terrorist attacks of September 11, 2001, the latter event exciting such formulations as "the worldflash of a coming future" and "I felt species grief, then species shame, then species fear" (a formula repeated in *Koba the Dread*).[23] The columns also contain critical observations that transcend genre considerations. His review of *Vermillion Sands*, for instance, demonstrates that matters of style, not science, ani-mate his admiration for Ballard. Noting that *The Atrocity Exhi-bition* and *Crash* "had the curious distinction of being at once rarefied, pornographic, tedious, puerile, and hauntingly well written," Amis concludes: "Ballard's prose may have its faults—monotony, ornateness, a glib serendipity—but its combination of precision and sonority, its exactness in recreating the exotic, has no equivalent in post-war fiction."[24]

In his review of *The Day of Creation,* which did find its way into *The War against Cliché,* Amis reveals Ballard's influence on his social concerns as well. He calls Ballard "our leading investigator of the effects of technology, pornography, and television" (108), a distinction many readers have awarded to Amis himself. Amis's interest in pornography first took fictional form in *Dead Babies,* but two years before this novel appeared he approached the subject in two *New Statesman* columns using a second pseudonym, "Bruno Holbrook."[25] The first, "Fleshpots," is a "review" of a London strip club; the second, "Coming in Handy," analyzes pornographic magazines.[26] Both present commodified sexuality as a sad spectacle of endlessly deferred desire. Taken together with Amis's other journalism concerning sex—from his reviews of pornographic films and his profile of Madonna to his 2001 essay on the pornographic film industry in southern California—they reveal his determination to unflinchingly document the devaluation of love and eroticism in the postmodern West. As he told an interviewer in 1990, "modern life . . . is so mediated that authentic experience is much harder to find. . . . We've all got this idea of what [life] should be like—from movies, from pornography."[27]

Interesting in their own right, Amis's reviews, essays, and profiles exploring the social implications of commodified sexuality illuminate his fictional preoccupations as well. John Self and Keith Talent are both self-confessed pornography addicts, driven and deformed by mass-mediated desire. Keith Talent, whose libido is "all factoid and tabloid," represents a reductio ad absurdum of such addictions, illustrating the observation of another character in the novel that "if love was dead or gone then the self was just self, and had nothing to do all day but work on sex. Oh, and hate. And death" (298). In his fiction, Amis's male characters ferociously pursue what a character in

Success calls "socio-sexual self-betterment," but fulfillment is always beyond their reach. Trapped in the echo chamber of self-consciousness, they instead testify to the ways in which the cultural logic of capitalism militates against intimacy. As *Experience* demonstrates, Amis himself is capable of celebrating the joys of romantic love and erotic passion.[28] But as he has filtered these experiences through the genre of satire, which requires and thrives on negative emotion, they have generated fiction in which characters are agents or objects of perverse desires and designs, and sexuality is the enemy of innocence. Sexuality typically appears in this fiction as another name for narcissism, for domination, for the corruption of innocence.[29]

Amis continued brooding on pornography at the dawn of the twenty-first century. In April 2000 he visited the set of a hard-core film in southern California, interviewed several porn stars, and published his responses as "Sex in America" in the February 2001 issue of *Talk* magazine. The essay analyzes the increasingly lucrative (and acceleratingly violent) sex film industry, and likens pornography to jokes as Nietzsche defined them: "epigraphs on the deaths of feelings." Amis notes that recent porn entrepreneurs have profited by proffering a graphic severity: "That is where the market is taking us: toward heat, intensity, a frenzied athleticism. More than this, porno, it seems, is a parody of love. It therefore addresses itself to love's opposites, which are hate and death."[30] Fetishistic perversity also permeates contemporary porn, and Amis's famous candor takes him into territory where few mainstream journalists had previously dared to tread.[31] Amis suggests with wry apprehension that the exploitation of aberrant urges risks unmasking a latent attraction in the viewer: "Porno services the 'polymorphous perverse':

the near-infinite chaos of human desire. If you harbor a perversity, then sooner or later porno will identify it. You'd better hope that this doesn't happen while you're watching a film about a coprophagic pig farmer—or an undertaker" ("Sex in America," 134).

As this formulation implies, Amis has not lost his impulse toward mordant satire. In 2000 he told reporter Richard Brooks that his novel-in-progress would intertwine pornography, pedophilia—and the British Royal Family. In this sense his visit to the heart of the American pornography industry also constituted "research" for this novel[32]—as did his review of two studies of the British monarchy published in May 2002.[33] This will not be the first time that Amis's journalism has anticipated and provided insights into his fiction. Nor will it be the last. He is one of those rare contemporary writers who moves comfortably from one mode of writing to the other without experiencing dissonance or disjunction. "How did the split between creation and response occur, and when did we stop thinking that they called on the same talents?" he asks in his (as yet uncollected) review of Philip Roth's *Reading Myself and Others*.[34] To the envy of his contemporaries, Martin Amis continues to write in defiance of such arbitrary distinctions.

CHAPTER 10

The Edifice of Masculinity
Yellow Dog

Thirty years after *The Rachel Papers* announced his emergence as a major talent, Martin Amis published *Yellow Dog* (2003), his most ambitious satire since *Money* and his most uneven novel since *London Fields*.[1] It knits together much of the journalism Amis wrote in the 1990s—on the terrorist attacks of September 11, 2001, on the royal family, on gender, on incest, on pornography, on Hitler and Stalin—into a variegated web of parallel and interconnecting plots. The central thread concerns Xan Meo, an actor-writer and doting father with a criminal lineage who suffers a head injury in a seemingly random act of violence and becomes a moral desperado. His return to goodness requires a descent into a world of nightmarish compulsion that pits him against his niece, a pornographic film actress-turned-director who tempts him to embrace his darkest urges, and Joseph Andrews, a vicious East End gangster semiretired in southern California. Xan's story is a model of social realism in comparison with the two baroque narratives that unfold above and below it: a blackmail threat against an imaginary royal family headed by Henry IX, and the sexual trials and tribulations of Clint Smoker, a supremely sleazy tabloid journalist who writes a misogynistic column called "Yellow Dog" for the *Morning Lark*. Hovering over all these plots—literally and figuratively—is the story of CigAir 101, a jetliner containing the corpse of

Royce Traynor, whose sexual jealousy and vengeful rage even death has not quelled.

Yellow Dog, like all his fiction since *Einstein's Monsters,* reflects Amis's apocalyptic imagination, his quest for what he once disparagingly called the "big illumination."[2] The novel diagnoses the toxic effects of misology, misogyny, and what Amis has called "the entire edifice of masculinity"—and proposes laughter as an antidote. The four part opening chapter of *Yellow Dog,* with its fugue-like structure announcing and reflecting the pattern of the novel as a whole, audaciously orchestrates these themes. As Alan Hollinghurst noted in one of the best early assessments of the novel:

> Here is Amis in all his shifting registers, his drolleries and ferocities, his unsparing comic drive, his aesthetic dawdlings and beguilements, his wry, confident relish of his own astonishing effects. The pace is smartish, and there are three strands of narrative, each with its particular social register and verbal colour, distinct as the worlds within a Dickens novel, and with a comparable sense of latent connectedness.[3]

The "shifting registers" of the novel—as well as the proliferation of fragmentary sentences and exchanges (ellipses dot the verbal surface of the narrative like "a series of failed SOS messages," as Robert Douglas-Fairhurst has written)[4]—limn the social fragmentation and disconnectedness Amis is diagnosing. But they also express an artistic discord within the author —between satirical magnification and emotional intimacy, between the social sage and the literary stylist. This becomes particularly acute in *Yellow Dog.* In this novel the emotional center is concerned with father-daughter incest that eludes the boundaries of satire, and the book's final sections lurch from satire to thinly veiled sermonizing to sentimentality.

As he was writing *Yellow Dog,* Amis described it as "a novel about what it feels like to be living in our current era, which established itself on September 11," an era in which "everything is qualified . . . everything is contingent."[5] Amis strikes a resonant chord of contingency in the novel's first paragraph, a cascade of grammatical fragments in which the antitheses and cadences echo the opening of Charles Dickens's *A Tale of Two Cities:*

> But I go to Hollywood but I go to hospital, but you are first but you are last, but he is tall but she is small, but you stay up but you go down, but we are rich but we are poor, but they find peace but they find . . .[6]

"War" is the missing, implied comparison in this last sequence; the reader is invited to supply it—and to supply the world-historical context out of which *Yellow Dog* emerged. The novel is not directly concerned with the September 11, 2001, terrorist attacks on New York and Washington, but the atavistic beliefs that Amis sees as having motivated them are everywhere apparent. The entire novel, in fact, can be read as an anatomy of and defiant campaign against those forms of unreason that unleash the dogs of destruction. In his June 2002 essay "The Voice of the Lonely Crowd," Amis claims that "the champions of militant Islam are, of course, misogynists, woman-haters; they are also misologists—haters of reason." He goes on to indict all religious doctrine as "a massive agglutination of stock response, of clichés, of inherited and unexamined formulations."[7] Such habitual responses smother meaningful modes of human communication, producing the substitute forms of connection and exchange (revenge, violence, exploitive forms of sexuality) that are poisoning the world of *Yellow Dog*.

Illness is introduced in the novel's first paragraph with the word "hospital," and it is linked to the word "Hollywood" in a causal chain. ("Hollywood" becomes a multivalent symbol in the novel for the increasing influence of celebrity, publicity, and pornography—as well as for the "reflexive exhibitionism" they engender.)[8] In the context of the first chapter, "Hollywood" and "hospital" apply literally to Xan Meo, who is divorced and remarried, with two small daughters from the second marriage (to an American academic named Russia Tannenbaum) and older boys from the first.[9] An insubstantial actor—"he was famous, and therefore in himself there was something specious and inflationary, something bigged-up" (8)—he leaves his north London home one evening for a short walk to a Camden Town bar called the Hollywood. He wants to be in a celebratory mood—he is observing the fourth anniversary of his divorce, and the success of his short story collection *Lucozade*—but as he approaches the bar, he hears ominous sounds above him: "Sometimes a descending aeroplane can sound a warning note: one did so, up above—an organ-chord, signalling its own doom" (10). Then he senses that something has poisoned the moral atmosphere, and the color of illness makes the first of many appearances in the novel:

> He stopped and thought: that feeling again. And he sniffed the essential wrongness of the air, with its fucked-up under-taste, as if all the sequiturs had been vacuumed out of it. A yellow-world of faith and fear, and paltry ingenuity. And all of us just flying blind. (10)[10]

Soon after, Xan is attacked by two thugs who advise him between blows that he is being beaten for mentioning Joseph Andrews in print.[11] One of Xan's attackers is Mal Bale, the "cuboid" bouncer who made his first appearance in Amis's short story "The State of England."[12] Here he is the novel's only sympathetic criminal, a character whose nascent recognition that violence is a "category error" (13) obliquely expresses one of the novel's insistent themes.

Xan is taken to the hospital, where he is treated for a head injury that turns his emotional and moral world upside down. He reverts to an atavistic form of masculinity—male power and presumption run amok.[13] He lapses into the argot and attitudes of his criminal ancestors, lusts after every woman he sees, and makes macho pronouncements about everything from food ("Seafood is bullshit. I want meat" [101]) to global politics ("Pakistan is plain bullshit. They just cobbled it together on the map" [136]). As he pursues revenge against the man who had him attacked, "he could feel the violence hormones . . . squirreling around in him: voluptuous killers of pain and reality" (228). When he realizes he is becoming sexually attracted to his four-year-old daughter, Billie, it is presented as a grotesque extension of male privilege: "her power, her rights (which depended on what? Civilisation?) had seemed to disappear; and his power, his rights—they had corrosively burgeoned" (252).

Xan's disturbing thoughts about his daughter link him with Henry IX, a virtual prisoner in a "Hollywood" of media obsession and unwanted publicity. (On the second anniversary of the Queen's incapacitating fall from her horse, Henry peers out the window at his French retreat and spies "Floodlights, cranes, gantries, retractable ladders: the firefighters of the Fourth Estate" [18–19]). Henry is infantile, dull, and "senescent with ennui" (54), but his approval rate hovers at 75 percent.[14] The sections of the novel devoted to his predicaments and pronouncements contain acute parodies of royal discourse and royal handlers, but Amis knows better than to join the long line of those who have directly satirized the royal family. He invests his monarch with what Hollinghurst has called a "sublime silliness," one that allows him to voice (in an admittedly banal register) some of the novel's serious concerns.[15] Here is Henry in a passage from one of his daily letters to his fifteen-year-old daughter about her mother's comatose condition, and the way in which his own emotions have been kidnapped by the cameras:

> The presence of the media simultaneously cheapens and confuses one's sufferings. Of course I am moved, of course I am shaken. But must I display my wounds to the camera? . . . More and more viscerally do I feel that the media are base violators who poison everything they touch. (52)

As the blackmailers' revelations about the compromising video of his daughter grow more disturbing, and the bloodhounds of the tabloid press begin baying, Hal contracts a raging case of "stress excema" on his backside ("a frenzy of formication, right up the root of you" [147]). He thus ends up "in hospital" with the rest of his circle—his comatose wife; his daughter, sick of the glare of publicity and plotting abdication; and his personal attendant Brendan Urquhart-Gordon Esquire, a.k.a. "Bugger," who has chosen chastity over "the reification of his schoolyard nickname" (84) and who is heartsick with another love that dare not speak its name—for Princess Victoria herself.[16]

Amis's wordplay in these sections of the novel creates a comically skewed atmosphere of gender confusion and polymorphous perversity. When they are alone together Henry calls Gordon "Bugger," and because Henry once portrayed Hotspur in a school production of *Henry IV, Part I,* Gordon calls him "Hotty."[17] When the two men first examine a still image of the naked Victoria sent by the blackmailers, Henry sighs "Oh Bugger," and Gordon replies, "Oh Hotty." Henry and Victoria's relationship is also uncomfortably close, and it infantilizes both parties. Henry often speaks to her as if they are siblings, except that with his wife bedridden, Victoria often functions as a surrogate wife. And Henry's Chinese mistress He Zhizen—"He" is pronounced "her" and "Zhizen" could be pronounced "jejeune"—is the dominant partner in their couplings, with Henry often represented as her infant: "Now in his grandfather's gazebo he lay back helplessly, like a child being changed" (121). The implicitly incestuous nature of these and other exchanges within the royal household mirrors what Gordon considers the "incestuous and narcissistic but essentially subliminal" relationship "between the English and the Englands" (55).

Gordon and the king spend much of their time immersed in "fantasies of protection" (135) in relation to Victoria, but like Russia Tannenbaum, she is a living repudiation of patriarchal dominance and control. Their patronizing and ineffectual efforts are no match for her own "robust indignation": "There was nothing regal in it—on the contrary, there was something severely republican and everywoman in her steep frown, her straight neck" (155). She is also a rationalist and a skeptic; after she praises Muslims, who she thinks "have much more feeling for each other than Christians," Gordon adopts his most obsequious third-person tone: "is the Princess . . . feeling herself 'drawn' to Mecca?" She replies "God no," adding, "I don't *think* I've got any faith in me. I just find it riveting" (153). Then

Henry intervenes, oblivious to the fact that she is not seriously considering conversion: "I expect you'd go a bit blank, my precious, if I told you to wear a uh, black *tepee* for the rest of your days" (154). Her response reveals that she is also a nascent feminist: "But think of the agonies that Western women go through because of their looks. The constant worries and comparisons. It's forced on you too. This stupid vanity is forced on you" (154). In a key exchange with Gordon, after she is informed of the still images showing her naked in the "Yellow House" (part of a vacation chateau in Nice), Victoria contemptuously rejects the patriarchal assumption that women are to be judged and granted moral dispensation by men:

> "He will forgive you anything and everything, you may be sure. Without a second thought. And so will I. He will always protect you. And so will I."
>
> "Forgive me?" she said. With the words evenly stressed, he thought, as he dropped her hand and backed away. (156)

Near the end of the novel, when Henry accedes to Victoria's desire for abdication, he intimates that this will involve more than releasing his paternalistic hold on Victoria: "The people will have to grow up. I'll have to grow up. And if I can grow up, *they* can grow up. And then *she* can grow up" (325).

Gordon also exercises a paternalistic hold on Victoria; one of his duties involves screening the salacious and sometimes threatening letters the Princess receives, letters that come from "the world of onanistic longing—and coarse sentimentality, and impotent sadism" (152). This precisely describes the readers of the *Morning Lark,* as well as the paper's guiding spirit, Clint Smoker.[18] Clint is spectacularly squalid, from his nostril ring shaped like a pair of handcuffs to his apartment in "Foulness, near Southend," which has long been reduced to "a condition of untouchable sordor" and is "saturated with pornography in all its forms" (30). His hyper-jaundiced view of the world is reflected not only in his complexion but in his workplace, which is

> turbid with emanations, spores, allergies. Everyone at the *Lark* was always sneezing, sniffing, coughing, yawning, retching. They knew they felt sick, but didn't know they felt sick because they worked in a certain kind of building: they thought they felt sick because of what they did in it all day long. . . . Today the sick building gave off an olive glow; a thin rain had fallen, and its face seemed to be dotted with sweat. (28–29)

Amis's rendering of Clint Smoker reveals the author's deep affinity with Dickens, especially what James Wood has called his "interest in grotesque portraiture and loud names, and in character as caricature, a vivid blot of essence."[19] In contrast to the precious style that Amis often deploys to parody royal-speak, the Clint sections of the novel read like a fever-dream of gutter press excess. The *Lark*, which evokes an actual London tabloid called the *Daily Sport*, boasts a vast all-male readership that its editorial staff refers to as "wankers"—British slang for masturbators. Breasts always trump breaking news ("no global cataclysm had yet the power to push the pin-up off the front page" [25]), and its writers transform all news into narratives of sexual exhibitionism, violence, or humiliation. While everyone at the paper is growing wealthy from the *Lark*'s ancillary enterprises—hardcore websites and sexlines so popular they "had caused the collapse of the local telephone network" (25)—sports coverage still dominates the paper's "news" pages. Not only does the *Lark* pay disgraced athletes for the rights to their stories, it contracts with them in advance and arranges for them to disgrace themselves. When the reader first meets Clint he is setting up an "exclusive" tryst between *Lark* staffer (and former pornographic actress) Donna Strange and a washed up soccer player named Ainsley Car. Clint also arranges to have Car's wife Beryl break in on this encounter and then to have Car beat her. In Clint's enthusiastic words: "we'll have Donna's tits and arse all over pages one to five, Beryl's black eyes all over pages five to ten, plus an eight-page pullout soul-searcher from the man himself, Ainsley Car" (45). Clint seals this deal with Car at a local restaurant. When the drunken Car asks about his fee, and Clint answers with a "jolting sum," Car inexplicably erupts in a stream of post-9/11 consciousness that links the *Lark*'s orchestration of premeditated violence with another, more catastrophic kind:

"*All passengers to the rear of the plane! . . . Stam back! Don't no one go near! Fuck amfrax—this geezer's got hepatitis G an an an-grenade up his arse!* OH MY GOD! IT'S THE TOWER! IT'S BIG BEN, IT'S OLD TOM, IT'S BUCK PAL! NO! THE UMFINKABLE! OH MY GOD, WE'RE ALL GONNA—" (45)

Amis uses Car and several *Morning Lark* editorial discussions to seriocomically represent many of the cultural anxieties spawned by the September 11 attacks. At one point Clint and his editor Desmond Heaf are discussing a bungled plot against the king by an extremist group called the "Legion of the Pure," whose "dirty bomb" blows up in an airport car park before the group can send it into the skies. Heaf asks, "So what was in this 'dirty bomb'?" Clint's answer, while reassuring on one level (this is clearly a group without access to high-tech bioterror labs), packs several plausible scenarios into a funny yet painful Pandora's box of a sentence: "Radioactive medical waste, Chief, plus ringworm, West Nile virus, liquid gangrene, and a cladding of mad cow" (160).

Although the Legion's dirty bomb never becomes airborne, CigAir 101 contains a menacing cargo of its own, which becomes a literally overarching metaphor for the malign and corrosive male energies in the novel. Bulletins on the airliner's troubled flight from England to America (part cockpit transcript, part disaster narrative) punctuate seven of the novel's eleven chapters, and they grow increasingly dire. Reynolds Traynor is on board, returning the corpse of her husband from England to America. She and the Hemingwayesque lead pilot, John Macmanaman, have been involved in a long-term affair, and they are both anticipating a future together. But her dead husband seems determined to replicate what Amis, in *Koba the Dread,* claims with regards to Joseph Stalin—that "he could kill people violently even from his coffin" (231). When atmospheric turbulence ("a beast of the upper air") loosens Royce Traynor's coffin from its position in the cargo hold, the corpse becomes preternaturally armed and dangerous: "He rolled on his side and pitched up against a rank of canisters marked HAZMAT (Hazardous Material): Class B and Class C-3 dynamite propellants and rocket motors for fighter-aircraft ejection seats" (131). The dead Traynor becomes increasingly animated as the flight continues—baring his teeth, edging toward the cargo door —like some spectral embodiment of sexual jealousy and vengeance.[20] Amis has said that male violence is "a kind of relief from humiliation; the human being, being as he is, always has to be answered, despite the proven inability of violence to ever solve anything."[21] In one of the last "101 Heavy" sections of the novel, Royce Traynor is preparing his final statement:

> Decompression, explosive decompression, was what he wanted to bring about, and the collapse, the catastrophic strangulation, of the cabin floor, with all its tubes and veins and arteries. Most proximately, the blown door would mean his own escape (he would be the first to go), his martyrdom, after death. (281)

The language of this passage links Traynor with a lengthening line of actual suicide bombers and suicide pilots.

By Part III of the novel, all four the novel's plots are moving west across America. CigAir 101 never reaches its destination, but the novel's three major plots converge in greater Los Angeles. Xan and Clint both travel to the San Sebastiano Valley, (a.k.a. "Little Hollywood," "Lovetown," "Sextown," "Fucktown"), drawn into the nexus of crime and debased sexuality whose presiding spirit is Joseph Andrews, a high-end producer in the pornographic film industry.[22] Each has arrived with a dual purpose. Xan has discovered that Joseph Andrews ordered him beaten, and he flies west seeking revenge. His trip is facilitated by his agent, who gets him a job "acting" in *Crown Sugar,* one of the industry's many "Anglophile" pornographic films. As his agent puts it, "what they like to do now is hire mainstream British actors to play so-called character parts" (250) in films with titles like *Anne of a Thousand Lays, Fallstiff, King Rear, Pump and Circumstance,* and an ongoing series of *Princess Lolita* films featuring a Princess Victoria look-alike. Such films are proliferating now that still images of the bare-breasted

Princess, hijacked from the blackmailer's video and circulated on the Internet, have appeared in the pages of the *Lark*. Clint Smoker arrives in town to report on this phenomenon and to conduct admiring interviews with the likes of Dork Bogarde and Hick Johnsonson. But he is also seeking relief from his "little problem" by enrolling in the "San Sebastiano Academy for Men of Compact Intromission." Clint hopes to improve his sexual performance because he has become involved in an increasingly intimate correspondence with a lexically-challenged "cyberpal" who sends him reassuring text messages like this one: "it's not size th@ m@ters, clint. It's love th@ m@ters" (103). Gordon doesn't physically travel to "Little Hollywood," but he immerses himself in its inverted world by watching a videotape of *Princess Lolita,* hoping for clues about the identity of the blackmailers. As he watches the tape, he realizes "my God: pornography turned the world upside down. You gave your head away, and what your mind liked no longer mattered; now the animal parts were in the driving seat—and tall in the saddle" (257). Gordon emerges from this experience "with a sense of himself revised dramatically downward" (258).

Xan spends much of his time in "Little Hollywood" in the company of his cousin Cora Susan, known in the industry as Karla White. She is directing *Crown Sugar,* and she is also helping Joseph Andrews carry out his vendetta against Xan. Virtually every Amis novel contains a radical nihilist, and Cora, who was raped by her father "between the age of six and nine, inclusive," (235) encourages Xan to embrace his inner atavist:

> "Look at the future. Us, us victims, we're not so frightened and repelled by the way the world is now: the end of normalcy. We always knew there was no moral order. So sleep with Billie, and introduce her to the void." (236)

Xan's conversations and entanglements with Cora (she attempts to seduce him so he will betray Russia and destroy his marriage) constitute an extended exploration of incest, linked to the novel's central theme because it defines the extreme limit of male malignity. This strand of the novel draws from both *Experience* and *Koba the Dread*, especially Amis's observation in *Koba* that "given total power over another, the human being will find that his thoughts turn to torture" (201).[23]

In the chapter that introduces him, Joseph Andrews's thoughts have already embraced torture: he has captured a motorist who insulted him and has been assaulting him for nearly a week with an assortment of "skewers" and "chisels." Throughout much of his narrative, Joseph is dictating his memoirs into a tape recorder, and these passages, which parody the hard-man autobiographies turned out by such British gangsters as Tony Parker and "Mad" Frankie Fraser, demonstrate Amis's remarkable facility at literary ventriloquism.[24] Much of Joseph's dramatic monologue details his enthusiasm for "doing" his associates' women, which reveals his sexual pathology and the ways in which his story contributes to the novel's thematic design. Here is Joseph recording (but not understanding) a conversation with his favorite lieutenant, Keith the Snake, in which Keith makes him an offer, then psychoanalyzes him on the fly: "Hey Jo. You want to stuff my bird so you can pretend you're me?" "Oi." "Hey Jo. You want to stuff my bird so you can pretend you're *her*?" . . . Well it was all off then. [Click] One of them uh, circular arguments. Blah blah blah (264). There is a resonant irony in Joseph's reference to "circular arguments" here, since virtually all the males in the novel are bent on (and by) reprisal and revenge. These endless and typically violent arguments constitute what Robert-Douglas

Fairhurst has called "pathological versions of the ordinary human need for reciprocity and exchange."[25]

After Xan has his final confrontation with Joseph—when he discovers Joseph, not Mick Meo, is his biological father—Amis spells out Joseph's pathology in a conversation Xan has with Cora: "He wants to have them so he does them. And has their wives." "Mm," replies Cora. "Hence the love of pain: he's correcting himself for it" (305). Besides betraying a lack of confidence in the reader's discernment, this exchange echoes Amis's analysis of fascist violence in *Koba the Dread:*

> Nazism, and also Bolshevism, exude the confusions of crypto-homosexuality, homosexuality enciphered and unacknowledged—the cult of hardness, with all the female qualities programmatically suppressed. Heterosexuality has clarity, and homosexuality has clarity; but much violence waits in the area in between. (132)

Joseph reveals in his memoirs that he was twice engaged, "but by an unfortunate coincidence, both of them've gone and took they own lives" (262). This coincidence echoes another: Russia Tannenbaum, "author of a university-press bestseller about the children of tyrants" (90), gives a lecture in Munich about "Geli Raubal and Eva Braun," two women in Hitler's life who famously committed suicide.

Given Joseph's abiding animus toward women, and given Amis's moral sympathies in the novel, it will come as no surprise that a violent death awaits Joseph at novel's end. What is surprising is that a novel dedicated to decentering masculinity and male power should end with so much moralizing by the novel's redeemed patriarch. Xan apologizes for this tendency—in a letter he composes to Russia on his flight back to England—by acknowledging that "general thoughts are not my strength" (306). But he offers them anyway, in flat-footed prose, all the while cribbing from a far wittier version of the ideas—Amis's essay on the poet Robert Bly and his book *Iron John*.[26] He notes that "men were in power for five million years," and while they now share it with women (at least in the West), "unconsciously, and not for long at a time, men miss women being tractable, and women miss men being decisive; but we can't *say* that." He continues: "it will take a century to work off those five billennia and consolidate the change. We pretend it is, but the change isn't yet intact and entire" (307). As this chapter has demonstrated, the thematic structure of *Yellow Dog* is heavily braced by "general thoughts," and the last thing the novel needs is an ending that spells them out.

Later, Xan imagines calling Cora with "avuncular advice" that suggests his own work of consolidation has only just begun: "it sounds soft, and trite—but have a baby. When I look at you I always look for your children. That's what your breasts are looking for too: they're looking for your children" (335). Unless this is meant to reflect Xan's persistent atavism, it is a serious artistic misstep. Too often in Amis's writing generalizations about the "universal" rely on culturally conditioned and insufficiently interrogated assumptions about essential differences between the sexes. This passage, which implies that women are by nature maternal, seems egregiously out of place in a novel whose most basic units of discourse—character names—intentionally blur gender distinctions. Female characters have names like "Russia," "He," and "Billie," and male characters have names such as "Xan" and "And." Xan's "general thoughts" dissipate the radical impulses within the novel's assault on the "edifice of masculinity."

When he is not lapsing from the picture to the diagram, Amis's imagery and figurative language convey his themes to powerful effect. This ranges from the way that green and yellow hues—the colors of envy and jaundice—spread throughout the narrative fabric like a stain, to the myriad birds, animals, and insects that populate its pages and offer a vivid counterpoint to the main action. These two patterns often converge, as when Clint Smoker is consumed with murderous rage and drives through sidestreets looking for his enemy, "buzzing round culs-de-sac like a hornet in a jamjar" (327). A much more complex commingling occurs when Xan Meo recalls a childhood encounter with a literal yellow dog in the novel's penultimate chapter. Xan has just learned that Joseph Andrews is dead, and this triggers a memory from Xan's childhood, when a sound brought him into the shed in his backyard: "The sound had a rhythm, like a murderous act of love: a grunt, then a muffled, slushy impact or convergence, then an answering moan. And over and above it the crying, the choric wail of the yellow dog" (337). In the shed he discovers Mick Meo beating Joseph Andrews, and he now realizes what he didn't then: Mick was revenging himself on Joseph because Joseph had told him that he was Xan's father (301–2). This memory entrains other memories of animalistic and animal encounters Xan witnessed in the backyard—his sister with a boyfriend "up against the wheelless van with her skirt round her waist"; a series of dogs "stoically stuck together in coition and awaiting the deliverance of the bucket"; "the hectic hen coming running to the screeching cock" (337).

This backyard, where Xan's "sentimental understanding had so far been formed" (337), represents the atavistic impulses and attitudes human beings throw off to become civilized.[27] The

last paragraph of this chapter, in which Xan remembers Mick
Meo turning on him and throwing him out of the shed after Xan
has interrupted his attack, transforms the title of the novel from
a label for a scurrilous journalist to a multivalent symbol:

> While it happened (and he didn't remember much: at one
> point he was in mid-air, and taking an intense interest in the
> nature and texture of his destination) you could hear the yel-
> low dog. Whining, weeping, and rolling its head as if to ease
> an aching neck, working its shoulders, trying to free itself of
> this thing—this thing on its back. (337)

This yellow dog is female, and "this thing" is literally the male
dog she is trying to shake off. But similar struggles—to shake off
the past, the patriarchy, sexual debasement, malignant cycles of
reprisal and revenge—have been enacted throughout the novel,
most obviously by Xan Meo. They are also enacted by Russia
Tannenbaum, Princess Victoria, the passengers of Flight 101,
and even the planet itself, which whips up a "rodeo of wind" at
one point: "the earth trying to throw its riders" (9).

Xan's story began with a ride to hospital—a ride that takes
him to his primitive self—in an ambulance whose siren pierced
the air with "choric howls of electrified distress" (3). The word
"choric," sounding both at the beginning and near the end of
Yellow Dog, recalls a passage in *Experience,* a passage which
reminds the reader that for Amis not everything that is "primitive" in humans is destructive. When Fernanda, Amis's first
daughter by his second wife, was born her heart briefly stopped
beating, "and from then on all thoughts were primitive and
choric—just a steady whine for mercy. But my faith in the cunning of babies was strong" (364). In the last chapter of *Yellow*

Dog, Amis places a great deal of faith in the "cunning of babies," trusting they will justify one last hard turn in the novel, this one from poetic peroration to sentimental coda. Xan's youngest daughter Sophie has just stood up on her own for the first time, and soon after she takes an inevitable tumble:

> As . . . he sat comforting her on the sofa, he looked at the lashes of her eyes, their tear-freshened zigzag—and he remembered her birth, and the zigzag, the frantic scribble of the heart-monitor as Sophie toiled within. . . . And minutes later, when Sophie came, for the first time in his life he was contemplating the human vulva with a sanity that knew no blindspots. . . . She slipped away from him now and started moving round the room, from handhold to handhold. And he thought, with numb tautology: in this project of their protection, the hopelessly painful thing, when they were small, was their size, their small size, their very small size. (339)

The thematic implications of this passage are unmistakable: Sophie ("Sophia" is Greek for "wisdom") has helped Xan regain his moral vision and reclaim his humanity. Whether it succeeds in transcending its origins in Amis's sentimental education is for the reader to decide.[28]

Notes

Chapter 1—Understanding Martin Amis

1. Martin Amis, *Experience: A Memoir* (London: Jonathan Cape, 2000) 7.

2. This autobiographical impulse continued in Martin Amis, *Koba the Dread: Laughter and the Twenty Million* (London: Jonathan Cape, 2002); see chapter 7.

3. For more on the autobiographical sources of the lost child in Amis's fiction, see Maureen Freely, "A Voyage around My Daughter," *Observer,* 23 June 1996, 6. Amis has acknowledged that Freely led him to see "what perhaps no writer should ever see: the place in the unconscious where my novels come from." See *Experience,* 7, 280.

4. Quoted by Stephen Moss in "After the Storm," *Guardian,* 3 October 1998, 22.

5. See especially Victoria Glendinning, "The Best of You Is Still Here and I Still Have It," *Daily Telegraph,* 20 May 2000, 3; James Wood, "The Young Turk," *Guardian,* 20 May 2000, 8; Michiko Kakutani, "For Writers, Father and Son, Out of Conflict Grew Love," *New York Times,* 23 May 2000; David Lodge, "Putting Down Good Words," *Times Literary Supplement,* 26 May 2000, 25–26; John Banville, "Sons and Lovers," *Irish Times,* 27 May 2000, 67; John Lanchester, "Be Interesting!" *London Review of Books,* 6 July 2000, 3–6. For a minority report see John Leonard, "His Father's Son," *New York Times Book Review,* 28 May 28 2000, 6.

6. Martin Amis, "A?" Review of *Abba Abba,* by Anthony Burgess, *New Statesman,* 17 June 1977, 821.

7. Quoted by John Haffenden in "Martin Amis," *Novelists in Interview* (London: Methuen, 1985) 16. Amis continues: "Mere psychological truth in a novel doesn't seem to me all that valuable a

commodity. I would sooner let the words prompt me, rather than what I am actually representing."

8. Adam Mars-Jones, "Fireworks at the Funeral," *Times Literary Supplement,* 1 May 1987, 457.

9. Quoted by Jason Cowley in "Portrait: Martin Amis," *Prospect,* August/September 1997, 53.

10. Martin Amis, "Fear and Loathing," *Guardian,* 18 September 18 2001, G2. Amis returned to this subject in his essay "The Voice of the Lonely Crowd," *Guardian Review,* 2 June 2002, 4–6, asserting that in the hours following the September 11 attacks "all the writers on earth were reluctantly considering a change of occupation." He goes on to elevate writers above every other social group, preposterously asserting that they are free from the ideological motivations that characterize religious believers, the politically committed, and other members of what he calls "the lonely crowd."

11. John Lanchester, "Be Interesting!" 5.

12. John Updike, "Jake and Lolly Opt Out," in *Hugging the Shore: Essays and Criticism* (New York: Knopf, 1983), 300. The review begins: "If the postwar English novel figures on the international stage as winsomely trivial, Kingsley Amis must bear part of the blame." In *Experience,* Martin Amis recounts asking his father if he had read this review (94), and later quotes from it (177). Martin Amis had previously noted that many of the pieces exhibit the American author's "worst vein: the rhapsodic, sub-Lawrentian, supersensual goo that so memorably coagulated in his worst novel, *Couples*" ("Christian Gentleman," review of *Hugging the Shore, Observer,* 15 January 1984, 48). Unaccountably, Amis left this review out of his collection *The War against Cliché: Essays and Reviews, 1971–2000* (London: Jonathan Cape, 2001), even though he includes his reviews of Updike's two other essay collections, *Picked Up Pieces* and *Odd Jobs: Essays and Criticism.*

13. Adam Mars-Jones, "Looking on the Blight Side," *Times Literary Supplement,* 24 March 1995, 19. Amis has said that "there are plenty of people writing novels about subtle gradations within one

mind," adding that "comedy comes into the gap that you create between people when you force them apart, when you make the division extreme . . . that's what I'm always in search of—the comedy of the disparity" ("Eleanor Wachtel with Martin Amis," *Malahat Review,* March 1996, 56). For the best sustained critique of Amis's insistent ironizing, see James Wood, "Martin Amis: The English Imprisonment," *The Broken Estate: Essays on Literature and Belief* (London: Jonathan Cape, 1999), 186–99.

14. "It was very shocking," Amis said of his parents' divorce. "A complete surprise. Numbness. It was in the days when not everyone's parents were divorced. Had it happened a few years later, I'd have probably thought: 'About time, too. Very feeble not to have divorced parents.' But I felt social shame" ("Martin Amis: Middle Age Is Drawing the Poison from His Pen," *Times* (London), 14 May 2000, 15). Kingsley married Elizabeth Jane Howard in 1962, but in 1980 this marriage also ended. Both marriages, and both breakups, are recounted in *Experience;* see especially 28, 105–6, 142–47, 214–16.

15. In *The Information,* the protagonist Richard Tull experiences a similar reversal when his marriage breaks up and he imagines his two young sons caring for him. The last bedtime story he tells his sons is one "in which they bravely rescued their daddy—rescued him, and then tended to his wounds" (475). Richard had earlier thought of the day when his wife, Gina, would ask him to leave, and "the children will have to come to love us separately" (448); now as he leaves the sleeping boys, they "looked like figures on a battlefield, arrested, abandoned" (476).

16. For his experience at the most important of these, the "Sussex Tutors" in Brighton, see *Experience,* 9–11, 19–21, 37–38, 55–57, 74–75, and 107–9. After passing his entrance exams, Amis recounts in *Experience* that he wrote Howard to thank her for "quite literally getting me into Oxford. Had you not favored my education with your interest and sagacity, I would now be a 3–O-levelled wretch with little to commend me" (150). Later in *Experience* he

writes of Howard: "She was generous, affectionate and resourceful; she salvaged my schooling and I owe her an unknowable debt for that. . . . As far as I am concerned she is, with Iris Murdoch, the most interesting female writer of her generation" (215).

17. Quoted by Charles Michener in "Britain's Brat of Letters," *Esquire,* January 1987, 110.

18. For more (from Amis) on his tenure at the *TLS,* see "The Coming of the Signature," *Times Literary Supplement,* 17 January 1992, 18; and *Experience* 34–35, 191. See also Derwent May, *Critical Times: The History of the 'Times Literary Supplement'* (New York: Harper Collins, 2001), 421.

19. Quoted by Vanessa Thorpe in "Daddy Dearest," *Observer,* 16 April 2000, 27.

20. See Ian Hamilton, ed., *The New Review Anthology* (London: Heinemann, 1985).

21. Quoted by Ian Parker in "Auden's Heir," *New Yorker,* 25 July 1994, 65. For more on the politics of this trio, see *Experience,* 191–92, 254–60; and *Koba the Dread,* 21–25, 245–54. For more on the *New Statesman* see the introduction to Christopher Hitchens, *Lines of Dissent: Writing from the New Statesman, 1913–1988* (London: Verso, 1988), 1–15. It is worth noting that the *New Statesman*'s reviews of Amis's work have been mainly negative since the late 1980s; they often seem indistinguishable from the hostile notices regularly published in the conservative weekly the *Spectator.*

22. Quoted by Michael Shnayerson in "Famous Amis," *Vanity Fair,* May 1995, 160.

23. Before he severed all ties with the *Times* after the paper published excerpts from Eric Jacobs's diary of Kingsley's last days (against the Amis family wishes), Amis was handsomely rewarded for appearing in its pages—£36,000 for the six book reviews he wrote for the *Sunday Times* between 10 September 1995 and 17 March 1996 (see bibliography for complete list).

24. *Talk,* edited by his longtime friend and former lover Tina Brown (who had earlier edited *Vanity Fair* and the *New Yorker*)

began publishing in September 1999. It ceased publication in January 2002. For more on the Amis-Brown relationship, see *Experience* 27, 49–50, 306n, and Judy Bachrach, *Tina and Harry Come to America: Tina Brown, Harry Evans, and the Uses of Power* (New York: Free Press, 2001).

25. In *Experience* Amis also had this to say about *The Rachel Papers* and the role of nepotism in his early career: "The single run was so tiny that an individual copy of the novel is now worth twice the original advance. For the record: Pat Kavanagh, and my chief publisher, Tom Maschler, also handled my father, and I had known both of them since youth. So, yes, the whole thing was tacitly nepotic" (25).

26. Quoted by Mira Stout in "Down London's Mean Streets," *New York Times Magazine,* 4 February 1990, 48.

27. David Flusfeder, "The Esquire Interview: Martin Amis," *Esquire,* October 1977, 23. Amis's influence on British writers who emerged in the 1980s and 1990s is one sign of this status. Elaine Showalter describes a fictional subgenre of "lad-lit" stretching from Kingsley to Martin Amis and beyond, and notes that the younger Amis has influenced such writers as Nick Hornby, Will Self, Stephen Fry, Ardal O'Hanlon, David Baddiel, Alexei Sayle, and Ben Elton. See "They Think It's All Over," *New Statesman,* 12 August 2002, 24–26; rpt. as "Ladlit," in *On Modern British Fiction,* ed. Zachary Leader (Oxford: Oxford University Press, 2002), 60–76.

28. Zachary Leader, ed., *The Letters of Kingsley Amis* (New York: Harper Collins, 2000), 871 (Kingsley to Larkin, 10 May 1979); 674–75 (Kingsley to Elizabeth Jane Howard, 13 August 1973); 951 (Kingsley to Larkin, 3 August 1982); and 969 (Kingsley to Larkin, 8 February 1984).

29. Since Kingsley's death, Martin has won the James Tait Black Memorial Prize for *Experience* and the Books Critics Circle Award for his collection *The War against Cliché.*

30. Craig Raine, who has been a friend since they met at Oxford in the late 1960s, insists Amis's media image is a myth: "As a person

he is very warm and has a real gift for friendship. He's careless but he's loyal. . . . He doesn't loll on his laurels or try to be grand—he's a great entertainer, he makes you laugh" (quoted by Stephen Moss in "After the Storm," 22).

31. Quoted by Jonathan Wilson in "A Very English Story," *New Yorker*, 6 March 1995, 99.

32. Chris Dignan, "Amis, Author With £20,000 Teeth, Has £106 Wedding," *Sunday Times* (London), 5 July 1998, 3. Martin and Isabel have had two daughters, Fernanda, born in 1996, and Clio, born in 1999.

33. See especially Harold Bloom, *The Anxiety of Influence: A Theory of Poetry* (New York: Oxford, 1973); *A Map of Misreading* (New York: Oxford, 1975); and *Poetry and Repression: From Blake to Stevens* (New Haven: Yale, 1976). Because Bloom's theory is transhistorical and mythic in emphasis, it obscures the generational and historically specific nature of the literary tension between Kingsley and Martin. Other influential discussions of writers' relationships to their predecessors include T. S. Eliot's 1917 essay "Tradition and the Individual Talent," reprinted in *The Sacred Wood: Essays on Poetry and Criticism* (London: Methuen, 1920), 1–18; George Levine's *The Realistic Imagination: English Fiction from Frankenstein to Lady Chatterley* (Chicago: University of Chicago Press, 1981); and Jerome Meckier's *Hidden Rivalries in Victorian Fiction* (Lexington: University Press of Kentucky, 1987).

34. Michener, "Britain's Brat," 110.

35. "Martin Amis," in *1990 Current Biography Yearbook*, ed. Charles Moritz (New York: H. W. Wilson, 1990), 20.

36. Lewis Burke Frumkes, "A Conversation with Martin Amis," *Writer*, October 2000, 14. See also Amis, *Experience*, 23–24.

37. Michener, "Britain's Brat," 110.

38. Barnes's assessment is quoted in Stout, "Down London's Mean Streets," 35; Hitchens claimed that Kingsley and Martin had "the most enviable father-son relationship I'd ever seen" (Christopher Hitchens, "Kingsley Amis and 'Little Shit' Martin," *Evening Standard*, 8 May 2000, 23).

39. Martin Amis, "Buy My Book, Please," *New Yorker,* 26 June and 3 July 1995, 97; Flusfeder, "The Esquire Interview," 29. It is also worth noting that in *Experience,* after detailing Kingsley's stinginess, Martin writes that with his own children "I intend to be more liberal in my praise" (25).

40. This quest has powerful extra-literary sources. In *Experience,* Amis recounts a conversation with Saul Bellow following Kingsley's death in which he said "You'll have to be my father now." He adds: "It worked, and still works. As long as you're alive I'll never feel fatherless" (360). As James Wolcott has written about this passage, "Martin Amis is a little old to be Brandon de Wilde chasing after Shane" ("The Amis Papers," *Vanity Fair,* July 2000, 181).

41. In *Experience,* Martin notes that Kingsley, "despite his real admiration for Iris Murdoch, Elizabeth Taylor and Elizabeth Jane Howard, . . . regarded women's writing as essentially occult. . . . Nabokov (no soulmate of Kingsley's) also confessed to being exclusively 'homosexual' in his literary tastes" (31).

42. David Lodge, *After Bakhtin: Essays on Fiction and Criticism* (London: Routledge, 1990), 26.

43. Kingsley Amis, *Lucky Jim* (Harmondsworth: Penguin, 1978), 128.

44. Susan Morrison, "The Wit and Fury of Martin Amis," *Rolling Stone,* 17 May 1990, 102. Amis explains and analyzes the political differences between himself and his father most fully in *Koba the Dread.* For more on the political and aesthetic relationship between Martin and Kingsley, see Gavin Keulks, *Father and Son: Kingsley Amis, Martin Amis, and the British Novel since 1950* (Madison: University of Wisconsin Press, 2003).

45. Quoted by Patrick McGrath in "Interview with Martin Amis," *Bomb,* winter 1987, 28; rpt. in *Bomb Interviews,* ed. Betsy Sussler (San Francisco: City Lights Books, 1992), 194.

46. Theodor Adorno and Max Horkheimer, *Dialectic of Enlightenment,* trans. John Cumming (New York: Herder and Herder, 1972), 179.

47. Ibid., 4, 6.

48. Sven Birkerts, "Postmodernism: Bumper-Sticker Culture," in *American Energies* (New York: William Morrow, 1992), 21–23.

49. Martin Amis, "Don Juan in Hull," *New Yorker*, 12 July 1993, 82; rpt. as "The Ending: Don Juan in Hull," in *The War against Cliché*, 471–90.

50. Quoted by Susan Morrison in "The Wit and Fury," 101.

51. Quoted by Haffenden in "Martin Amis," 5.

52. Michel Foucault, *The History of Sexuality, Volume I: An Introduction* (Harmondsworth: Penguin, 1981). Foucault posits a continually fluctuating cultural unconscious which directs and determines class distinctions, truth value, gender relations, and the nature of all knowledge. Foucauldian analysis itself is, of course, indebted to psychoanalytic notions of unconscious determination and schemes of unconscious mechanisms, especially as they have been reinterpreted by Jacques Lacan. See especially Jacques Lacan, *Écrits: A Selection*, trans. Alan Sheridan (New York: Norton, 1977), *The Language of the Self: The Function of Language in Psychoanalysis*, trans. Anthony Wilden (Baltimore: Johns Hopkins University Press, 1968). Following Juliet Mitchell's *Psychoanalysis and Feminism: Freud, Reich, Laing, and Women* (New York: Vintage Books, 1975) and *Feminine Sexuality: Jacques Lacan and the Ecole Freudienne*, ed. Mitchell with Jacqueline Rose (London: Macmillan, 1982) feminist theorists have applied Lacanian insights to gender issues. Amis's career-long preoccupation with masculinity—especially as it has been shaped/misshaped by late capitalism—makes his work particularly amenable to feminist and gender analysis.

53. Martin Amis, *The War against Cliché*, 467; *Experience*, 121; "A Tale of Two Novels," *Observer*, 19 October 1980, 27.

54. Jameson, Frederic. *Postmodernism; or, The Cultural Logic of Late Capitalism* (Durham, N.C.: Duke University Press, 1992).

55. Among the former, Mark Sanderson is representative; see "The Amis Way of Saying Things," *Sunday Telegraph*, 8 April 2001, 11. John Fuller is an example of the latter; see "Yob Action," *Village Voice*, 1 December 1987, 66.

56. Linda Hutcheon, "Postmodernism," in *Encyclopedia of Contemporary Literary Theory,* ed. Irena R. Makaryk (Toronto: University of Toronto Press, 1993), 612.

57. Quoted by Susan Morrison in "The Wit and Fury," 99.

58. Quoted by Haffenden in "Martin Amis," 9–10.

59. Quoted by McGrath in "Interview," 193.

60. Adam Mars-Jones, "Looking on the Blight Side," 19.

61. Ibid., 19.

62. See especially Mikhail Bakhtin, "Discourse in the Novel," in *The Dialogic Imagination,* trans. Caryl Emerson and Michael Holquist (Austin: University of Texas Press, 1981), 259–422.

63. Lawrence, D. H. *The Rainbow* (New York: Viking, 1975), 1–2.

Chapter 2—Nasty Things Are Funny

1. Amis himself indicted his first two novels in these terms: "I am no great admirer of my first novel, or indeed of my second, regarding them as a mixture of clumsy apprenticeship and unwarranted showing off" ("A Tale of Two Novels," *Observer,* 19 October 1980, 26). Ironically, they were the first of his novels to be adapted for the screen—*The Rachel Papers* in 1989 (directed by Damian Harris, and starring A-list actors James Spader, Ione Skye, Jonathan Pryce, and Dexter Fletcher as Charles); *Dead Babies* in 2000 (directed by first-timer William Marsh, and released straight to video in the United States under the title *Mood Swingers*). The first received middling reviews, the second was excoriated by everyone but Martin Amis.

2. Amis has called his first three novels "not antifeminist but prefeminist" (Susan Morrison, "The Wit and Fury," 101).

3. Adam Phillips, "Cloud Cover," *London Review of Books,* 16 October 1997, 3.

4. Henri Bergson, *Laughter: An Essay on the Meaning of the Comic,* trans. Cloudesley Brereton and Fred Rothwell (London: Macmillan, 1911).

5. Quoted by Susan Morrison in "The Wit and Fury," 17 May 1990, 101. In *Experience*, Amis complains that in his review of *The Rachel Papers*, Peter Prince "saw no irony, no stylization—no difference at all between me and my narrator, with his 'cheesy little *bon mots*' and 'dingy little *apercus*'" (34).

6. Jonathan Swift, *The Poems of Jonathan Swift*, ed. Harold Williams (London: Oxford University Press, 1958), 597.

7. Amis discussed the autobiographical matrix of *The Rachel Papers* in an interview with Charles Michener, "Britain's Brat," 110; and, more recently, in *Experience* (5, 15, 24–25, 34–35, 45, 173n, 231n, 264, 293n, 309n, 342).

8. Kingsley Amis, *Lucky Jim*, 140.

9. Martin Amis, "A Tale of Two Novels," *Observer*, 19 October 1980, 26. Jacob Epstein's letter to Amis admitting the plagiarism appeared the following week. See "Tale of Two Novels," *Observer*, 26 October 1980, 32.

10. Amis was well aware of the pitfalls of this form of satire. Less than two years before he published *Dead Babies*, he reviewed Philip Roth's novel *The Breast*, calling it "his second attempt at Menippean satire—and his second emphatic dud—in a row" (*Observer*, 25 March 1973, 36). Roth's first foray into the form was *The Great American Novel* (New York: Holt, 1973).

11. As Martin was at work on *Dead Babies*, Kingsley was himself writing a variation on the country house novel—*Ending Up* (see *Experience*, 349).

12. Martin Amis, "Many Voices," review of *Problems of Dostoevsky's Poetics*, by Mikhail Bakhtin, *Times Literary Supplement*, 29 March 1974, 346.

13. Mikhail Bakhtin, *Problems of Dostoevsky's Poetics*, trans. R. William Rotsel (Ann Arbor: Ardis Press, 1973), 94.

14. Ibid.

15. Ibid.

16. Adorno and Horkheimer, *Dialectic of Enlightenment*, 118. The year he was writing *Dead Babies*, the *TLS* published a review

of three books by and two books about Adorno. See Jeremy Shapiro, "The Critical Theory of Frankfurt," 4 *October* 1974, 734.

17. Amis himself is a harsh critic of *Dead Babies*: "I'd give it a really blistering, unfavorable review. I can see what's contrived about it, what's plagiarized; I'm a great lifter of phrases, at least of how they're constructed" ("Martin Amis," *1990 Current Biography Yearbook*, ed. Charles Moritz, 21). The influence of J. G. Ballard and William S. Burroughs weighs heavily on the novel; see Amis's reviews of Ballard and Burroughs in Martin Amis, *The Moronic Inferno* (London: Penguin Books, 1986), 144–46; and *The War against Cliché*, 95–112, 299–307.

18. Martin Amis, "Translucent Salamanders," *Observer*, 11 June 1972, 29; rpt. in *The War against Cliché*, 299–307. The larger social satire in *Dead Babies* is indebted to Burroughs, specifically *Exterminator!* which Amis reviewed in the *Observer* in 1974. When the novel was (anonymously) reviewed in the *TLS* the same year, during Amis's tenure there as literary editor, it was described, like *Dead Babies* could be, as "a series of statements about the contemporary West; about the moral evisceration of a post-Hiroshima, post-Vietnam world, and the frenetic, fragmented sub-cultures which caper in the vacuum left behind" ("Under the Mattress," *Times Literary Supplement*, 22 March 1974, 282).

19. Karl Miller, *Doubles: Studies in Literary History* (Oxford: Oxford University Press, 1985), 409.

20. For Kingsley's relationship to Larkin, see Kingsley Amis, *Memoirs* (New York: Summit, 1991), especially 51–64; Leader, ed., *The Letters of Kingsley Amis;* and Richard Bradford, *Lucky Him* (Chester Springs, Pa.: Peter Owen, 2002). In a 1993 interview, Philip Amis remembers being angry when *Success* originally appeared; he clearly assumed that he was the only "Philip" alluded to in the dedication. "You could say I was the taller one who got his come-uppance in the end. . . . But that's simplistic. It was probably about Martin and someone else, a friend, say. I happen to be taller than Martin but there the resemblance ends. When he

dedicated the book to me I was outraged, but it's water off a duck's back now" (Andrew Billen, "On a Whimsical Carousel Ride Back to Boyhood," *Observer,* 28 November 1993, 8).

21. See Martin Amis, "Philip Larkin, 1922–1985," in *Visiting Mrs. Nabokov and Other Excursions* (New York: Harmony, 1993) 201–6; and "Don Juan in Hull," 74–82.

22. Philip Larkin, *Collected Poems,* ed. Anthony Thwaite (New York: Farrar, Strauss, and Giroux, 1989), 180. *Success* contains a plethora of additional Larkinian allusions—as do a great many of Amis's novels. For a thorough exploration of these subtextual appropriations and echoes, see Bill Jarmell, "Amis is a Larkinholic" (http://martinamis.albion.edu/larkinholic.htm).

23. Martin Amis, "The Sublime and the Ridiculous: Nabokov's Black Farces," in *Vladimir Nabokov, His Life, His Work, His World: A Tribute,* ed. Peter Quennell (New York: William Morrow, 1980), 76.

24. Martin Amis, "Lolita Reconsidered," 111; rpt. as "Nabokov's Grand Slam," *The War against Cliché,* 471–90.

25. My thanks to Professor John Nash of Trinity College Dublin for explaining the etymology and connotations of the word "yob."

26. Passages like this one anticipate *Other People,* which is informed throughout by the imagery and perspective of "Martian School" poets Craig Raine and Christopher Reid, whose poems Amis published in the *New Statesman* in the late 1970s. See chapter 2.

27. Graham Fuller, "Yob Action," *Village Voice,* 1 December 1987, 66.

28. Tom Paulin, "Fantastic Eschatologies," *Encounter,* 3 September 1978, 78. Paulin's claim is given some support in *Experience,* where Amis himself admits that in the early 1970s he often experienced what Christopher Hitchens called "tramp dread": "the suspicion . . . that you would not only fail but go under. Perhaps everybody has this" (35, 53).

29. Fuller, "Yob Action," 69.

30. Amis writes that "great novels are shocking; and then, after the shock dies down, you get aftershocks" ("Lolita Reconsidered," 111).

Chapter 3—Entering the "Martian School"

1. "What you're always looking for is a way to see the world differently. So you do it through the eyes of a drunk [as in *Money*] or an amnesiac [as in *Other People*]." Quoted by Susan Morrison in "The Wit and Fury," 99. More recently, Amis cited "the Martian School of poets" as a direct influence on his quest to "see the world as if you've never seen it before. As if you'd never really got used to living here on this planet" (Francesca Riviere, "Martin Amis," *Paris Review* 146 (1998): 121.

2. Many elements of *No Exit* are echoed in *Other People*. Most importantly, the play, like the novel, is about characters consigned to a hell-like limbo of eternal recurrence. Its triangular dialogue is implicitly echoed in the relationship Amis establishes among Mary/ Amy, the narrator/Prince, and the reader. Amis wrote *Other People* during a seven month stay in Paris (*Experience*, 250).

3. Amis has called his few attempts at poetry "chopped-up prose, not a different vein." Quoted by Haffenden in "Martin Amis," 16.

4. Martin Amis, "Point of View," *New Statesman*, 14 December 1979, 954. It is worth noting that Amis published one other poem with a "Martian School" feel, even though it was published two years before that phrase was coined: "An American Airman Looks Ahead," *Observer*, 5 June 1977, 28. Like "Point of View," this poem, whose speaker is an astronaut, reflects Amis's familiarity with the poetry of Christopher Reid and Craig Raine.

5. James Fenton, "The Martian School," *New Statesman*, 20 October 1978, 520. Fenton also reviewed *A Martian Sends a Post-card Home* (along with Christopher Reid's *Arcadia* and three other volumes of poetry) in the *London Review of Books*, 6 December

1979, 16. See also "Beautiful Objects," *New York Review of Books,* 29 November 2001, 49–50, where Fenton concedes that he invented the idea of "The Martian School": "I was fibbing: there was no Martian School. There were two poets, friends, whose aesthetic somewhat overlapped, and whose careers have since been similar."

6. Craig Raine, *A Martian Sends a Postcard Home* (Oxford: Oxford University Press, 1979), 1–2.

7. See *Experience,* 9, 110, 150, 335. Amis also reviewed three books about, and one by, Coleridge: *Coleridge, The Damaged Archangel,* by Norman Fruman, *Times Literary Supplement,* 1 December 1972, 1463; *Coleridge: Poet and Revolutionary 1772–1804,* by John Cornwell, *New Statesman,* 23 March 1973, 426–28, rpt. in *The War against Cliché,* 175–78; *A Voyage in Vain: Coleridge's Journey to Malta in 1804,* by Aleth Hayter, *Observer,* 16 September 1973, 37; *Coleridge's Verse: A Selection,* ed. William Empson and David Pirie, *Times Literary Supplement,* 12 January 1973, 40–41, rpt. in *The War against Cliché,* 178–81.

8. Samuel Taylor Coleridge, *The Collected Works of Samuel Taylor Coleridge,* ed. James Engell and W. Jackson Bate (Princeton: Princeton University Press, 1983), vol. 7, part 2: 7.

9. Quoted by Haffenden in "Martin Amis," 17.

10. Ibid.

11. Quoted by Susan Morrison in "The Wit and Fury," 98.

12. Alan Hollinghurst, "Opening Eyes," *New Statesman* 13 March 1981, 21.

13. "I am absolutely with [V. S.] Pritchett in the idea that the most extraordinary, magical thoughts are in people. . . . I do think people's thoughts are infinite and dormant" (Martin Amis, quoted by Haffenden in "Martin Amis," 9).

14. Evan Hunter, "Mary Lamb and Mr. Wrong," *New York Times Book Review,* 26 July 1981, 9.

15. Quoted by McGrath in "Interview," 27.

16. Quoted by Susan Morrison in "The Wit and Fury," 98.

17. Samuel Taylor Coleridge, "Dejection: An Ode," in *Samuel Taylor Coleridge Poems,* ed. John Beer (London: J. M. Dent, 1991), 280.

18. Victoria Glendinning, "Lamb's Tale from Amis," *Listener,* 5 March 1981, 320.

Chapter 4—I Am All You Never Had of Goods and Sex

Philip Larkin, "Money," in *Collected Poems,* ed. Anthony Thwaite (New York: Farrar, Strauss, and Giroux, 1989), 180. Amis quotes this (the first) and the last four stanzas of the sixteen-line poem in *Experience,* calling it "a favourite of mine" (243).

1. David E. Larson, M.D., ed., *Mayo Clinic Family Health Book* (New York: William Morrow, 1990), 687.

2. For more on this aspect of the novel, see Patrick Brantlinger, *Fictions of State: Culture and Credit in Britain, 1694–1994* (Ithaca: Cornell University Press, 1996), 234–63; and Tamás Bényei "Allegory and Allegoresis in Martin Amis's *Money,*" The Proceedings of the First Conference of the Hungarian Society for the Study of English, vol. 1 (Debrecen, Hungary: Institute of English and American Studies, 1995), 182–87.

3. Quoted by Haffenden in "Martin Amis," 13–14. See also Martin Amis, "A Bowl of Cat Food for Breakfast," *Observer,* 8 May 1983, 40: "Money has cheerfully survived its identification as the root of all evil. There is always an undertow of revulsion, however, waiting to bubble to the surface." It should be noted that the full title of the novel, with its pun on the word "note" (referring both to the British term for paper currency and a written statement) expresses this revulsion, implying that money is life-destroying.

4. Quoted by Haffenden in "Martin Amis," 13–14.

5. Quoted by McGrath in "Interview," 27. See also *Experience,* where Amis claims that every person has at least one novel in them, and in *Money* he was writing the novel that John Self "had in him but would never write" (6).

6. Ian Hamilton, "Martin and Martina," *London Review of Books,* 20 September–3 October 1984, 3. In an interview with Jean W. Ross (for *Contemporary Authors,* New Revision Series 27 [Detroit: Gale Research, 1987], 23), Amis said that throughout the first two drafts of the novel, John Self was named John Sleep. Amis then considered the name John Street before settling on Self. The analog for Self's name is most likely Nabokovian, derived from John Shade in *Pale Fire.* Self's distinctively charged voice, however, stems from Bellow, especially *The Adventures of Augie March* and *Henderson the Rain King.* As Amis explained to John Haffenden shortly after the publication of *Money,* "I learned from Bellow's *Henderson the Rain King* that you can have a great dolt of a character who says completely realistic things like, 'Thanks, Prince. I wish you all kinds of luck with your rain ceremony, but I think right after lunch my man and I had better blow,' after a beautifully long, complicated paragraph about all his warring responses and yearnings." Cf. *Novelists in Interview* (New York: Methuen, 1985), 8.

7. *Simulacra and Simulation,* trans. Sheila Faria Glaer (Ann Arbor: University of Michigan Press, 1994).

8. This and other aspects of the intricate pattern of doubling in *Money* are discussed in Miller, *Doubles,* 411–15.

9. Hamilton, "Martin and Martina," 3.

10. Ibid.

11. It is worth noting that Self's "Fiasco" originates from the same imaginary garage as Kingsley Amis's "Apfelsine" in *Stanley and the Women.*

12. Samuel Taylor Coleridge, *Lectures on Shakespeare, Collected Works 5, Lectures, 1808–1819 on Literature II,* ed. R. A. Foakes (Princeton: Princeton University Press, 1987), 315. Coleridge's assessment of Roderigo is also worth noting, since it applies equally to John Self: "the want of character and the power of the passions, like the wind loudest in empty houses, forms his character" (313).

13. John Bayley, "Being Two Is Half the Fun," *London Review of Books,* 4 July 1985, 13.

14. Laura L. Doan, "'Sexy Greedy' *Is* the Late Eighties: Power Systems in Amis's *Money* and Churchill's *Serious Money,*" *Minnesota Review* (spring/fall): 73. Doan's essay is a cautionary example of how *not* to practice ideological criticism. She demonstrates little sensitivity to the nuances of Amis's novel, favoring crudely formulated charges of classism and sexism that cannot withstand close critical scrutiny. John Haffenden anticipated Doan in supposing that Amis wrote himself into *Money* so readers would not mistake him for Self—an interpretation that Amis rejects (Haffenden, "Martin Amis," 11).

15. A separate essay could be written on the autobiographical matrix of *Money,* the extent of which this chapter can only suggest. Self, like Amis, had an American mother, and spent some of his childhood in New Jersey. Self's relationship with Martina Twain, who is knowledgeable about aesthetics, alludes to Antonia Phillips, the American professor of aesthetics Amis married in 1984 (on the very day *Money* was published—see *Experience,* 177n). The fact that Martina functions as the American double of the British character Martin Amis takes on added significance in light of this fact.

16. "I must say I find them pretty difficult to get on with . . . It's his style. I can't get to the end of a paragraph. It's too ornate" (Kingsley Amis quoted by Michener in "Britain's Brat," 110). See chapter 1 for an extended discussion of Amis's relationship to his father.

17. Quoted in "Martin Amis," *Contemporary Authors* 27, 1989, 21. Shanti Padhi has called the scatological elements in Amis's novels of the 1970s the "pranks of a young writer trying with utmost panache to outdo his rivals in porno-peddling." See "Bed and Bedlam: The Hard-Core Extravaganzas of Martin Amis," *Literary Half-Yearly* 23 (January 1982): 36.

18. Amis's wickedly comic portrait of Lorne Guyland owes something to Kirk Douglas. Guyland wants to rewrite his role in the film so that he dies sacrificing himself for the two female leads (while they look on, naked and weeping)—a variation on the Kirk Douglas character's sacrificial death at the end of *Saturn 3*. Shortly after

returning from Hollywood and his *Saturn 3* scripting work, Amis told a reporter that "Kirk Douglas was only interested in a script that made him seem young and attractive," adding that he kept calling Amis to suggest that the robots in the film say "That man is so virile" when Douglas ran past" (*Sunday Times* [London], 13 July 1980, 32).

19. In his review of Saul Bellow's *The Dean's December,* Amis wrote that "nowadays, our protagonists are a good deal lower down on the human scale than their creators: they are anti-heroes, non-heroes, sub-heroes." (See *The Moronic Inferno,* 5). He recycles this trope in *The Information.*

20. Susan Morrison, "The Wit and Fury," 98.

21. See the discussion of *The Rachel Papers* in chapter 1 for a summary of this case.

22. The parallels between *Money* and *1984* are extensive. Like Winston Smith, Self is under constant surveillance. In place of O'Brien, the state operative who slowly initiates Smith into the truth of his utter imprisonment, *Money* has Goodney, who shadows and psychologically terrorizes Self. Martina Twain offers Self love and hope, which is also what Julia gives Smith. But just as Smith finally turns in Julia, so Self betrays Martina.

23. Walter Benjamin, *Reflections* (New York: Schocken Books, 1986), 85–86.

Chapter 5—Apocalypse Now

1. John Updike, "Nobody Gets Away with Everything," *New Yorker,* 25 May 1992, 86.

2. Martin Amis, "Saul Bellow and the Moronic Inferno," in *The Moronic Inferno,* 200.

3. Martin Amis, "Norman Mailer," in *The Moronic Inferno,* 60.

4. John Lanchester, "As a Returning Lord," *London Review of Books,* 7 May 1987, 12.

5. As if to make up for this oversight, ten years later Amis has detective Mike Hoolihan, the female narrator of his novella *Night*

Train, evoke this very group in her rant about murder: "I kept saying out loud: 'Where are the women?' Where WERE the women? I'll tell you: they were witnesses. Those straggly chicks in their tents on Greenham Common, England, making the military crazy with their presence and their stares—they were witnesses" (22).

6. Adams Mars-Jones, "Fireworks at the Funeral," 457. I am also indebted to Mars-Jones for bringing the importance of the Greenham Common Peace Camp to my attention.

7. Lanchester, "As a Returning Lord," 11.

8. This fact is obscured in the Vintage paperback edition of the novel, which mistakenly prints the opening note by "M. A." *before* the second title page, wrongly indicating it was written by Martin Amis. In a BBC Radio 4 Book Club discussion of *London Fields* (13 September 2001), Amis called this mistake "disastrous" to the meaning of the novel. He goes on to explain the relationship between Samson's narrative and Asprey's intervention: "What's happened is that Mark Asprey has come back to the flat, found the novel, and found the intervening material, which is the narrator's little chapters between the chapters, stitched it all together, and brought it out under the name of Martin Amis."

9. Graham Fuller, "Murder He Wrote: Martin Amis's Killing Fields," *Village Voice,* 24 April 1990, 75.

10. Interview with Martin Amis, *New York Times Book Review,* 4 March 1990, 42.

11. Fuller, "Murder He Wrote," 75. Novelist David Lodge chaired the 1989 Booker Prize committee, when committee members Maggie Gee and Helen McNeil lobbied successfully to keep *London Fields* off the shortlist on the grounds of the novel's supposed misogyny. Lodge later wrote that he "deeply regretted" this decision. See David Lodge, "Diary," *New Statesman,* 6 November 1998, 7; and Blake Morrison, "Why Nicola Got Knocked for Six," *Observer,* 24 September 1989, 45. For a devastating critique of this decision, and the awarding of the prize to Kazuo Ishiguro, see George Walden, "A Butler's Tale That By-Passes Brutal Reality," *Daily Telegraph,* 1 January 1990, 12. About Ishiguro's novel

Walden writes: "It is not a bad book. In fact it has everything the English mind at its most inert most admires: it is elegant, elegiac, escapist, untaxing, melancholic to the point of tedium and limp to the point of death. . . . Taken together with the rejection of Amis's brutally vital book about the here, now and future, it is possible to see the success of *The Remains of the Day* as a literary portent: yet another sign that, after the rude upsets of the 1980s, the underlying consensus for immobilism in British society is re-congealing."

12. Fuller, "Murder He Wrote," 75.

13. *London Fields* is the third of Amis's novels to borrow from Vladimir Nabokov's *Despair* (the other two are *Success* and *Money*). Like Nicola, the protagonist of *Despair* arranges his own death; like Samson, he ends his narrative with a suicide note. He has also "failed in art and love," but this is left for the reader to infer. Amis wrote about *Despair* in his essay "The Sublime and the Ridiculous: Nabokov's Black Farces," in *Vladimir Nabokov, His Life, His Work, His World: A Tribute,* ed. Peter Quenell (London: Weidenfeld and Nicolson, 1980), 73–86.

14. In the 13 September 2001 BBC Radio 4 Book Club discussion Amis said he locates the moral center of the novel in Kim and Samson's feeling for her.

15. Quoted by Anthony DeCurtis in "Britain's Mavericks," *Harper's Bazaar,* November 1991, 146.

16. M. John Harrison, "Speeding to Cradle from Grave," *Times Literary Supplement,* 20 September 1991, 21. For more on the symbolic "reach" of *Time's Arrow,* see Richard Menke, "Narrative Reversals and the Thermodynamics of History in Martin Amis's *Time's Arrow,*" *Modern Fiction Studies* (winter 1998): 959–80.

17. Other antecedents include *Sylvie and Bruno* by Lewis Carrol; *Alice's Adventures in Wonderland,* where the White Queen claims that she lives backwards in time; *Le Testament d'Orphée* by Jean Cocteau; *An Age* by Brian Aldiss; *Counter-Clock World* by Philip K. Dick; "The Curious Case of Benjamin Button," by F. Scott Fitzgerald, in which a man is born at the age of seventy and proceeds

backward to a state of infancy; and "Mr. F is Mr. F" by J. G. Ballard. In his afterword to *Time's Arrow*, Amis refers obliquely to the Dresden firebombing description in *Slaughterhouse Five* while discussing influences on his own novel (168). Maya Slater notes that *Time's Arrow* takes up the challenge posed by Nabokov in *Look at the Harlequins!*: "Nobody can imagine in physical terms the act of reversing the order of time. Time is not reversible" ("Problems When Time Moves Backwards," *English: The Journal of the English Association* [summer 1993]: 141).

18. Some critics have attacked Amis for what they call his narrative "trickery" in *Time's Arrow*, suggesting that his technical brilliance is an affront to the memory of the murdered six million. See especially Rhoda Koenig, "Holocaust Chic," *New York*, 21 October 1991, 117; and James Buchan, "The Return of Dr. Death," *Spectator*, 28 September 1991, 38. Amis was so incensed by Buchan's assertion that he used the Holocaust for literary profit—and by the *Spectator*'s cover headline "Designer Gas Ovens"—that he wrote a rare reply ("Creepier than Thou," *Spectator*, 5 October 1991, 25). He continued the quarrel with Buchan in *Experience* (94–95), where he calls Buchan "a humourless worthy" (toned down from something harsher at the suggestion of the publisher's lawyers).

19. Martin Amis, "Blown Away," *New Yorker*, 30 May 1994, 48; rpt. as "I Am in Blood Stepp'd in So Far," *The War against Cliché*, 11–17.

20. Robert Jay Lifton, *The Nazi Doctors: Medical Killing and the Psychology of Genocide* (New York: Basic Books, 1986), 15. Subsequent references will cite page numbers to this edition.

21. As the following discussion suggests, virtually every aspect of *Time's Arrow*—historical setting, plot, characterization, even language—is informed by *The Nazi Doctors*. The reader who consults Lifton's book will find more parallels than I have space to discuss here. See also Susan Vice, "Form Matters: Martin Amis, *Time's Arrow*," in *Holocaust Fiction* (London: Routledge, 2000), 11–37.

22. His first name has a more precise historical provenance: one of the high SS officials in the eastern killing bureaucracy was named Odilo Globlocnik.

23. Sigmund Freud, "The Uncanny," trans. Alex Strachey, in *The Standard Edition of the Works of Sigmund Freud* (London: The Hogarth Press, 1953), 7, 219–56.

24. Harrison, "Speeding to Cradle from Grave," 21.

25. Frank Kermode, "In Reverse," *London Review of Books,* 12 September 1991, 11.

Chapter 6—Amis Agonistes

1. In April 2002, for instance, Random House announced that it had offered Charles Frazier, author of *Cold Mountain,* an $8 million advance for his second novel—the result of a closed auction organized by his newly acquired agent, International Creative Management. The advance was based on a one-page synopsis.

2. Quoted in Wilson, "A Very English Story," 99.

3. Harper Collins spent approximately £100,000 promoting *The Information,* which sold for £16 in hardback and £7 in paper, so the book clearly "earned back" Amis's advance. For a detailed discussion of the marketing of *The Information,* and the political economy of contemporary publishing, see "'What is an Author?' Contemporary Publishing Discourse and the Author Figure," *Publishing Research Quarterly* (spring 2000): 63–77.

4. Both statements are quoted in Wilson, "A Very English Story," 102, 106.

5. Readers seeking significant fictional antecedents for *The Information* are advised to consult George Orwell's novel *Keep the Aspidistra Flying* (1936), in which the protagonist is a bitter, envious, and failed poet.

6. Amis, "Lolita Reconsidered," *Atlantic,* September 1992, 112.

7. In his essay on James Joyce's *Ulysses,* Amis praises Joyce for eliciting "the authentic shiver, the sense of pregnant arrest," at the

end of that novel (*The War against Cliché*, 445). Amis took the phrase from the critic F. R. Leavis, and in his review of Don DeLillo's *Underworld* he attributes it to him (*The War against Cliché*, 320).

8. This title, with its echo of Milton, hints at one of the other webs of literary reference in *The Information*. Amis re-read *Paradise Lost*, which he considers the greatest non-dramatic poem in the English language, before writing the last draft of *The Information*; the novel alludes to Milton's epic in myriad ways. For more on the importance of the poem for Amis, see *Experience*, 133–34, 193, 281–82, 335.

9. Like so much else in Richard's existence, this has a precise parallel in his author's life. In *Experience*, Amis recounts that the morning after a fierce argument with Salman Rushdie about the merits of Samuel Beckett's prose: "I was to be found at the Paddington Sports Club, working out on the quiz machine with my friends Steve and Chris" (82).

10. In 1974 and 1975 Amis published a series of reviews (and an interview with Joseph Heller) for a similarly "little" journal: Ian Hamilton's Arts Council-supported *New Review*.

11. Jorge Luis Borges, *The Aleph and Other Stories, 1933–1969*, trans. Norman Thomas di Giovanni (New York: Dutton, 1970), 23, 26.

12. I am indebted to Bill Jarmell for pointing out this allusion —and dozens of additional Larkin echoes in *The Information*. See "Amis is a Larkinholic," http://martinamis.albion.edu/larkinholic.htm.

13. See Wilson, "A Very English Story," 97.

14. Quoted by Haffenden in "Martin Amis," 16.

15. In his essay on James Joyce's *Ulysses*, Amis calls Joyce "the exemplary Modern, fanatically prolix, innovative and recondite, and free of any obligation to please a reading public" (*The War against Cliché*, 442).

16. When he was a child Martin imagined that he and his brother Philip, one year his senior, were twins. See *Experience*, 97n.

17. Lucy Partington was abducted and killed in 1973; her remains were exhumed in 1994. *Experience* is haunted by Partington's murder and murderers; see esp. 53–77, 65–71, 108–12, 130–35, 139–41, 147–49, and 347–50.

18. See Amis, "Blown Away," *New Yorker,* 30 May 1994, 49.

19. In *Experience* Amis recounts that as a child he was often asked to tend to his father when Kingsley experienced late-night panic attacks (180).

20. In the midst of writing *The Information*, Amis learned that his cousin Lucy Partington had been murdered by a serial killer, and it increased his anxiety about his own children. "I would imagine each of my sons finding themselves, as their distant cousin had, in such a violent force field, and I would imagine the moment when they sensed the magnitude of the undifferentiated hatred that was ranged against them" (*Experience,* 66).

21. Susan Morrison, "The Wit and Fury," 99.

Chapter 7—Thiz Zdrange Resizdanze

1. When this story first appeared in print it was accompanied by a photograph of Elias Fawcett and dedicated to him (Martin Amis, "What Happened to Me on My Holiday," *New Yorker,* 21 July 1997, 64). This dedication is retained in *Heavy Water.*

2. John Updike strenuously objected to Amis's representation of identity in *Night Train*, claiming that Amis "writes out of a sensibility uncomfortably on the edge of the post-human. His characters strikingly lack the soulful, willful warmth that he admires in Saul Bellow; they seem quick-moving automata, assembled of mostly disagreeable traits." See "It's a Fair Cop," *Sunday Times* (London), 21 September 1997, Books 1.

3. Amis's appropriation of the detective genre elicited a scathing review from fellow novelist Anita Brookner, who accused Amis of "an assault on the reader's good faith," calling *Night Train* "streetwise, and without a trace of honest intention" ("Farewell, My Lovely," *Spectator,* 27 September 1997, 36, 37). Mostly inured to

criticism, Amis was stung by this review, as well as by John Buchan's 1991 review of *Time's Arrow* ("The Return of Dr. Death," *Spectator,* 28 September 1991, 38). "Both were questioning my integrity in a way I would never accuse Danielle Steele of doing. I wouldn't accuse her of being cynical; cynics don't write novels." See Stephen Moss, "The Mick Jagger of Literature?" *Guardian,* 19 February 1999, 22. The conservative British weekly the *Spectator,* where Buchan's and Brookner's reviews were printed, has always reserved special scorn for Amis.

4. Phillips, "Cloud Cover," 7.

5. Ibid. Other critics who joined Phillips in admiring *Night Train* and arguing that it marks an important stage in Amis's career include Frank Kermode, "A Thriller with Something on Its Mind" (*Atlantic Monthly,* February 1998, 100–104); Patrick McGrath, "Her Long Goodbye" (*New York Times Book Review,* 1 February 1998, 6); Natasha Walter, "Dark Side of the Tracks" (*Guardian Weekly,* 28 September 1997, 29–30); and James Wood, "An American in Amis" (*Observer,* 21 September 1997, 17).

6. Martin Amis, "Heavy Water," *New Statesman,* 22 & 29 December 1978, 874–76.

7. In addition to the autobiographical resonance of this revision, Amis may have wanted to suggest a parallel between a father who abandons his family and the Labour party's abandonment of its principles and thus its constituents.

8. In the final paragraph of the story Amis cements the symbolic connection between John's physical condition and the moral state of those who patronize him by revealing that the bottles that Mother regularly provides him to quell his fitfulness contain water and gin—the same alcohol consumed in such large quantities by the vacationers on board ship. It is possible to read the relationship between Mother and John allegorically, to see John as symbolizing working class dependence on the British welfare state. The fact that gin has long been the favored drink of the poor in England (primarily because it was plentiful and cheap) reinforces this reading.

9. In his introduction to *Lines of Dissent: Writing from the New Statesman, 1913–1988* (London: Verso, 1988), Christopher Hitchens writes of the Labour Party in the 1970s that it possessed "all the elements . . . of post-imperial dudgeon: of the romancing of outdated industry; . . . of the constipated conception of the nation-state—that have brought us to the present slough" (8). Two years after "Heavy Water" was originally published the Labour Party was voted out of office for the next 18 years. In *Koba the Dread*, Amis notes that in 1978 he and his brother voted Labour and adds "the social effect of trade-union—they used to say trades-union—ascendancy was everywhere apparent" (23).

10. Martin Amis, "Blackpool Diary," *New Statesman*, 14 October 1977, 504.

11. Martin Amis, "Action at Sea." *Sunday Telegraph Magazine*, 21 January 1979, 46. Amis's observation here may have been influenced by this comment by Philip Larkin: "I wouldn't mind seeing China if I could come back the same day. Generally speaking, the further one gets from home the greater the misery" (*Required Writing: Miscellaneous Pieces, 1955–1982* [London: Faber and Faber, 1983], 55).

12. Ibid., 46.

13. Commenting on this addition to the 1998 version of the story, Peter Stothard wrote that "*New Statesman* readers at Christmas 1978 did not need, of course, to be informed about how trade union leaders ran the country in the intervals between Soviet-style fraternal holidays. Those who had been to Blackpool two months before knew well that Joe Gormley and Arthur Scargill were calling the shots, that the Labour Prime Minister had seen his economic policy torn apart by his own brothers and that Neil Kinnock was looking greedily at the spoils which might be left." (*Times* [London], 1 October 1998, 22).

14. John Lanchester, "Be Interesting!" 5.

15. Martin Amis, "Saul Bellow's December," *Observer*, 11 December 1983, 25; rpt. as "Saul Bellow in Chicago," in *The*

Moronic Inferno and Other Visits to America (London: Jonathan Cape, 1986), 199.

16. In a 1997 interview, Amis told Barbie Dutter that "America is . . . where history is being written. . . . It is more like a world than a country, and that would be an exciting place for a writer to be." See "Amis looks set to book his passage to America," *Telegraph,* 13 October 1997, 2.

17. Martin Amis, "Madonna Exposed," *Observer Magazine,* 11 October 1992, 37; rpt. in *Visiting Mrs. Nabokov and Other Excursions,* 255–64. In his foreword to *The War against Cliché,* Amis extends this conceit: "you can become famous without having any talent (by abasing yourself on some TV nerdothon: a clear improvement on the older method of simply killing a celebrity and inheriting the aura)"(xii).

18. A. O. Scott, "Trans-Atlantic Flights," *New York Times Book Review,* 31 January 1999, 5.

Chapter 8—Patriarchy and Its Discontents: *Experience*

1. Sally Amis died on 8 November 2000; she was 46.

2. Gayle Rubin's influential definition of patriarchal heterosexuality as one or another form of the "traffic in women" applies here. See "The Traffic in Women: Notes Toward a Political Economy of Sex," in *Toward an Anthropology of Women,* ed. Rayna Reiter (New York: Monthly Review Press, 1975), 157–210. In this connection it is worth noting that Sally Amis also appears intermittently in *Experience* as a diminished figure desperately devoted to her father (353–55, 365–66, 375–80).

3. In *Experience,* Amis writes that a son's struggle with his father constitutes "an argument that is never over" (191).

4. *Experience* was awarded the James Tait Black Memorial Prize for Nonfiction in 2001.

5. Joan Acocella, "Family Romance," *New Yorker,* 19 & 26 June 2000, 186.

6. In a 10 May 1979 letter to Philip Larkin, Kingsley wrote: "Did I tell you that Martin is spending a year abroad as a TAX EXILE? Last year he earned £38,000. Little shit. 29, he is. Little shit." See Leader, ed., *The Letters of Kingsley Amis,* 871.

7. Elizabeth Jane Howard, "Breaking Point," *Sunday Times,* 23 June 2002.

8. Amis does not sentimentalize the brutal facts of Lucy's fate: "We know what happened to her after death. She was decapitated and dismembered, and her remains were crammed into a shaft between leaking sewage pipes, along with a knife, a rope, a section of masking-tape and two hair grips" (*Experience,* 62).

9. Richard Brooks, "Amis Accused of Exploiting Fred West Link," *Sunday Times* (Sunday), 11 June 2000, 3.

10. Joan Acocella, "Family Romance," 184. Amis's dislike of Acocella's review—which he voiced during the question and answer period following his reading from *Experience* in Seattle on 15 June 2000—suggests the appositeness of her analysis.

11. See especially "Green with Envy," *Observer,* 19 June 1977, 13; "Blackpool Diary," *New Statesman,* 14 October 1977, 504; "A New Sheriff Rides in from the West," *Observer,* 9 November 1980, 11; and most of the essays and profiles collected in *The Moronic Inferno.*

12. Hitchens's response to *Koba* was scathing. He told journalist Tim Rutten that Amis is guilty of "solipsism" and of "insulting" not only the memories of Stalinism's many heroic left-wing opponents, but also history itself. "Hard work is involved in the study of history. Hard moral work, too. We don't get much assistance in that task from mushy secondhand observations." See "Friendship Doesn't Get in the Way of a Feud, and Vice Versa," *Los Angeles Times,* 2 August 2002, 1. See also Hitchens's two public responses to Amis: "Don't Be Silly," *Guardian,* 4 September 2002, G2.6, and "Lightness at Midnight: Stalinism without Irony," *Atlantic,* September 2002, 144–53, which was reprinted in *Unacknowledged Legislation,* paperback ed. (London and New York: Verso, 2002), 272–85.

13. Stalin's indictment of his second wife sounds eerily similar to Kingsley's interpretation of his own second wife's departure. See Elizabeth Jane Howard, "Breaking Point."

14. Quoted by Allan Brown in "Laughter and Lost Daughters," *Scotsman on Sunday,* 3.

15. Paul Berman, "*Koba the Dread:* A Million Deaths Is Not Just a Statistic," *New York Times Book Review,* 28 July 2002, 7.

16. Allan Brown, "Amis Breaks Silence," *Scotsman on Sunday,* 3. Amis objected to Brown's treatment of Sally Amis's life in a letter to the *Scotsman* on 16 December 2001: "I HAVE only just seen your Sunday Encounter piece of October 28, 2001. Your correspondent, Allan Brown, has looked into the clippings file and has reproduced some ungenerous inaccuracies about my sister. My sister's baby daughter was not the result of "a one-night stand"; in fact, she cohabited for some time with the father. More generally, the impression is given that my sister lived in penury and neglect. Not so. She was in full contact with every member of her family, and her will disposed of a considerable legacy."

17. Ibid.

Chapter 9—The Novelist as Critic

Martin Amis, "In Praise of Pritchett," *The War against Cliché,* 65.

1. James Wood, "Paradox Pile-Up," *Times Literary Supplement,* 15 October 1993, 21.

2. Quoted by Haffenden in "Martin Amis," 16.

3. Jason Cowley, "Talking Heads," *New Statesman,* 24 June 2002, 50.

4. Amis's first published comments on AIDS came in a 1983 review of a British television documentary on the AIDS crisis. See "Mother Nature and the Plague," *Observer,* 1 May 1983, 36. Following the publication of "Making Sense of AIDS," Amis took another step in sympathetic understanding, and ceased calling homosexuality a "condition" (*The Moronic Inferno,* 197). In

Hockney's Alphabet (New York: Random House, 1991), Amis contributed the entry "H is for Homosexual," which concludes with these sentences: "I call homosexuality not a 'condition' (and certainly not a 'preference'). I call it a destiny. Because all I know for certain about homosexuality is that it asks for courage. It demands courage" (24).

5. Martin Amis, "The American Eagle," *Observer,* 25 August 1984, 17.

6. In his foreword to *The War against Cliché* Amis writes that in looking back over his reviews of these writers, "I am . . . struck by how hard I sometimes was on writers who (I erroneously felt) were trying to influence me: Roth, Mailer, Ballard" (xv).

7. Michener, "Britain's Brat," 108–11.

8. Personal interview, 7 March 2000. The plan included writing a postgraduate thesis on Shakespeare.

9. Amis's appearance in a 2002 Oxford University Press anthology of critical essays on fiction served to emphasize his continuing ties both to the literal institution and the institutional study of literature. See "Against Dryness," in *On Fiction in Britain, 1950–2000,* ed. Zachary Leader (Oxford: Oxford University Press, 2002), 265–69.

10. Actually, 1948 is rather late to be "inaugurating" the Age of Criticism. *The Great Tradition* was published after Leavis's own *New Bearings in English Poetry* and *Revaluation,* Q. D. Leavis's *Fiction and the Reading Public,* and William Empson's *Seven Types of Ambiguity.* In addition, T. S. Eliot's *Criterion* magazine (on which Leavis's own *Scrutiny* was partly modeled), had its heyday in the 1920s.

11. Amis's first published review, "What the People Sing"; a review of *The Faber Book of Popular Verse,* ed. Geoffrey Grigson, was published in the *Daily Telegraph,* 4 November 1971, 8. On 14 January 1969, Amis submitted the winning entry (No. 2,031) in the *New Statesman*'s "Weekend Competition" under the name "M. L. Amis." His winning entry was announced in the 14 February 1969 issue (236).

12. *Sunday Times Magazine,* 7 November 1993, 20–24. Amis makes a similar point in *Experience* (241).

13. The first statement comes from Martin Amis, "Corrective Force," review of *Nor Shall My Sword: Discourses on Pluralism, Compassion and Social Hope,* in *Times Educational Supplement,* 25 August 1972, 14; the second from Martin Amis, "Life, Literature and Leavis," review of *The Living Principle: English as a Discipline of Thought* in *Observer,* 14 September 1975, 25. See also Martin Amis, "Thankless Tasker,"review of *Letters in Criticism* in the *New Statesman,* 31 May 1974, 774–75. In *Experience,* Amis writes that "when F. R. Leavis died in 1978 I assembled a valuation of his career, by various hands, in the *New Statesman,* and called the thing 'F. R. Leavis: A Symposium'" (335). For more Amis references to Leavis in *The War against Cliché,* see esp. xii–xiii, 78–79, 320, 445. It is also worth noting that it was Leavis who objected to Kingsley's appointment at Peterhouse, Cambridge, calling him a "pornographer."

14. Martin Amis, introduction to *The Moronic Inferno,* x.

15. McGrath, "Interview," 29.

16. Martin Amis, "Queasy Rider," *New Statesman,* 22 March 1974, 414.

17. Amis omitted his review of Updike's nonfiction collection *Hugging the Shore* from *The War against Cliché,* possibly because it contains Updike's damning review of Kingsley's fiction. See Martin Amis, "Christian Gentleman," *Observer,* 15 January 1984, 48.

18. See *The Postmodern Condition: A Report on Knowledge,* trans. Brian Massumi (Minneapolis: University of Minnesota Press, 1985).

19. Amis's zealous defense of Nabokov's rigorous narrative control is rooted in his long-running dispute with Kingsley about the merits of *Lolita.* In 1958 Kingsley wrote what Martin calls a "willfully philistine review" of the novel (later collected in *What Became of Jane Austen?*), in which he wholly identified Humbert with Nabokov (*Experience,* 121n).

20. See bibliography for complete references.

21. Amis, "Christian Gentleman," 48.

22. See John Updike, "Nobody Gets Away with Everything," 86; and "It's a Fair Cop," *Sunday Times* (London), 21 September 1997, Books 1.

23. See Amis, "Fear and Loathing," G2, and *Koba the Dread,* 92.

24. Martin Amis, "Science Fiction," *Observer,* 3 March 1974, 37.

25. This pseudonym, along with Henry Tilney and multiple other personas, reappears in the playful and pseudonymous contributions to the *New Statesman*'s "Weekend Competition" feature, to which he and Julian Barnes contributed during the 1970s.

26. The second column is accompanied by a contributor's note on the fictitious author, claiming that Bruno Holbrook "is at present engaged in a study of Wayland Young," author of *Eros Denied: Sex in Western Society* (1964). "Coming in Handy," *New Statesman,* 14 December 1973, 922. By adopting the surname "Holbrook," Amis is alluding to David Holbrook, an acclaimed poet and an indignant opponent of pornography who contributed to *Pornography: The Longford Report* (1972), which sought through a propaganda campaign to provide support for a parliamentary bill designed to redefine obscenity as an affront to community standards. Six months before Amis adopted his "Bruno Holbrook" pseudonym, Holbrook singled out the *New Statesman* for rebuke while censuring left-wing journalists for failing to report his views regarding pornography and "cultural nihilism." See David Holbrook, "Seduction of the People," *Spectator,* 30 March 1974, 384–85.

27. Quoted by Susan Morrison, "The Wit and Fury," 101.

28. At the same time, *Experience* broods on the murder of Amis's cousin Lucy Partington by the pedophile and serial murder Fred West (61–65, 139–40).

29. In a 1996 interview, Amis compared his "moral scheme" to that of his father, observing that while his father prizes decency, the positive values in his books "are always represented by innocence, by a child" (quoted in Eleanor Wachtel, "Eleanor Wachtel with Martin Amis," *Malahat Review,* March 1996, 49).

30. Martin Amis, "Sex in America," *Talk,* February 2001, 135.

31. When "Sex in America" was reprinted as "A Rough Trade," 17 March 2001, in the *Guardian,* the newspaper received dozens of letters attacking its decision to publish the piece. A representative sample was published in the *Guardian Saturday Review,* 24 March 2001, 5.

32. Richard Brooks, "Amis Writes Royals into a Porno Plot," *Sunday Times,* 28 May 2000, 5.

33. Martin Amis, "The Queen's Heart," *New Yorker,* 20 May 2002, 106–10.

34. Martin Amis, "Being Serious in the Fifties," *New Statesman,* 7 November 1975, 578.

Chapter 10—The Edifice of Masculinity

1. As with *The Information, Yellow Dog* entered bookstores trailing clouds of prepublication controversy. Tibor Fischer, whose novel *Voyage to the End of the Room* was published on the same day as *Yellow Dog,* attacked the book in "Someone Needs to Have a Word with Amis," *Telegraph,* 4 August 2003, 18. This scathing review itself became a major news story and influenced subsequent reviews. It also confirmed the jaundiced view of the tabloid press expressed in *Yellow Dog.* As George Walden wrote in "Back to Blighty," *New Statesman,* 8 September 2003, 49, "it is a sign of the galloping contamination of tabloid ethics that Amis's book should have been widely and lovingly trashed before it appeared—celebrity 'failure' makes irresistible copy." Eleven days after Fischer published his screed, on 15 August, *Yellow Dog* was named one of twenty-three finalists for the Man Booker Prize, but it did not make the shortlist, announced on 16 September. The prepublication tempest surrounding *Yellow Dog* is summarized in John Walsh, "Twilight of the Idol?," *Independent,* 15 August 2003, 3, and Sarah Lyall, "For a British Novelist, Tornadoes in August," *New York Times,* 26 August 2003, E1

2. In his 1981 essay on Norman Mailer, Amis claims that Mailer fell prey "to the novelist's fatal disease: ideas. His naivete about 'answers,' 'the big illumination,' 'the secret of everything,' persists to this day" ("Norman Mailer," in *The Moronic Inferno,* 60). In my introduction I speculate on the sources of Amis's post-1984 turn toward the apocalyptic; see chapter four for an analysis of the ways in which this impulse is manifested in his fictions of the late 1980s.

3. Alan Hollinghurst, "Leader of the Pack," *Guardian,* 6 September 2003, 9.

4. Robert Douglas-Fairhurst, "Dickens With a Snarl," *Observer Review,* 24 August 2003, 15.

5. Jonathan Curiel, "Working with Words on All Fronts," *San Francisco Chronicle,* 4 November 2001, Sunday Review 2.

6. Martin Amis, *Yellow Dog* (London: Jonathan Cape, 2003), 3. Subsequent references will cite page numbers to this edition. Amis is here echoing Dickens's famous opening paragraph: "It was the best of times, it was the worst of times, it was the age of wisdom, . . ." (Oxford: Oxford University Press, 1996, 1). Despite this allusion—and another to *Bleak House*—*Yellow Dog* resembles *Great Expectations* more than any other Dickens novel in its preoccupation with recurrence and return, in its fascination with criminality, in its emphasis on the corrosive effects of envy.

7. Martin Amis, "The Voice of the Lonely Crowd," *Guardian Review,* 2 June 2002, 6. For an account of the backlash Amis experienced after publishing this essay, see Jack Malvern, "Amis Aims Below the Belt in Attack on Islam," *Times* (London), 21 October 2002, 3.

8. Amis explained the phrase "reflexive exhibitionism" in a September 2003 interview. "At one extreme is pornography. On a lesser scale there's that loss of inhibition, that shading of the boundary between the public and the private that can be seen in everything from mobile phone chat (conversational denuding in public) to *Big*

Brother and reality TV. Everybody feels they have to have a lively personality, even when they haven't got one. There's a . . . kind of forced ebullience, to them" (Nick Rennison, "The Influence of Anxiety," *Waterstone's Books Quarterly* 10 [2003]: 24).

9. Xan's surname derives from Duane Meo, John Self's "whizzkid editor" in *Money,* and it also hints at the many ways in which he is an authorial alter ego (Xan Meo = "me"). "Xanthic" means "yellow," thus linking Xan, who was treated for jaundice in the hospital after his birth, to the novel's symbolic palette of colors related to illness.

10. Speaking with Mark Lawson on "Front Row" (BBC4, 1 September 2003), Amis said that "in the days following September 11, . . . one's feeling about the planet changed. It went from being a blue or a grey planet, to something like a yellow planet. And that feeling hasn't gone away."

11. By giving this name to the most vicious character in *Yellow Dog,* Amis is evoking Henry Fielding, the first great satirical novelist in English literature, whose 1742 novel *Joseph Andrews* also features male duplicity, sexual violence, and near-incest. Fielding's protagonist, however, is an icon of innocence and virtue. *Yellow Dog*'s Joseph Andrews owes more to Ben Kingsley's performance as Don Logan in the 2000 film *Sexy Beast* than he does to Fielding's novel. It is also worth noting that Xan Meo's acting portfolio recalls actor Ray Winstone, who portrays Gary "Gal" Dove in *Sexy Beast.*

12. The word "Lucozade," the title of Xan's short story collection, is the brand name of a sports drink sold in Britain; it is also British rhyming slang for "spade," which in turn is slang for a person of African descent. The word is woven into the sociolinguistic satire of "The State of England," where both Mal and Joseph Andrews make their first appearances.

13. Symbolically, the blows Xan suffers—unexpected and unprecedented—reenact at the personal and individual level the terrorist attacks of September 11, 2001. And his posttraumatic mental

state—subrational and violent—comes to represent what Amis has described as the mentality of terrorists.

14. Although he is an imaginary monarch, Henry IX's vapidity often suggests parallels with both the current Prince of Wales and Edward VIII.

15. Hollinghurst, "Leader of the Pack," 9. Amis's portrait of Henry IX recalls the bemused monarch in Ronald Firbank's novel *The Flower Beneath the Foot;* his depiction of Henry's household draws on Evelyn Waugh and P. G. Wodehouse. Amis said the major challenge in these sections of the novel was "finding a voice for the royal characters—one somewhere between P. G. Wodehouse and Evelyn Waugh" (Rennison, "The Influence of Anxiety," 22). Amis's 2002 review-essay on Queen Elizabeth II and the royal family ("The Queen's Heart," *New Yorker,* 20 May 2002, 106–10), is a surprisingly sympathetic treatment.

16. "Bugger" is British slang for a male homosexual. The name Brendan-Urquhart Gordon is a nod to Julius Gore-Urquhart in Kingsley Amis's *Lucky Jim,* a rich patron of the arts and occasional literary journalist. Gordon himself, whose views at times echo those of Martin Amis, is hyper-fastidious and has a special fondness for the novels of Henry James, whom Amis has called "tirelessly fastidious" (*Experience,* 154n.).

17. American slang for someone who is "hot," i.e. sexually attractive.

18. Clint Smoker's surname also comes from an earlier Amis novel: Dirk Smoker is the ghostwriting hack who ghostwrites the autobiography of Kim Twemlow, Keith Talent's darting hero in *London Fields.*

19. James Wood, "V. S. Pritchett and English Comedy," in *On Modern British Fiction,* ed. Zachary Leader (Oxford: Oxford University Press, 2002), 11.

20. The Royce Traynor plot serves as a master-trope for the theme of male malignity that suffuses the novel. As Robert Douglas-Fairhurst has written, the "itch of vengeance" motivates all the plots in *Yellow Dog"* ("Dickens With a Snarl," 15).

21. Martin Amis, interview by Mark Lawson, *Newsnight,* BBC, 8 September 2003.

22. These sections often repeat verbatim Amis's nonfiction analysis of the San Fernando Valley pornographic film industry. See Martin Amis, "Sex in America," *Talk,* February 2001, 8–103, 133–35.

23. Some readers will be put off by Amis's handling of this theme, but as Robert MacFarlane has noted, "like Nabokov in *Lolita,* Amis squares up to a taboo and tries to acknowledge and analyse its existence without ever condoning it" ("Martin Amis Versus the Modern World," *Evening Standard,* 1 September 2003, A36). In *Experience,* Amis discusses the fact that Frederick West, the serial killer who murdered Amis's cousin Lucy Partington, raped and sexually tortured his own children (139–40n.). The subject of incest first appears in Amis's fiction in *Success* (see chap. 2).

24. As Amis writes in a note at the end of the novel, his portrait of Andrews draws in part from the life of "Mad Frank" (Frankie Fraser), one of London's most notorious criminals (see especially Frankie Fraser and James Morton, *Mad Frank's Diary,* Time Warner, 1995); and on the interviews contained in Tony Parker, ed., *Life after Life: Interviews with Twelve Murderers* (London: Secker & Warburg, 1990).

25. Douglas-Fairhurst, "Dickens With a Snarl," 15.

26. In many ways *Yellow Dog* is a novel-length antidote to Robert Bly's mythopoeic hymn to male empowerment, which Amis skewered in a 1991 review that can be found in *The War against Cliché,* 3–9. As James Ley has written, the novel is "a treatise on the ugly absurdity of male desires, and a guide to disempowerment and personal invalidation" ("A Mellower Amis Barks Back," *The Age* [Melbourne], 6 September 2003, 4).

27. As Amis wrote in his 1983 profile of Saul Bellow, "'being human' isn't the automatic condition of every human being. Like freedom or sanity, it is not a given but a gift, a talent, an accomplishment, an objective." See "Saul Bellow in Chicago," in *The Moronic Inferno* (London: Penguin, 1987), 208.

28. Reviewing a new edition of Evelyn Waugh's *Brideshead Revisited* in 1981, Amis equated sentimentality with artistic failure: "Waugh's snobbery is revealed here as a failure of imagination, an artistic failure; it is stock-response, like sentimentality" (*The War against Cliché*, 202).

Bibliography

Books by Amis

(This list includes English, American, and Canadian first editions of all books written by Amis and important later editions)

The Rachel Papers. London: Jonathan Cape, 1973; New York: Alfred A. Knopf, 1974; New York: Vintage, 1992.

Dead Babies. London: Jonathan Cape, 1975; New York: Alfred A. Knopf, 1976; New York: Vintage, 1992. Republished as *Dark Secrets,* St. Albans: Triad/Panther, 1977.

Success. London: Jonathan Cape, 1978; New York: Harmony, 1987; New York: Vintage, 1992.

Other People: A Mystery Story. London: Jonathan Cape, 1981; New York: Viking, 1981; New York: Vintage, 1994.

Invasion of the Space Invaders: An Addict's Guide. London: Hutchinson, September 1982; Millbrae, California: Celestial Arts, 1982; Toronto: Methuen, 1982.

Money: A Suicide Note. London: Jonathan Cape, 1984; New York: Viking, 1985; New York: Penguin, 1986.

The Moronic Inferno and Other Visits to America. London: Jonathan Cape, 1986; New York: Viking, 1987; New York: Penguin, 1987.

Einstein's Monsters. London: Jonathan Cape, 1987; New York: Harmony, 1987; New York: Vintage, 1990.

London Fields. London: Jonathan Cape, 1989; New York: Harmony, 1990; Toronto: Lester & Orpen Dennys, 1989; New York: Vintage, 1991.

Time's Arrow, or, The Nature of the Offense. London: Jonathan Cape, 1991; New York: Harmony, 1991; Toronto: Viking, 1991; New York: Vintage, 1992.

Visiting Mrs. Nabokov and Other Excursions. London: Jonathan Cape, 1993; New York: Harmony, 1994; Toronto: Alfred A. Knopf Canada, 1993.

Two Stories. London: Moorhouse & Sørensen, 1994. Contains "Denton's Death" and "Let Me Count the Times." Small press limited edition, total run of 326 copies.

God's Dice. London: Penguin, 1995. Contains "God's Dice" (alternate title of "Bujak and the Strong Force") and "The Little Puppy That Could" (both from *Einstein's Monsters*).

The Information. London: Harper Collins, 1995; New York: Harmony, 1995; Toronto: Alfred A. Knopf Canada, 1995; New York: Vintage, 1996.

Night Train. London: Jonathan Cape, 1997; New York: Harmony, 1998; Toronto: Alfred A. Knopf Canada, 1997; New York: Vintage, 1999.

Heavy Water and Other Stories. London: Jonathan Cape, 1998; New York: Harmony, 1999; New York: Vintage, 1999.

The Coincidence of the Arts. Paris: Coromandel Express, 1999. Short story from *Heavy Water,* individual pages housed in a metal container, is illustrated by seven original prints by Peruvian photographer Mario Testino. Limited to fifty-five copies, each signed by M. A. and Testino.

Experience: A Memoir. London: Jonathan Cape, 2000; New York: Hyperion/Talk Miramax Books, 2000; Toronto: Alfred A. Knopf Canada, 2000; New York: Vintage, 2002.

The War against Cliché: Essays and Reviews, 1971–2000. London: Jonathan Cape, 2001; New York: Hyperion/Talk Miramax Books, 2001.

Koba the Dread: Laughter and the Twenty Million. New York: Hyperion/Talk Miramax Books, 2002; London: Jonathan Cape, 2002.

Yellow Dog. New York: Hyperion/Talk Miramax Books, 2003; London: Jonathan Cape, 2003.

Uncollected Works

Fiction
"Debitocracy." *Penthouse,* November 1974, 50–58, 62. Dystopian
   short story about a future world where sexual passion has been
   vanquished.

Poetry and Drama
It's Disgusting at Your Age. In *New Review,* September 1976,
   19–24; rpt. in *The New Review Anthology,* edited by Ian Hamil-
   ton, 216–30. London: Heinemann, 1985. One-act play that
   anticipates *Success.*
"An American Airman Looks Ahead." *Observer,* 5 June 1977, 28.
   Poem reflecting Amis's association with "the Martian School."
"Point of View." *New Statesman,* 14 December 1979, 954. Another
   "Martian School" poem which reappears in *Other People: A
   Mystery.*

Produced Screenplay
Saturn 3. Dir. Stanley Donen. ITC Films, 1980.

Uncollected Essays
"Chalk and Cheese." *Times Educational Supplement,* 21 September
   1973, 58. Essay on Thom Gunn and Ted Hughes.
"How Awful Goodness Is." *Times Educational Supplement,* 21 Sep-
   tember 1973, 61. Essay on *Bleak House,* by Charles Dickens.
"Joseph Heller in Conversation with Martin Amis." *New Review,*
   November 1975, 55–59.
"Enigma and Variations." *Radio Times,* 13–19 December 1975,
   7–9. Essay on the varied and passionate responses Jane Austen
   elicits from readers.
"Problem City." *New Statesman,* 6 February 1976, 156. Essay on
   New York City.

"My Oxford." In *My Oxford,* edited by Ann Thwaite, 203–13. London: Robson, 1977. Essay on Amis's undergraduate experience at Exeter College, Oxford University.

"On the Wagon." *Sunday Times,* 22 May 1977, 35. Report on the Cannes film festival

"Dark Laughter." *New Statesman,* 8 July 1977, 55–56. Essay on Nabokov.

"Blackpool Diary." *New Statesman,* 14 October 1977, 504. Notes from Blackpool Tory conference.

"The State of Fiction: A Symposium." *New Review,* Summer 1978, 18.

"The Bodies in Question." *Observer,* 18 February 1979, 11. "Private Line" column on pornography.

"Shower of Gold." *Observer,* 22 April 1979, 34. Profile of Joseph Heller.

"A Tale of Two Novels." *Observer,* 19 October 1980, 26. Essay accusing Jacob Epstein of plagiarizing from *The Rachel Papers.*

"A New Sheriff Rides in from the West." *Observer,* 9 November 1980, 11. Essay on "Reagan's World" examining the screen image of Ronald Reagan and his mastery of the television medium in his presidential campaign.

"The Sublime and the Ridiculous: Nabokov's Black Farces." In *Vladimir Nabokov, His Life, His Work, His World: A Tribute,* edited by Peter Quenell. New York: William Morrow, 1980. Essay on Nabokov's *Despair; King, Queen, Knave; Laughter in the Dark;* and *Lolita.*

"London Literary Life: Let Me In, Let Me In!" *New York Times Book Review,* 5 April 1981, 9, 28. Essay on the London literary scene.

"The Novelist Cast as Mendacious Wrecker." *Times,* 8 September 1982, 9. Essay on *Despair,* by Vladimir Nabokov.

"Tabloid Tactics: Martin Amis in New York." *Observer,* 12 September 1982, 28. Essay on New York tabloid newspapers.

"Tough Nut to Crack." *Observer,* 31 October 1982, 27. Essay on being expelled from a Battersea grammar school at age thirteen.

"Letter from London." *Vogue*, April 1985, 216, 221–22. Comments on Prince Andrew and the tabloid journalism of Fleet Street.

"The Great American Mix." *Observer*, 16 February 1986, 29. Essay on "sex, drink and celebrity" among American writers, including Saul Bellow, Joseph Heller, Norman Mailer, Philip Roth, and Gore Vidal.

"*Goodfellas:* Blowing Away the Romantic Myth of the Mobster." *Premiere*, October 1987, 76, 79. Appreciation of Martin Scorsese's *Goodfellas*

"The Worst Review." *New Statesman & Society*, 31 March 1989, 29. Amis's contribution to symposium "Words for Salman Rushdie," published for the anniversary of the *fatwa* against Rushdie.

"Relative Values: Deux Amis." *Sunday Times Magazine*, 3 December 1989, 11, 14. Kingsley and Martin Amis on their relationship.

"Second Thoughts: Crying for the Light." *Independent*, 29 September 1990, Weekend Books, 29. Essay on the "unexpected growth and difficult birth" of *London Fields*.

"H is for Homosexual." In *Hockney's Alphabet: Drawings by David Hockney*, edited by Stephen Spender, 23–24. New York: Random House, 1991. A short (two page) rumination on homosexuality, emphasizing Amis's evolving attitudes.

"The Coming of the Signature." *Times Literary Supplement*, 17 January 1992, 18. Essay on Amis's tenure at the *TLS*.

"Mark Boxer." In *The Collected and Recollected Marc*, edited by Mark Amory, 49–51. London: Fourth Estate, 1993. Amis's elegy for his friend, the caricaturist Mark Boxer.

"A Defence of the Writer's Realm." *Sunday Times*, 4 April 1993, 7. Essay supporting Salman Rushdie, text taken from Amis's acceptance speech for the *Sunday Times* Award for Excellence in Writing (28 March 1993).

"The Heat of Wimbledon." *New Yorker*, 26 July 1993, 66–70. Essay on Wimbledon tennis tournament.

"At the Wide-Open Open." *New Yorker,* 4 October 1993, 173–78. Essay on the U.S. Open tennis tournament.

"The Thugs Have Taken Over." *Evening Standard,* 25 October 1993, 27. Personal essay on crime and society.

"The Fuck-It Generation." Review of *Living Dangerously: Young Offenders in Their Own Words* and *Talking Blues,* by Roger Graef. *Esquire* (U.K.), November 1993, 92–95, 220.

"My Imagination and I." In *Power and the Throne: The Monarchy Debate,* edited by Anthony Barnett, 79–80. London: Vintage, 1994. Amis writes of a "sex dream" about the Duchess of York.

"Tennis Personalities." *New Yorker,* 5 September 1994, 112. Tennis essay in "Shouts and Murmurs" section.

"Travolta's Second Act." *New Yorker,* 20 & 27 February 1995, 212–18. Profile of actor John Travolta.

"Buy My Book, Please." *New Yorker,* 26 June & 3 July 1995, 96–99. Essay on U.S. book tour for *The Information.*

"The Games Men Play." *New Yorker,* 14 August 1995, 40–47. Tennis essay on the U.S. Open.

"Jane's World." *New Yorker,* 8 January 1996, 31–35. Essay on Jane Austen's present-day popularity.

"My Ad." *New Yorker,* 9 September 1996, 98. Tennis essay in "Shouts & Murmurs" section.

"The Mirror of Ourselves." *Time,* 15 September 1997, 64. Essay on the death of Princess Diana.

"Books I Wish I'd Written." *Guardian,* 2 October 1997, T18. On Amis's "research" for *Night Train.*

"Of Cars and the Man." *The Republic of Letters,* March 1998, 2–3; rpt. as "Road Rage and Me," *Guardian,* 7 March 1998, Features, 1. Essay on road rage.

"Peter Porter." In *Paeans for Peter Porter: A Celebration for Peter Porter on His Seventieth Birthday by Twenty of His Friends,* edited by Anthony Thwaite, 13–15. London: Bridgewater Press, 1999. Amis's brief, affectionate appreciation of the Australian expatriate poet.

"The Shock of the Nou." *Observer Review,* 30 May 1999, 1–2. Essay on football crowd at a match between Manchester United and Barcelona.

"Sex in America." *Talk,* February 2001, 98–103, 133–35. Essay on the Los Angeles pornography industry.

"Fear and Loathing." *Guardian,* 18 September 2001, G2. Essay on the terrorist attacks in the U.S., part of the *Guardian* series "Special Report: Terrorism in the U.S."

"Remembering a Life." Review of *Iris* (film). *Talk,* December 2001/January 2002, 131–33. Reprinted as "Against Dryness." In *On Modern British Fiction,* edited by Zachary Leader (Oxford Press, 2002), 265–69. Oxford: Oxford University Press, 2002. Essay on Richard Eyre's film about the novelist Irish Murdoch, her battle against Alzheimer's disease, and her husband John Bayley's devotion.

"The Voice of the Lonely Crowd." *Guardian Review,* 2 June 2002, 4–6. Essay on the implications for writers and literature of the September 11, 2001, terrorist attacks.

"Window on a Changed World." *Daily Telegraph,* 11 September 2002, 17. Essay analyzing how the terrorist attacks in New York on 11 September 2001 have changed America and the world.

"The Palace at the End." *Guardian,* 4 March 2003, 23. Essay on the global implications of the war in Iraq.

"The World: An Explanation." *Daily Telegraph,* 8 March 2003, 29. Brief commentary on contemporary global politics and terrorism.

Uncollected Book Reviews

"What the People Sing." Review of *The Faber Book of Popular Verse,* ed. Geoffrey Grigson. *Daily Telegraph,* 4 November 1971, 8.

"Language, Truth and Politics." Review of *Public Voices: Literature and Politics with Special Reference to the Seventeenth Century,* by L. C. Knights. *Observer,* 14 November 1971, 33.

"Reviews in Brief." Review of *Aleksander Solzhenitsyn: the Major Novels,* by Abraham Rothberg. *New Society,* 2 March 1972, 461–62.

"Science Fiction." Reviews of *What's Become of Screwloose?,* by Ron Goulart; *Conscience Interplanetary,* by Joseph Green; *Out of Their Minds,* by Clifford Simak; *Dread Companion,* by André Norton; and *Orbit 6,* ed. Damon Knight. *Observer,* 16 April 1972, 32. Published under the pseudonym Henry Tilney.

"Science Fiction." Reviews of *The Day after Judgement* by James Blish; *Nighwtings,* by Robert Silverberg; *Children of Tomorrow,* by A. E. Van Vogt; and *Timescoop,* by John Brunner. *Observer,* 28 May 1972, 33. Published under pseudonym Henry Tilney.

"The Shrug of Resignation." Review Of *Another World,* by James Hanley. *The Times,* 8 June 1972, 10.

"The Dragon." Review of *The Dragon,* short stories by Yevgeny Zamyatin. *The Times,* 13 July 1972, 10.

"Science Fiction." Reviews of *You Feel Anything When I Do This?* by Robert Sheckley; *Other Days, Other Eyes,* by Bob Shaw,; *Dimension X,* ed. Damon Knight; *Nine Princes in Amber,* by Roger Zelazny; and *The Time Stream,* by Eric Temple Bell. *Observer,* 16 July 1972, 30. Published under pseudonym Henry Tilney.

"Organ Duets." Review of *Hermaphrodeity,* by Alan Friedman. *Times Literary Supplement,* 4 August 1972, 909. Published anonymously.

"Corrective Force." Review of *Nor Shall My Sword: Discourses on Pluralism, Compassion and Social Hope,* by F. R. Leavis. *Times Educational Supplement,* 25 August 1972, 14.

"Science Fiction." Reviews of *Who Needs Men?,* by Edmund Cooper; *Ipomea,* by John Rackham; *Un-Man,* by Poul Anderson; *Welcome to the Monkey House,* by Kurt Vonnegut; and *The Big Win,* by Jimmy Miller. *Observer,* 3 September 1, 972, 33. Published under the pseudonym Henry Tilney.

"Circling Around." Review of *Raw Material,* by Alan Sillitoe, and *Trust an Englishman* by John Knowler. *Observer,* 5 November 1972, 38.

"Science Fiction." Reviews *Of Time and Stars, The Wind from the Sun,* and *Lost Worlds of 2000* by Arthur C. Clarke; *The Gods Themselves, An Isaac Asimov Double,* and *The Space Merchants* by Isaac Asimov; and *The Dreaming Earth* by John Brunner. *Observer,* 12 November 1972, 37. Published under pseudonym Henry Tilney.

"The Deviousness of STC." Review of *Coleridge, The Damaged Archangel,* by Norman Fruman, *Times Literary Supplement,* 1 December 1972, 1463. Published anonymously.

"Society and the Superego." Review of *Sincerity and Authenticity,* by Lionel Trilling. *Times Educational Supplement,* 1 December 1972, 18.

"Second Thoughts." Review of *The Gates* by Jennifer Johnston; *Full Moon,* by Caradog Prichard; and *How She Died,* by Helen Yglesias. *New Statesman,* 19 January 1973, 96.

"Science Fiction." Reviews of *A Transatlantic Tunnel, Hurrah!,* by Harry Harrison; *The Mistress of Downing Street,* by Walter Harris; *Clone,* by Pierre Boulle; *Broke Down Engine,* by Ron Goulart; and *Pstalemate,* by Lester del Rey. *Observer,* 28 January 1973, 35. Published under pseudonym Henry Tilney.

"Precious Little." Review of *The Abortion: An Historical Romance,* by Richard Brautigan. *Times Literary Supplement,* 2 February 1973, 113. Published Anonymously.

"MacPosh." Reviews of *Mungo's Dream* by J. I. M. Stewart; *The Autobiography of Miss Jane Pittman,* by Ernest J. Gaines; *The Taxi,* by Violette Leduc, translated by Helen Weaver; *One of Our Own,* by Frank Norman; and *Birchwood,* by John Banville. *New Statesman,* 9 February 1973, 205–06.

"Alas, Poor Bradley." Review of *The Black Prince* by Iris Murdoch; *Through the Dark and Hairy Wood,* by Shaun Herron; and *Botchan,* by Natsume Soseki. *New Statesman,* 23 February

1973, 278–79 (the review of *The Black Prince* is reprinted in *The War against Cliché* 83–85).

"A Big Boob." Review of *The Breast,* by Philip Roth. *Observer,* 25 March 1973, 36.

"Formidable Wit." Review of *Epistle to a Godson and Other Poems,* by W. H. Auden. *Times Educational Supplement,* 6 April 1973, 27.

"Science Fiction." Reviews of *Tomorrow Lies in Ambush,* by Bob Shaw; *Inconstant Moon,* by Larry Niven; *Machines and Men,* by Keith Roberts; *The Best of John W. Campbell,* by John W. Campbell; *The Early Asimov,* by Isaac Asimov; *Out of this World,* ed. Amabel Williams-Ellis and Michael Pearson; *The Ruins of Earth,* by Thomas Disch; *Killer Pine,* by Lindsay Gutteridge; *Grey Matters,* by William Hjorstberg; *Heart Clock,* by Dick Morland; and *Panic O'Clock* by Christopher Hodder-Williams. *Observer,* 10 May 1973, 37. Published under the pseudonym Henry Tilney.

"Nabokov in Switzerland." Review of *Transparent Things,* by Vladimir Nabokov. *Spectator,* 12 May 1973, 591.

"Cultivating a Cult." Review of *Breakfast of Champions* and *Happy Birthday, Wanda June,* by Kurt Vonnegut Jr. *Observer,* 15 July 1973, 33.

"Eliot Made Easy." Reviews of *George Eliot,* by T. S. Pearce, and *George Eliot: Middlemarch,* ed. Patrick Swinden. *Times Literary Supplement,* 17 August 1973, 950. Published anonymously.

"Science Fiction." Reviews of *Rendezvous with Rama* by Arthur C. Clarke; *The Embedding,* by Ian Watson; *Time out of Mind,* by Richard Cowper; *Age of Miracles,* by John Brunner; *Star Trek 7,* by James Blish. *Observer,* 2 September 1973, 35. Published under pseudonym Henry Tilney.

"Coleridge in Malta." Review of *A Voyage in Vain: Coleridge's Journey to Malta in 1804,* by Aleth Hayter. *Observer,* 16 September 1973, 37.

"The Dialect of the Tribe." Review of *The Survival of English: Essays in Criticism of Language,* by Ian Robinson. *New Statesman,* 19 October 1973, 564–65.

"Circling Around." Review of *Raw Material,* by Alan Sillitoe; and *Trust an Englishman,* by John Knowler. *Observer,* 5 November 1973, 38.

"Science Fiction." Reviews of *The Stainless Steel Rat Saves the World,* by Harry Harrison; *Frankenstein Unbound,* by Brian Aldiss; *The Invincible,* by Stanislaw Lem; *The Oak & the Ram,* by Michael Moorcock; *Midsummer Century,* by James Blish; *Robert Sheckley Omnibus, The Best of Arthur C. Clarke, The Best of Isaac Asimov,* and *The Best of Robert Heinlein,* ed. Robert Conquest; *The 1973 World's Best SF,* ed. Donald Wollheim; and *Best SF Stories of the Year,* ed. Lester del Rey. *Observer,* 11 November 1973, 36. Published under pseudonym Henry Tilney.

"Verse Vocation." Review of inaugural issue of *Poetry Nation,* ed. C. B. Cox and Michael Schmidt. *Times Literary Supplement,* 23 November 1973, 1452. Published anonymously.

"Science Fiction." Reviews of *Vermillion Sands,* by J. G. Ballard; *Mindfogger,* by Michael Rogers; *The Tenth Planet,* by Edmund Cooper; and *Where Do We Go from Here?* ed. Isaac Asimov. *Observer,* 23 December 1973, 23. Published under pseudonym Henry Tilney.

"Rhetoric of Ghosts." Review of *Exterminator!,* by William Burroughs. *Observer,* 3 March 1974, 37.

"Science Fiction." Reviews of *The Twilight of Briareus,* by Richard Cowper; *Dying Inside,* by Robert Silverberg; *Brainrack,* by Kit Pedler and Gerry Davis; *Bad Moon Rising,* ed. Thomas Disch; *The Darkness on Diamondia,* by A. E. Van Vogt; *Guns of Avalon,* by Roger Zelzny; and *SF Monthly. Observer,* 17 March 1974, 37. Published under pseudonym Henry Tilney.

"For His Pains." Review of *Thieves of Fire,* by Denis Donoghue. *New Review,* April 1974, 91–92.

"Isadora's Complaint." *Observer,* 21 April 1974, 37. Review of *Fear of Flying,* by Erica Jong.

"Science Fiction." Reviews *Casey Agonistes,* by Richard McKenna; *The 80–Minute Hour,* by Brian Aldiss; *Time Enough for Love,* by

Robert Heinlein; *Friends Come in Boxes,* by Michael Coney; *The Hephaestus Plague,* by Thomas Page; and *The Rats,* by James Herbert. *Observer,* 5 May 1974, 37. Published under pseudonym Henry Tilney.

"Science Fiction." Reviews of *Inverted World,* by Christopher Priest; *The Continuous Katherine Mortenhoe,* by D. C. Compton; *Halcyon Drift,* by Brian Stableford; *Beyond Apollo,* by Barry Malzburg; *The Sheep Look Up,* by John Brunner. *Observer,* 18 August 1974, 28.

"Catcher in the Sty." Review of *Something Happened,* by Joseph Heller. *New Review,* December 1974, 64–65.

"Science Fiction." Reviews of *Flow My Tears, The Policeman Said,* by Philip K. Dick; *Worlds Apart,* by Richard Cowper; *Star Smashers and the Galaxy Rangers,* by Harry Harrison; *Albion! Albion!,* by Dick Morland; *The Moving Snow,* by Ian Weekley; *Winter's Children,* by Michael Coney; *Stationary Orbit,* by Peter Macey; *The Parasaurians,* by Robert Wells; *Singularity Station,* by Brian N. Ball; *The Swarm,* by Arthur Herzog; *Nebula Award Stories 9,* ed. Kate Wilhelm; *The John W. Campbell Memorial Anthology,* ed. Harry Harrison; *Before the Golden Age,* ed. Isaac Asimov. *Observer,* 8 December 1974, 31.

"Each Dawn They Die." Review of *The Last Hours Before Dawn,* by Reg Gladney. *Times Literary Supplement,* 17 January 1975, 48.

"Tour de Farce." Review of *The Glory of the Hummingbird,* by Peter De Vries; *Death, Sleep and the Traveler,* by John Hawkes; and *About Harry Townes,* by Bruce Jay Friedman. *New Statesman,* 21 February 1975, 250.

"Science Fiction." Reviews *Orbitsville,* by Bob Shaw; *Unfamiliar Territory,* by Robert Silverberg; *Real-Time World,* by Christopher Priest; *Rhapsody in Black,* by Brian Stableford; *To Ride Pegasus,* by Anne McCaffrey; *The Men from PIG and ROBOT,* by Harry Harrison; *Into Deepest Space,* by Geoffrey Hoyle. *Observer,* 23 February 1975, 28.

"Fellow Fans." Reviews of *Beyond the Words: Eleven Writers in Search of a New Fiction,* ed. Giles Gordon, and *Farewell, Fond Dreams,* by Giles Gordon. *New Statesman,* 7 March 1975, 315–16.

"Left-Handed Backhand." Reviews of *Wampeters, Foma and Granfalloons,* by Kurt Vonnegut; and *Myron,* by Gore Vidal. *Observer,* 6 April 1975, 30.

"Out of Style." Review of *Look at the Harlequins!* by Vladimir Nabokov. *New Statesman,* 25 April 1975, 555–56.

"Science Fiction." Reviews of *The Jonah Kit,* by Ian Watson; *The Quincunx of Time,* by James Blish; *To Live Again,* by Robert Silverberg; *10,000 Light Years from Home,* by James Tiptree Jr.; *Antigrav,* ed. Philip Strick; *The Man from Beyond,* by John Wyndham. *Observer,* 18 May 1975, 30.

"Science Fiction." Reviews of *Hell's Cartographers,* ed. Brian Aldiss and Harry Harrison; *Space Odysseys,* by Brian Aldiss; *The Man in the High Castle,* by Philip K. Dick; *City in the Sky,* by Curt Slodmak; *Cemetery World,* by Clifford Simak. *Observer,* 8 June 1975, 26.

"Life, Literature and Leavis." Review of *The Living Principle: "English" as a Discipline of Thought,* by F. R. Leavis. *Observer,* 14 September 1975, 25.

"Being Serious in the Fifties." Review of *Reading Myself and Others,* by Philip Roth, and *Mountains and Caverns,* by Alan Sillitoe. *New Statesman,* 7 November 1975, 577–78.

"Up!" Review of *High-Rise,* by J. G. Ballard; *Vote to Kill,* by Douglas Hurd; and *Freedom for Mr. Mildrew and Nigel Someone,* by Clive Murphy. *New Statesman,* 14 November 1975, 618. The review of *High Rise* is reprinted in *The War against Cliché* 102–03.

"Science Fiction." Reviews *Things Fall Apart,* by Ron Goulart; *Extrou,* by Alfred Exter; *The Mote in God's Eye,* by Larry Niven and Jerry Pournelle; *Imperial Earth,* by Arthur Clarke; *Shipwreck* by Charles Logan; *The Dynostar Menace,* by Kit Pedler and Gerry Davis; *Fade-Out,* by Patrick Tilley; *Monument* and

The Light That Never Was by Lloyd Biggle Jr. *Observer,* 16 November 1975, 30.

"Science Fiction." Reviews of *Wandering Stars,* ed. Jack Dann; *Night Walk,* by Bob Shaw; *Charisma,* by Michael Coney; *To Die in Italbar,* by Roger Zelazny; *Terminus,* by Peter Edwards; *High Destiny,* by Dan Morgan; and *The Best of E. E. 'Doc' Smith,* by E. E. Smith. *Observer,* 8 February 1976, 27.

"Soft Cor." Reviews of *Erotic Movies* and *Life Goes to the Movies,* by Richard Wortley. *New Statesman,* 13 February 1976, 199–200.

"Science Fiction." Reviews of *Buy Jupiter, Earth Is Room Enough* and *The Foundation Trilogy* by Isaac Asimov; *The Wind's Twelve Quarters* by Ursula K. le Guin; *A Cure for Cancer* and *The Lives and Times of Jerry Cornelius* by Michael Moorcock; *The Space Machine* by Christopher Priest; *Early Writings in Science and Science Fiction by H. G. Wells,* ed. Robert Philmus and David Y. Hughes; *The Brains of Earth* and *The Moon Moth* by Jack Vance; *The Wizard of Linn* A. E. Van Vogt; and *Glory Road* by Robert Heinlein. *Observer,* 4 April 1976, 27.

"Cover Up." Reviews of *Louie's Snowstorm,* by E. W. Hildick; *Rumble Fish,* by S. E. Hinton; *The Prince of Central Park,* by Evan H. Rhodes; *Me and My Million,* by Clive King; and *Operation Cobra,* by Anders Bodelsen. *New Statesman,* 21 May 1976, 690.

"Science Fiction." Reviews of *The Status Civilization,* by Robert Sheckley; *The Stochastic Man,* by Robert Silverberg; *The Custodians,* by Richard Cowper; *The Prayer Machine,* by Christopher Hodder Williams; *Badge of Infamy,* by Lester del Ray; *Eve Among the Blind,* by Robert Holstock; *No Direction Home,* by Norman Spinrad. *Observer,* 13 June 1976, 27.

"Science Fiction." *Observer,* 8 August 1976, 22. Reviews of *Wreath of Stars* by Bob Shaw; *Brontomed!,* by Michael Coney; *The Book of Philip Jose Farmer,* by Philip Jose Farmer; and *Anita,* by Keith Robert.

"Science Fiction." Reviews of *Skyfall,* by Harry Harrison; *Children of Dune,* by Frank Herbert; *The Feast of St. Dionysus* by Robert Silverberg; *New Dimensions 6,* ed. Robert Silverberg; *The Beast That Shouted Love at the Heart of the World,* by Harlan Ellison; *Again, Dangerous Visions,* ed. Harlan Ellison; *The Exile Waiting,* by Vonda N. McIntyre; *The Man With Two Memories,* by J. B. S. Haldane; and *The Grain Kings,* by Keith Roberts, *Observer,* 3 October 1976, 24.

"The Jokers in the Pack." Reviews of *Slapstick,* by Kurt Vonnegut, and *I Hear America Swinging,* by Peter De Vries. *Observer,* 7 November 1976, 27.

"Nice and Nasty." Review of *Four Crowded Years: The Diaries of Auberon Waugh 1972–1976; The Book of Bores,* by Richard Ingrams, Michael Heath and Barry Fantoni; and *Lord Gnome of the Rings: The Best of Private Eye. New Statesman,* 26 November 1976, 760–61.

"Science Fiction." Reviews of *Low-Flying Aircraft,* by J. G. Ballard; *Cosmic Kaleidoscope,* by Bob Shaw; *Man Plus,* by Frederick Pohl; *The Space Vampires,* by Colin Wilson; *The Lost Traveler,* by Steve Wilson; *Who's Who in Science Fiction,* by Brian Ash; *Science Fiction at Large,* ed. Peter Nicholls. *Observer,* 5 December 1976, 30.

"Science Fiction." Reviews of *The Martian Inca,* by Ian Watson; *J. G. Ballard: The First Twenty Years,* ed. James Goddard and David Pringle; *The Bicentennial Man,* by Isaac Asimov; *The Hellhound Project,* by Ron Goulart; *Nebula Maker,* by Olaf Stapledon; and *The Paradise Game* by Brian Stableford. *Observer,* 13 February 1977, 35.

"Science Fiction." Reviews of *Medusa's Children,* by Bob Shaw; *Out of Time,* by Larry Niven,; *Shadrach in the Furnace,* by Robert Silverburg; *Mindbridge,* Joe Haldeman; *The King is Dead,* by Alexander Thynn; *Wonderworlds,* by William F. Nolan; and *Long after Midnight,* by Ray Bradbury. *Observer,* 8 May 1977, 26.

"Electric Ladyland." Review of *Crackpot,* by Ron Goulart. *New Statesman,* 14 April 1978, 503.

"The 'Me' Machine." Review of *In Our Time,* by Tom Wolfe. *Observer,* 21 December 1980, 26.

"In the Hot Seat." Review of *Six Problems for Don Isidro Parodi,* by Jorge Luis Borges and Adolfo Bioy-Casares, trans. Norman Thomas di Giovanni. *Observer,* 19 July 1981, 28.

"Young, Gifted and Funny." Review of *Lantern Lecture,* by Adam Mars-Jones. *New Statesman,* 2 October 1981, 21–22.

"In the Jungle, the Mighty Jungle." Review of *The Mosquito Coast,* by Paul Theroux. *New York,* 8 March 1982, 84–85.

"Room with a Viewer." Review of *Television: The Medium and its Manners,* by Peter Conrad, and *Ah! Mischief: The Writer and Television,* ed. Frank Pike. *Observer,* 16 May 1982, 31.

"Laughter in the Dark." Review of *Nabokov: The Critical Heritage,* ed. Norman Page. *Observer,* 20 June 1982, 31.

"Don't Leave 'Em Laughing, Just Leave." Review of *The Breaks,* by Richard Price. *New York,* 24 January 1983, 56.

"Kafka Renewed." Review of *Stories 1904–1924,* by Franz Kafka, translated by J. A. Underwood. *Observer,* 24 April 1983, 30.

"Christian Gentleman." Review of *Hugging the Shore,* by John Updike. *Observer,* 15 January 1984, 48.

"Ghost at the Feast." Review of *Roman,* by Roman Polanski. *Observer,* 22 January 1984, 53.

"American Nightmare." Review of *The Place of Dead Roads,* by William S. Burroughs. *Observer,* 29 April 1984, 23.

"Chequered Careers." Review of *Total Chess,* by David Spanler; *Chess: The History of a Game,* by Richard Eales; and *The Oxford Companion to Chess,* by David Hooper and Kenneth Whyld. *Observer,* 23 December 1984, 28.

"He Likes it There." Review of *Sunrise with Seamonsters,* by Paul Theroux. *Observer,* 16 June 1985, 22.

"The American Eagle." Review of a collected uniform edition of Saul Bellow's works. *Observer,* 25 August 1985, 17.

"Californian Lifeniks." Review of *The Golden Gate,* by Vikram Seth. *Observer,* 22 June 1986, 23

"A Bolt Out of the Blue." Review of *No Laughing Matter,* by Joseph Heller and Speed Vogel. *Observer,* 7 September 1986, 26.

"The Breasts." Review of *The Dying Animal,* by Philip Roth. *Talk,* May 2001, 111–12.

"Voices of Revolution." Review of *Voices of Revolution, 1917,* by Mark D. Steinberg. *Times Literary Supplement,* 16 January 2002, 10.

"The Queen's Heart." Review of *Monarch: The Life and Reign of Elizabeth II,* by Robert Lacey; and *The Monarchy: An Oral Biography of Elizabeth,* by Deborah Hart Strober and Gerald S. Strober. *New Yorker,* 20 May 2002, 106–10.

Selected Film, Television, and Concert Reviews

"Unisex Me Here." Review of David Bowie concert at the Hammersmith Odeon. *New Statesman,* 6 July 1973, 28–29.

"Fleshpots" Review of London strip clubs. *New Statesman,* 14 September 1973: 362. Published as Bruno Holbrook, the pseudonym Amis used for two pieces on pornography in the *New Statesman.*

"Coming in Handy." Review of pornographic magazines. *New Statesman,* 14 December 1973, 922–23. Published as Bruno Holbrook.

"Miss Emmanuelle." Review of French soft-core film. *New Statesman,* 23 August 1974, 264–65.

"Pot Luck." Review of *Success Story: Interview with Gore Vidal* on *Horizon* (BBC-2). *New Statesman,* 15 August 1975, 208–09.

"Potter Platter." Review of *Play for Today,* by Dennis Potter (BBC-1). *New Statesman,* 9 April 1976, 481–82.

"I Didn't Get No . . ." Review of The Rolling Stones at Earls Court. *New Statesman,* 28 May 1976, 712–13.

"The Mild Bunch." Reviews of three films: *The Last Hard Men; The Human Factor;* and *What's Up Tiger Lily? New Statesman,* 18 June 1976, 823–24.

"Socket to Her." Reviews of two films: *The Tenant* and *Murder by Death*. *New Statesman*, 27 August 1976, 286–87.

"X to Grind." Review of *From Noon Till Three* (film). *New Statesman*, 3 September 1976, 321. Review of pornographic film.

"Crassroads." Review of *Dorian Gray*, adapted by John Osborne (BBC-1). *New Statesman*, 24 September 1976, 427–28.

"Capitalism and the Camera-Angle." Reviews of *The Age of Uncertainty*, presented by John Kenneth Galbraith, and *Eleanor Marx*, presented by Andrew Davies (BBC-2). *Sunday Times*, 16 January 1977, 35.

"Till the Ratings Do Us Part." Review of *The Man Alive Report: The American Way of Wedlock*. *Sunday Times*, 23 January 1977, 38.

"The Week Rape Came into Its Own." Review of *Act of Rape* (BBC-2). *Sunday Times*, 30 January 1977, 38.

"Punchbags." Review of *Pilger Report: Nuclear Power* (ATV) and *Professional Foul*, by Tom Stoppard (BBC-2). *New Statesman*, 30 September 1977, 454–55.

"Somebodaddy." Reviews of two films: *Heaven Can Wait* and *The Silent Partner*. *New Statesman*, 8 September 1978, 307–08.

"Chicken Raunch." Reviews of *At the Chicken Ranch* (ITV); *Clive James on Television* (LWT); cohabitation documentary *Couples* (BBC-1). *Observer*, 3 October 1982, 40. Reviews drive-in brothel documentary.

"Mother Nature and the Plague." Review of *Killer in the Village* (Horizon). *Observer*, 1 May 1983, 36. Reviews AIDS documentary.

"A Bowl of Catfood for Breakfast." Reviews of *Swindle!* (Channel 4), and *Inside China* (ITV). *Observer*, 8 May 1983, 40.

"Inside Charles's Marriage." Review of *At Home with Alastair Burnet: The Prince and Princess of Wales* (ITN). *Observer*, 27 October 1985, 28.

"Ronbo and the Arms Habit." *Observer*, 13 April 1986, 28. Reviews of programs featuring or concerning violence: *Magnum* (ITV); *Miami Vice* and *Film 86;* (BBC-1), *MOD: Keepers of the Threat* BBC-2); *Viewpoint 86: The Four Horseman* (ITV); and *Our Bomb—The Secret Story* (Channel 4).

Works about Martin Amis

Books

Dern, John A. *Martians, Monsters, and Madonna: Fiction and Form in the World of Martin Amis.* New York: Peter Lang, 2000.

Reynolds, Margaret, and Jonathan Noakes. Martin Amis: *The Rachel Papers, London Fields, Time's Arrow, Experience.* London: Vintage, 2003.

Tredell, Nicolas *The Fiction of Martin Amis: A Reader's Guide to Essential Criticism.* Cambridge: Icon Books, 2000.

Articles and Sections of Books

Alexander, Victoria. "Between the Influences of Bellow and Nabokov." *Antioch Review* 52 (fall 1994): 580–90.

Asher, Kenneth. "The Lawrentian Vision of Martin Amis's *London Fields.*" *Journal of Comparative Literature and Aesthetics* 24 (2001): 15–25.

Bellow, Janis Freedman. "Necropolis of the Heart." *Partisan Review* (fall 1995): 699–718 (essay on *The Information* and Philip Roth's *Sabbath's Theater*).

Bényei, Tamás. "Allegory and Allegoresis in Martin Amis's *Money,*" In *Proceedings of the First Conference of the Hungarian Society for the Study of English,* vol. 1 (Debrecen, Hungary: Institute of English and American Studies, 1995), 182–87.

Bernard, Catherine. "Disrembering/Remembering Mimesis: Martin Amis, Graham Swift." In *British Postmodern Fiction.* Edited by Theo D'haen and Hans Bertens, 121–44. Amsterdam and Atlanta: Rodopoi, 1993.

———. "A Certain Hermeneutic Slant: Sublime Allegories in Contemporary English Fiction." *Contemporary Literature* 38 (spring 1997): 164–84.

Brantlinger, Patrick. *Fictions of State: Culture and Credit in Britain, 1694–1994.* Ithaca, N.Y.: Cornell University Press, 1996.

Brown, Richard. "Postmodern Americas in the Fiction of Angela Carter, Martin Amis and Ian McEwan." In *Forked Tongues? Comparing Twentieth-Century British and American Literature*, edited by Ann Massa and Alistair Steed, 92–110. London: Longman, 1994.

Diedrick, James. "The Fiction of Martin Amis: Patriarchy and Its Discontents." In *Contemporary British Fiction*, edited by Richard J. Lane, Rod Mengham, and Philip Tew, 239–55. Cambridge: Polity, 2003.

Doan, Laura L. "'Sexy Greedy Is the Late Eighties': Power Systems in Amis's *Money* and Churchill's *Serious Money*." *Minnesota Review* 34–35 (1990): 69–80.

Easterbrook, Neil. "'I Know That It Is to Do with Trash and Shit, and That It Is Wrong in Time': Narrative Reversal in Martin Amis's *Time's Arrow*." *Conference of College Teachers of English Studies* 55 (1995): 52–61.

Finney, Brian. "Narrative and Narrated Homicides in Martin Amis's *Other People* and *London Fields*." *Critique* 37 (1995): 3–15.

Francois, Pierre. "Lethal Forms: Martin Amis's *Other People*." In *Inlets of the Soul: Contemporary Fiction in English and the Myth of the Fall*. Amsterdam and Atlanta: Rodopoi, 1999.

Holmes, Frederick. "The Death of the Author as Cultural Critique in *London Fields*." In *Powerless Fictions? Ethics, Cultural Critique, and American Fiction in the Age of Postmodernism*. Edited by Ricardo Miguel Alfonso, 53–62. Amsterdam and Atlanta: Rodopoi, 1996.

Howard, Gerald. "Slouching towards Grubnet: The Author in the Age of Publicity." *Review of Contemporary Fiction* 16 (1996): 44–53. Reprinted in Birkerts, Sven, ed. *Tolstoy's Dictaphone: Technology and the Muse*. St. Paul, Minn.: Graywolf, 16–27.

Keulks, Gavin. *Father and Son: Kingsley Amis, Martin Amis, and the British Novel since 1950*. Madison: University of Wisconsin Press, 2003.

Lodge, David. *The Art of Fiction*. New York: Viking Penguin, 1993.

Mallon, Thomas. *Stolen Words: Forays into the Origins and Ravages of Plagiarism*. New York: Ticknor and Fields, 1989. Contains an extended discussion of the controversy surrounding Jacob Epstein's novel *Wild Oats*, which plagiarized from *The Rachel Papers*.

Mars-Jones, Adam. *Venus Envy: On the WOMB and the BOMB*. London: Chatto & Windus, 1990. Focuses on changing representations of gender in contemporary fiction, with special emphasis on *Einstein's Monsters*.

Menke, Richard. "Narrative Reversals and the Thermodynamics of History in Martin Amis's *Time's Arrow*." *Modern Fiction Studies* 44 (winter 1998): 959–80.

Miller, Karl. *Doubles: Studies in Literary History*. London: Oxford University Press, 1985.

Mills, Sara. "Working with Sexism: What can Feminist Text Analysis Do?" In *Twentieth-Century Fiction: From Text to Context*, edited by Peter Verdonk and Jean Jacques Weber, 206–19. London: Routledge, 1995.

Miracky, James J. "Hope Lost or Hyped Lust? Gendered Representations of 1980s Britain in Margaret Drabble's *The Radiant Way* and Martin Amis's *Money*." *Critique: Studies in Contemporary Fiction* 44 (winter 2003): 136–43.

Moran, Joe. "Artists and Verbal Mechanics: Martin Amis's *The Information*." *Critique: Studies in Contemporary Fiction* 41 (summer 2000): 307–17.

Moyle, David. "Beyond the Black Hole: The Emergence of Science Fiction Themes in the Recent Work of Martin Amis." *Extrapolation: A Journal of Science Fiction and Fantasy* 36 (1995): 304–15.

Nash, John. "Fiction May be a Legal Paternity: Martin Amis's *The Information*." *English: The Journal of the English Association* 45 (1996): 213–24.

Rawson, Claude. "The Behaviour of Reviewers and their Response to Martin Amis's Novel, *Other People*." *London Review of Books*, 7–20 May 1981, 19–22.

Ryan, Kiernan. "Sex, Violence, and Complicity: Martin Amis and Ian McEwan." In *An Introduction to Contemporary Fiction:*

International Writing in English since 1970, edited by Rod Mengham, 203–18. Cambridge: Polity, 1999.

Slater, Maya. "Problems When Time Moves Backwards: Martin Amis's *Time's Arrow*." *English: The Journal of the English Association* 42 (1993): 141–52.

Smith, Penny. "Hell Innit: The Millenium in Alisdair Gray's Lanar, Martin Amis's *London Fields*, and Shena Mckay's *Dunedin*." *Essays and Studies* 48 (1995): 115–28.

Stevenson, Randall. "Recent and Contemporary: the Novel since the Nineteen Fifties." In *The British Novel since the Thirties: An Introduction*. Athens: The University of Georgia Press, 1986.

Stokes, Peter. "Martin Amis and the Postmodern Suicide: Tracing the Postnuclear Narrative at the Fin de Millenium." *Critique* 38 (1997): 300–311.

Taylor, D. J. *A Vain Conceit: British Fiction in the 1980s*. London: Bloomsbury, 1989.

———. "The Search for Value." In *After the War: The Novel and England since 1945*. London: Chatto & Windus, 1993.

Todd, Richard. "The Intrusive Author in British Postmodernist Fiction: The Cases of Alisdair Gray and Martin Amis." In *Exploring Postmodernism*, edited by Matei Calinescu and Douwe Fokkema, 123–37. Amsterdam: Benjamins, 1987.

———. "Resisting Dead Ends: Martin Amis." In *Consuming Fictions*. London: Bloomsbury, 1996.

Vice, Susan. "Form Matters: Martin Amis, *Time's Arrow*." In *Holocaust Fiction*. London: Routledge, 2000.

Wood, James. "Martin Amis: The English Imprisonment." In *The Broken Estate: Essays on Literature and Belief*. London: Jonathan Cape, 1999.

Selected Reviews

The Rachel Papers

Ackroyd, Peter. "Highway of Good Intentions," *Spectator*, 24 November 1973, 674.

Glueck, Grace. "Not the Son of Lucky Jim." *New York Times Book Review*, 26 May 1974, 4.

Miller, Karl. "Gothic Guesswork." *New York Review of Books*, 18 July 1974, 26.

Morrison, Blake. "Nice and Nasty." *Times Literary Supplement*, 16 November 1973, 1389.

Thwaite, Anthony. "The Way of the Warrior." *Observer*, 18 November 1973, 39.

Dead Babies

Feinstein, Elaine. "Killing Time." *New Statesman*, 17 October 1975, 479–80.

Lehmann-Haupt, Christopher. "Two Kinds of Metaphysical Joke." *New York Times Book Review*, 16 January 1976, 27.

Mason, Michael. "Post-Permissive Blues." *Times Literary Supplement*, 17 October 1975, 1225.

Mellors, John. "Raw Breakfast." *Listener*, 30 October 1975, 582.

Success

Ableman, Paul. "Sub-Texts." *Spectator*, 15 April 1978, 23–24.

Buchan, James. "An Unsuccessful Likeness." *Spectator*, 20 July 1991, 25–26.

Hepburn, Neil. "Tonto." *Listener*, 13 April 1978, 482–83.

Parini, Jay. "Men Who Hate Women." *New York Times Book Review*, 6 September 1987, 8.

Paulin, Tom. "Fantastic Eschatologies." *Encounter*, 3 September 1978, 73–78.

Thwaite, Anthony. "Sour Smell of Success." *Observer*, 16 April 1978, 27.

Other People: A Mystery Story

Ableman, Paul. "Fairies and Violence." *Spectator*, 21 March 1981, 22.

Ballard, J. G. "First Things Last." *Tatler*, March 1981, 111.

Glendinning, Victoria. "Lamb's Tale from Amis." *Listener*, 5 March 1981, 319–20.

Hollinghurst, Allan. "Opening Eyes." *New Statesman*, 13 March 1981, 21.

Hunter, Evan. "Mary Lamb and Mr. Wrong." *New York Times Book Review*, 26 July 1981, 9.

Levin, Bernard. "Forgetfulness of Things Past." *Sunday Times*, 8 March 1981, 43.

Morrison, Blake. "In the Astronomical Present." *Times Literary Supplement*, 6 March 1981, 247.

Sutherland, John. "Making Strange." *London Review of Books*, 19 March-1 April 1981, 21–22.

Invasion of the Space Invaders: An Addict's Guide
Korn, Eric. "Space Bores." *Sunday Times*, 26 September 1982, 33.

Money: A Suicide Note
Bayley, John. "Being Two is Half the Fun." *London Review of Books*, 4 July 1985, 13.

Burgess, Anthony. "Self Possessed." *Observer*, 30 September 1984, 20.

Geng, Veronica. "The Great Addiction." *New York Times Book Review*, 24 March 1985, 36.

Hamilton, Ian. "Martin and Martina." *London Review of Books*, 20 September–3 October 1984, 3–4. Rpt. in *Walking Possession* (London: Bloomsbury, 1994), 190–97.

Huth, Angela. "Stateside Scenes." *Listener*, 27 September 1984, 32.

Wilson, A. N. "Young Scumbag." *Spectator*, 20 October 1984, 29–31.

Yardley, Jonathan. "The Comic Madness of Martin Amis." *Washington Post Book World*, 24 March 1985, 3.

The Moronic Inferno and Other Visits to America
Bawer, Bruce. "What's Wrong with the English? Martin Amis on America." *New Criterion*, February 1987, 20–26.

Kermode, Frank. "J'Accuzi." *London Review of Books*, 24 July 1986, 5.

Einstein's Monsters

Imlah, Mick. "A Dart in the Heart." *Times Literary Supplement*, 29 September–5 October 1989, 1051.

King, Francis. "The Sin of the Fathers." *Spectator*, 2 May 1987, 31.

Lanchester, John. "As a Returning Lord." *London Review of Books*, 7 May 1987, 11–12.

Mars-Jones, Adam. "Fireworks at the Funeral." *Times Literary Supplement*, 1 May 1987, 457.

Penman, Ian. "Scumming It." In *Vital Signs*. London: Serpent's Tail, 1998.

See, Carolyn. "Humanity is Washed Up—True or False?" *New York Times Book Review*, 17 May 1987, 28.

London Fields

Hislop, Ian. "Six of the Best." *Literary Review*, September 1984, 14.

Kakutani, Michiko. "A Post-Mod Scheherazade In a Funky, Fearful London." *New York Times*, 13 February 1990, C17.

King, Francis. "A Thing Plot in a Fat Sandwich." *Spectator*, 23 September 1989, 36–37.

Lahr, John. "Books." *Vogue*, April 1990, 274–76.

McInerney, Jay. "Men on High Heels." *Observer*, 24 September 1989, 47.

Packer, George. "Something Amis." *Nation*, 23 April 1990, 565–66.

Pesetsky, Bette. "Lust Among the Ruins." *New York Times Book Review*, 4 March 1990, 1, 42.

Sante, Luc. "Cheat's Tale." *New Republic*, 30 April 1990, 45–46.

Szamuely, George. "Something Amiss with Martin." *National Review*, 28 May 1990, 46–48.

Wolcott, James. "Cool Hand Nuke." *Vanity Fair*, March 1990, 62, 68, 72.

Time's Arrow, or, The Nature of the Offense

Buchan, James. "The Return of Dr. Death," *Spectator*, 28 September 1991, 38.

Clifford, Andrew. "Fudging the Event Horizon." *New Scientist*, 30 November 1991, 55.

Harrison, M. John. "Speeding to Cradle from Grave." *Times Literary Supplement*, 20 September 1991, 21.

Kakutani, Michiko. "Time Runs Backward To Point Up a Moral." *New York Times*, 22 October 1991, C17.

Kermode, Frank. "In Reverse." *London Review of Books*, 13 September 1991, 11.

Koenig, Rhoda. "Holocaust Chic." *New York*, 21 October 1991, 117–18.

Lehman, David. "From Death to Birth." *New York Times Book Review*, 17 November 1991, 15.

Muchnick, Laurie. "Trading Places." *Village Voice Literary Supplement*, October 1991, 31.

Taylor, D. J. "Backward Steps." *New Statesman*, 27 September 1991, 55.

Updike, John. "Books: Nobody Gets Away with Everything." *New Yorker*, 25 May 1992, 85–88.

Wilson, A. N. "Books." *Vogue*. October 1991, 186, 188.

Visiting Mrs. Nabokov and Other Excursions

King, Chris Savage. "Bits of Rough." *New Statesman*, 1 October 1993, 39–40.

Mallon, Thomas. "Disarming Martin." *Gentleman's Quarterly*, March 1994, 124, 128.

Prose, Francine. "Novelist at Large." *New York Times Book Review*, 27 February 1994, 17.

Shone, Tom. "Brief Encounters of a Sobbing Martian." *Spectator*, 16 October, 1993, 38.

Wood, James. "Paradox Pile-Up." *Times Literary Supplement*, 15 October 1993, 21.

The Information

Bradbury, Malcolm. "Forget the Hype, Feel the Breadth." *Times* (London), 23 March 1995, 33.

Buckley, Christopher. "The Inflammation." *New York Times Book Review*, 23 April 1995, 3.

Kakutani, Michiko. "Raging Midlife Crisis as Contemporary Ethos." *New York Times*, 2 May 1995, C17.

Kaveney, Roz. "Energy and Entropy." *New Statesman*, 24 March 1995, 24.

Loose, Julian. "Satisfaction." *London Review of Books*, 11 May 1995, 9–10.

Mars-Jones, Adam. "Looking on the Blight Side." *Times Literary Supplement*, 24 March 1995, 19–20.

Ratcliffe, Michael. "What Little Boys Are Made Of." *Observer*, 26 March 1995, 17.

Ward, David C. "A Black Comedy of Manners." *Virginia Quarterly Review* (summer 1996): 561–64.

Wood, James. "Little Big Man." *New Republic*, 14 August 1995, 28–34.

Night Train

Brookner, Anita. "Farewell, My Lovely." *Spectator*, 27 September 1997, 36–37.

Kakutani, Michiko. "Detective Mike Hoolihan? She's Tough." *New York Times*, 27 January 1998, E7.

Kermode, Frank. "A Thriller With Something On Its Mind." *Atlantic Monthly*, February 1998, 100–104.

Lanchester, John. "Death Becomes Her." *New Yorker*, 16 February 1998, 80–81.

McGrath, Patrick. "Her Long Goodbye." *New York Times Book Review*, 1 February 1998, 6.

O'Brien, Geoffrey. "The Big Sleep." *New Republic*, 16 March 1998, 32–35.

O'Brien, Sean. "Choo-Choo Time." *Times Literary Supplement*, 19 September 1997, 22.

Page, Ra. "Superior Trash." *New Statesman*, 14 November 1997, 54.

Philips, Adam. "Cloud Cover." *London Review of Books*, 16 October 1997, 3–7.

Updike, John. "It's a Fair Cop." *Sunday Times Books* (London), *Sunday Times* (London), 21 September 1977, Books 1.

Walter, Natasha. "Dark Side of the Tracks." *Guardian Weekly*, 28 September 1997, 29–30.

Wolcott, James. "Synthetic Grit." *New Criterion*, March 1998, 64–66.

Wood, James. "An American in Amis." *Observer*, 21 September 1997, 17.

Heavy Water and Other Stories

Annan, Gabriele. "Taking the Whip to Language." *Spectator*, 3 October 1998, 50–51.

Birkerts, Sven. "The Twentieth Century Speaks." *Esquire*, February 1999, 64, 70.

Cowley, Jason. "A Small World." *Literary Review*, October 1998, 51.

Kakutani, Michiko. "Nine Easy Pieces: A Writer's Exercises." *New York Times*, 29 January 1999, E42.

Scott, A. O. "Trans-Atlantic Flights." *New York Times Book Review*, 31 January 1999, 5.

Walter, Natasha. "Fat Men, Thin Lives." *New Statesman*, 25 September 1998, 81–82.

Experience: A Memoir

Banville, John. "Sons and Lovers." *Irish Times*, 27 May 2000, E1.

Glendinning, Victoria. "The Best of You Is Here and I Still Have It." *Daily Telegraph*, 20 May 2000, 3.

Hamilton, Ian. "The New Model Martin Amis." *Sunday Telegraph*, 21 May 2000, 12.

Kakutani, Michiko. "The Amises, Two Writers in Discord, With Love." *New York Times*, 23 May 2000, B1, B7.

Lanchester, John. "Be Interesting!" *London Review of Books*, 6 July 2000, 3–6.

Lodge, David. "Putting Down Good Words." *Times Literary Supplement*, 26 May 2000, 25–27.

Walsh, John. "Night Train through a Dark Wood." *Independent*, 20 May 2000, 10.

Wood, James. "The Young Turk." *Guardian*, 20 May 2000, 8.

The War against Cliché: Essays and Reviews, 1970–2000

Cowley, Jason. "Mart for Mart's Sake." *Observer*, 8 April 2001, 17.

Dyer, Geoff. "Critical Velocity." *Guardian*, 14 April 2001, 10.

Kermode, Frank. "Nutmegged." *London Review of Books*, 10 May 2001, 27–8.

Kakutani, Michiko. "Writers Martin Amis Admires, and He Should Know." *New York Times*, 11 December 2001, E7.

Rainey, Lawrence. "The Most Uncommon Reader." *Independent*, 21 April 2001, 11.

Sanderson, Mark. "The Amis Way of Saying Things." *Sunday Telegraph*, 8 April 2001, 11.

Thorne, Matt. "Trainwreck in a Literary Time Machine." *Independent on Sunday*, 15 April 2001, 42.

Koba the Dread: Laughter and the Twenty Million

Acheson, Neil. "Nervous Laughter, in the Dark." *Guardian*, 7 September 2002, 10.

Berman, Paul. "A Million Deaths Is Not Just a Statistic." *New York Times Book Review*, 7.

Cowley, Jason. "Catastrophe Theories." *Observer*, 8 September 2002, 18.

Figes, Orlando. "A Shocking Lack of Decorum." *Sunday Telegraph*, 1 September 2001, 11.

Hitchens, Christopher. "Lightness at Midnight: Stalinism Without Irony." *Atlantic Monthly* (September 2002): 144–54.

Mount, Harry. "Stalin and the Death of a Sister." *Telegraph*, 31 August 2002, 3.

Thubron, Colin. "Martin vs. Stalin." *Times* (London) 4 September 2002, 2, 11.

Yellow Dog

Douglas-Fairhurst, Robert. "Dickens With a Snarl" *Observer Review*, 24 August 2003, 15.

Hollinghurst, Alan. "Leader of the Pack," *Guardian*, 6 September 2003, 9.

Hunter-Tilney, Ludovic. "Gr8 expectations." *Financial Times*, 5 September 2003, W5.

Jones, Lewis. "Surrounded by Broken Myths," *Telegraph*, 30 August 2003, 8.

Kemp, John. "A Burnt-Out Case," *Sunday Times*, 31 August 2003, Features, 41.

Shilling, Jane. "Fear and Loathing," *Sunday Telegraph*, 31 August 2003, 11.

Tait, Theo. "Yobs and Royals." *Times Literary Supplement*, 5 September 2003, 3–5.

Tayler, Christopher. "High on His Own Supply." *London Review of Books*, 11 September 2003, 11–12.

Thorne, Matt. "Let Me Introduce You to the Void," *Independent*, 31 August 2003, 17.

Walden, George. "Back to Blighty," *New Statesman*, 8 September 2003, 48–50.

Selected Interviews and Profiles

Cowley, Jason. "There Is a Kind of Mean-Spiritedness of Which I Am the Focus." *Times* (London), 4 August 1997, 15.

Frumkes, Lewis Burke. "A Conversation With . . . Martin Amis." *Writer*, October 2000, 14–16.

Haffenden, John. "Martin Amis." In *Novelists in Interview*. London: Methuen, 1985.

Hamilton, Ian. "The Company He Keeps." *Sunday Times*, 8 March 1981, 43.

Heawood, Jonathan. "It's the Death of Others That Kills You." *Observer*, 8 September 2002, 18.

James, Clive. "N. V. Rampant Meets Martin Amis." *London Review of Books* 6 (18–31 Oct. 1984): 14. Rpt. in *Snake Charmers in Texas: Essays, 1980–87*. London: Jonathan Cape, 1988, 203–6.

McGrath, Patrick. "Interview with Martin Amis. *Bomb* (winter 1987): 26–29. Rpt. in *Bomb Interviews*. Edited by Betsy Sussler. San Francisco: City Lights Books, 1992, 187–97.

Michener, Charles. "Britain's Brat of Letters." *Esquire*, January 1987, 108–11.

Morrison, Susan. "The Wit and Fury of Martin Amis." *Rolling Stone*, 17 May 1990, 95–102.

Moss, Stephen. "After the Storm." *Guardian*, 3 October 1998, 22.

Orr, Deborah. "England is Great, but America Has Real Chaos, and That's What Writers Like." *Independent*, 19 May 2000, 7.

Preston, John. "Posterity Counts, Critics Don't." *Sunday Telegraph*, 7 September 2003, 3.

Riviere, Francesca. "Martin Amis." *Paris Review* 146 (1998): 108–35.

Self, Will. "An Interview with Martin Amis." *Mississippi Review*, October 1993, 3, 143–69.

Shnayerson, Michael. "Famous Amis." *Vanity Fair*, May 1995, 133–40, 160–62.

Stout, Mira. "Down London's Mean Streets." *New York Times Magazine*, 4 February, 1990, 32–36, 48.

Wachtel, Eleanor. "Eleanor Wachtel With Martin Amis." *Malahat Review*, March 1996, 43–58.

Wolcott, James. "The Amis Papers." *Vanity Fair*, July 2000, 142–47, 181–82.

Index